THE CHRONOLOGY OF THE KINGS OF ISRAEL AND JUDAH

STUDIES IN THE HISTORY AND CULTURE OF THE ANCIENT NEAR EAST

EDITED BY

B. HALPERN AND M.H.E. WEIPPERT

VOLUME IX

THE CHRONOLOGY OF THE KINGS OF ISRAEL AND JUDAH

BY

GERSHON GALIL

E.J. BRILL
LEIDEN · NEW YORK · KÖLN
1996

The paper in this book meets the guidelines for permanence and durability of the Committee on Production Guidelines for Book Longevity of the Council on Library Resources.

Library of Congress Cataloging-in-Publication Data

Galil, Gershon.
The chronology of the kings of Israel and Judah / by Gershon Galil.
p. cm.—(Studies in the history and culture of the ancient Near East, ISSN 0169-9024 ; v. 9)
Includes bibliographical references and indexes.
ISBN 9004106111 (cloth)
1. Bible. O.T. Kings—Chronology. 2. Jews—History—953–586 B.C.—Chronology. I. Title. II. Series.
BS1335.5.G36 1996
222'.5095—dc20 96-13663
CIP

Die Deutsche Bibliothek – CIP-Einheitsaufnahme

Galil, Gershon:
The chronology of the kings of Israel and Judah / by Gershon Galil.. - Leiden ; New York : Köln : Brill, 1996
(Studies in the history and culture of the ancient Near East ; Vol. 9)
ISBN 90-04-10611-1
NE: GT

ISSN 0169-9024
ISBN 90 04 10611 1

PRINTED IN THE NETHERLANDS

To my mother
Malca Galil née Schäfler
and to the memory of my father
Jacob Galil (Gross)
(1926–1992)

CONTENTS

... et erit mihi magnus Apollo ...

Benedicti de Spinoza,
Tractatus Theologico-Politicus, 135

ACKNOWLEDGEMENTS

I consider it a great privilege that this book is published in the *Studies in the History and Culture of the Ancient Near East* series. I wish to express my deep gratitude to Prof. B. Halpern and to Prof. M. H. E. Weippert, the editors of the series. Prof. Halpern also contributed many helpful remarks.

Chapters V and VII appeared in an earlier form in the articles: "A New Look at the Chronology of the Last Kings of Judah," *Zion* 56 (1991), 5–19 (Hebrew); "The Babylonian Calendar and the Chronology of the Last Kings of Judah," *Biblica* 72 (1991), 367–378; "The Last Years of the Kingdom of Israel and the Fall of Samaria," *The Catholic Biblical Quarterly* 57 (1995), 52–65. I would like to thank the editors of these publications for permission to incorporate this material into the present volume.

I owe a special debt of gratitude to Professor B. Oded, my colleague in the Department of Jewish History in the University of Haifa, who has kindly read the manuscript and made significant comments.

My appreciations for their efforts are also due to the editors of E. J. Brill: Dr. F. Th. Dijkema; Mrs. Peri Bearman, senior editor for Near Eastern and Islamic studies; Ms. Gera van Bedaf, Production Editor; and Ms. Patricia Radder, Editorial Assistant for Ancient Near Eastern and Asian Studies.

I also wish to express my thanks to Mr. Edward Levin for improving my English style, and to Ms. Haya Schreiber, who contributed to the successful completion of this book with friendship and knowledge.

Last but not the least, I wish to thank Sigal, Shahaph and Ido, for their patience.

University of Haifa — G. Galil
May 1996

ABBREVIATIONS

Bibliographical Abbreviations

AB	*The Anchor Bible*
Ackroyd	P. R. Ackroyd, *Israel under Babylon and Persia*, Oxford 1979 (2nd ed.)
AfO	*Archiv Für Orientforschung*
Aharoni	Y. Aharoni, "The Chronology of the Kings of Israel and Judah," *Tarbiz* 21 (1950), 92–100 (Hebrew)
AION	*Annali dell'istituto Orientale di Napoli*
AJBA	*Australian Journal of Biblical Archaeology*
AJSL	*American Journal of Semitic Languages and Literature*
Albright	W. F. Albright, "The Chronology of the Divided Monarchy of Israel," *BASOR* 100 (1945), 16–22
Albright 1953	idem, "New Light from Egypt on the Chronology and History of Israel and Judah," *BASOR* 130 (1953), 4–11
Albright 1956	idem, "Further Light on Synchronisms between Egypt and Asia in the Period 935–685 B.C.," *BASOR* 141 (1956), 23–27
Albright 1963	idem, *The Biblical Period from Abraham to Ezra*, New York 1963
Albright 1970	idem, "Prolegomenon," in: C. F. Burney, *The Book of Judges with Introduction and Notes on the Hebrew Text of the Books of Kings*, New York 1970, 1–38
Alt, KS	A. Alt, *Kleine Schriften zur Geschichte des Volks Israel*, I–III, München 1953–1959
Andersen	K. T. Andersen, "Die Chronologie der Könige von Israel und Juda," *ST* 23 (1969), 69–114
Andersen 1989	idem, "Noch einmal: Die Chronologie der Könige von Israel und Juda," *Scandinavian Journal of the Old Testament* 1 (1989), 1–45
AcOr	*Acta Orientalia*
ARRIM	*Annual Review of the Royal Inscriptions of Mesopotamia Project*
AUSS	*Andrews University Seminary Studies*
BA	*The Biblical Archaeologist*
Barnes	W. H. Barnes, *Studies in the Chronology of the Divided Monarchy of Israel* (Ph.D. diss.), Ann Arbor, Michigan 1986
BASOR	*Bulletin of the American Schools of Oriental Research*
Becking	B. Becking, *The Fall of Samaria: An Historical and Archaeological Study* (*SHANE* 2), Leiden 1992
Begrich	J. Begrich, *Die Chronologie der Könige von Israel und Juda*, Tübingen 1929
BJRL	Bulletin of the John Rylands Library
Borger and Tadmor	R. Borger and H. Tadmor, "Zwei Beiträge zur alttestamentlichen Wissenschaft aufgrund der Inschriften Tiglatpilesers III," *ZAW* 94 (1982), 244–251

Bright	J. Bright, *A History of Israel*, Philadelphia 1981 (3rd ed.)
BZAW	*Beihefte zur Zeitschrift für die Alttestamentliche Wissenschaft*
Cameron	G. G. Cameron, "The Annals of Shalmaneser III, King of Assyria: A New Text," *Sumer* 4 (1950), 6–26
Cazelles	H. Cazelles, "587 au 586?," in: C. L. Meyers and M. O'Connor (eds.), *The Word of the Lord Shall Go Forth: Essays in Honor of D. N. Freedman*, Winona Lake 1983, 427–435
CB	*Cambridge Bible*
CBQ	*Catholic Biblical Quarterly*
Clines 1972	D. J. A. Clines, "Regnal Year Reckoning in the Last Years of the Kingdom of Judah," *AJBA* 2 (1972), 9–34
Clines 1974	idem, "The Evidence for an Autumnal New Year in Pre-Exilic Israel Reconsidered," *JBL* 93 (1974), 22–40
Cody	A. Cody, "A New Inscription from Tell āl-Rimah and King Jehoash of Israel," *CBQ* 32 (1970), 325–340
Cogan 1973	M. Cogan, "Tyre and Tiglath-pileser III: Chronological Notes," *JCS* 25 (1973), 96–99
Cogan 1980	idem, "Tendentious Chronology in the Book of Chronicles," *Zion* 45 (1980), 165–172 (Hebrew)
Cogan 1985	idem, "The Chronicler's Use of Chronology as Illuminated by Neo-Assyrian Royal Inscriptions," in: J. H. Tigay (ed.), *Empirical Models of Biblical Criticism*, Philadelphia 1985, 197–209
Cogan and Tadmor, II Kings	M. Cogan and H. Tadmor, *II Kings* (*AB*), Garden City, New York 1988
Cook	H. J. Cook, "Pekah," *VT* 14 (1974), 121–135
Curtis	E. L. Curtis, "Chronology of the Old Testament," in: J. Hastings (ed.), *A Dictionary of the Bible*, I, Edinburg and New York 1900, 397–403
Curtis and Madsen	E. L. Curtis and A. A. Madsen, *A Critical and Exegetical Commentary on the Books of Chronicles* (*ICC*), New York 1910
Dalley 1968	S. Dalley [Page], "A Stela of Adad-nirari III and Nergal-ereš from Tell al-Rimah," *Iraq* 30 (1968), 139–153
Dalley 1969	idem, "Adad-nirari III and Semiramis: the Stelae of Saba'a and Rimah," *Orientalia* 38 (1969), 457–458
Dalley 1985	idem, "Foreign Chariotry and Cavalry in the Armies of Tiglath-pileser III and Sargon II," *Iraq* 47 (1985), 31–48
Dalley 1990	idem, "Yahweh in Hamath in the 8th Century BC: Cuneiform Material and Historical Deductions," *VT* 60 (1990), 21–32
de Vries	see Vries, de
Donbaz	V. Donbaz, "Two Neo-Assyrian Stelae in the Antakya and Kahramanmaraṣ Museums," *ARRIM* 8 (1990), 5–24
Donner	H. Donner, "The Separate States of Israel and Judah," in: J. H. Hayes and J. M. Miller (eds.), *Israelite and Judaean History*, Philadelphia 1977, 381–434
EB	*Encyclopaedia Biblica*
EHAT	*Exegetisches Handbuch zum Alten Testament*
Elat	M. Elat, "The Campaigns of Shalmaneser III against Aram and Israel," *IEJ* 25 (1975), 25–35

Finegan	J. Finegan, *Handbook of Biblical Chronology*, Princeton, New Jersey 1964
Freedy and Redford	K. S. Freedy and D. B. Redford, "The Dates in Ezekiel in Relation to Biblical, Babylonian and Egyptian Sources," *JAOS* 90 (1970), 462–485
Freedman 1956	D. N. Freedman, "The Babylonian Chronicle," *BA* 19 (1956), 50–60
Freedman	idem and E. F. Campbell, "The Chronology of Israel and the Ancient Near East," in: G. E. Wright (ed.), *The Bible and the Ancient Near East: Essays in Honor of W. F. Albright*, Garden City, New York 1961, 203–228
FRLANT	*Forschungen zur Religion und Literatur des Alten und Neuen Testaments*
Galil 1988	G. Galil, "Sennacherib versus Hezekiah: A New Look at the Assyrian Campaign to the West in 701 BCE," *Zion* 53 (1988), 1–12 (Hebrew)
Galil 1991	idem, "The Babylonian Calendar and the Chronology of the Last Kings of Judah," *Biblica* 72 (1991), 367–378
Galil 1992a	idem, "Judah and Assyria in the Sargonid Period," *Zion* 57 (1992), 111–133 (Hebrew)
Galil 1992b	idem, "Conflicts Between Assyrian Vassals," *SAAB* 6 (1992), 55–63
Gooding	D. W. Gooding, Review of J. D. Shenkel, *Chronology and Recensional Development in the Greek Text of Kings*, Cambridge, Massachusetts 1968, *JTS* N. S. 21 (1970), 118–131
Gray 1964	J. Gray, *I and II Kings* (*OTL*), London 1964
Gray 1970	idem, *I and II Kings* (*OTL*), London 1970 (2nd ed.)
Green 1982	A. R. Green, "The Chronology of the Last Days of Judah: Two Apparent Discrepancies," *JBL* 101 (1982), 57–73
Hallo	W. W. Hallo, "From Qarqar to Carchemish: Assyria and Israel in the Light of New Discoveries," *BA* 23 (1960), 34–61
Halpern, Chronology	B. Halpern, "A Historiographic Commentary on Ezra 1–6: A Chronological Narrative and Dual Chronology in Israelite Historiography," in: W. H. Propp, B. Halpern and D. N. Freedman (eds.), *The Hebrew Bible and its Interpreters*; vol. 1: *Biblical and Judaic Studies*, Winona Lake 1990, 81–142
Halpern, Yaua, son of Omri	idem, "Yaua, son of Omri, yet again," *BASOR* 265 (1987), 81–85
Halpern and Vanderhooft	B. Halpern and D. S. Vanderhooft, "The Editions of Kings in the 7th–6th Centuries B.C.E.," *HUCA* 62 (1991), 179–244
HAT	*Handbuch zur Alten Testament*
Harrison	R. K. Harrison, *Introduction to the Old Testament*, London 1970
Hayes and Hooker	J. A. Hayes and P. K. Hooker, *A New Chronology for the Kings of Israel and Judah*, Atlanta 1988
Herrmann	S. Herrmann, *A History of Israel in Old Testament Times*, Philadelphia 1975
Horn	S. H. Horn, "The Babylonian Chronicle and the Ancient Calendar of the Kingdom of Judah," *AUSS* 5 (1967), 12–27
Horn 1964	idem, "The Chronology of King Hezekiah's Reign," *AUSS* 2 (1964), 40–52

HTR	*Harvard Theological Review*
HUCA	*Hebrew Union College Annual*
Hughes	J. Hughes, *Secrets of the Times: Myth and History in Biblical Chronology* (*JSOT* supp. 66), Sheffield 1990
IB	*Interpreter's Bible*
ICC	*The International Critical Commentary*
IEJ	*Israel Exploration Journal*
Jagersma	H. Jagersma, *A History of Israel in the Old Testament Period*, Philadelphia 1983
JAOS	*Journal of the American Oriental Society*
Japhet	S. Japhet, *The Ideology of the Book of Chronicles and its Place in Biblical Thought*, Jerusalem 1977 (Hebrew)
JBL	*Journal of Biblical Literature*
JCS	*Journal of Cuneiform Studies*
JEA	*Journal of Egyptian Archaeology*
Jenkins	A. K. Jenkins, "Hezekiah's Fourteenth Year: A New Interpretation of 2 Kings xviii 13–xix 37," *VT* 26 (1976), 284–298
Jepsen	A. Jepsen, "Zur Chronologie der Könige von Israel und Juda: Eine Überprüfung," in: A. Jepsen and R. Hanhart, *Untersuchungen zur israelitisch-jüdischen Chronologie* (*BZAW* 88), Berlin 1964, 1–48
Jepsen 1968	idem, "Noch einmal zur israelitisch-jüdischen Chronologie," *VT* 18 (1968), 31–46
JNES	*Journal of Near Eastern Studies*
Jones	G. H. Jones, *1 and 2 Kings* (*NCB*), Grand Rapids and London 1984
JTS	*Journal of Theological Studies*
JSOT	*Journal for the Study of the Old Testament*
KAI	H. Donner and W. Röllig, *Kanaanäische und aramäische Inschriften*, I–III, Wiesbaden 1971–1976 (3rd ed.)
KAT	*Kommentar zum Alten Testament*
Katzenstein	H. J. Katzenstein, *The History of Tyre*, Jerusalem 1973
Kitchen	K. A. Kitchen, *The Third Intermediate Period in Egypt* (*1100–650 BC*), Warminster 1973
Kleber	A. M. Kleber, "The Chronology of 3 and 4 Kings and 2 Paralipomenon," *Biblica* 2 (1921), 3–29, 170–205
Kutsch 1974	E. Kutsch, "Das Jahr der Katastrophe: 587 v. Chr.: kritische Erwägungen zu neueren chronologischen Versuchen," *Biblica* 55 (1974), 520–545
Kutsch 1985	idem, *Die Chronologischen Datuen des Ezekielbuches*, Göttingen 1985
Lay.	A. H. Layard, *Inscriptions in the Cuneiform Character from Assyrian Monuments*, London 1851
Lemche	N. P. Lemche, *Ancient Israel: A New History of Israelite Society*, Sheffield 1988
Levine	L. D. Levine, *Two Neo-Assyrian Stelae from Iran*, Toronto 1972
Lewy	J. Lewy, *Die Chronologie der Könige von Israel und Juda*, Giessen 1927
Lie	A. G. Lie, *The Inscription of Sargon II, King of Assyria, I: The Annals*, Paris 1929

Lipinski 1979	idem, "Aram et Israël du Xe au VIIIe siècle av. n.è.," *Acta Antiqua* 27 (1979), 49–102
Liver	J. Liver, *Studies in Bible and Judean Desert Scrolls*, Jerusalem 1971 (Hebrew)
Loretz and Mayer	O. Loretz and W. Mayer, "Pulu-Tiglatpileser III. und Menahem von Israel nach assyrischen Quellen und 2 Kön 15, 19–20," *UF* 22 (1990), 222–231
Malamat	A. Malamat, *Israel in Biblical Times: Historical Essays*, Jerusalem 1983 (Hebrew)
Mazar, Canaan and Israel	B. Mazar, *Canaan and Israel: Historical Essays*, Jerusalem 1974 (Hebrew)
Mazar, Cities and Districts	B. Mazar, *Cities and Districts in Eretz-Israel*, Jerusalem 1975 (Hebrew)
Michel	E. Michel, "Die Assur-Texte Shalmassars III. (858–824)," *WO* 2 (1954–1956), 27–45; 137–157; 221–233
Millard 1973	A. R. Millard, "Adad-nirari III, Aram, and Arpad," *PEQ* 105 (1973), 161–164
Millard, Eponyms	idem, *The Eponyms of the Assyian Empire 910–612 BC* (*State Archives of Assyria Studies* 2), Helsinki 1994
Millard and Tadmor	A. R. Millard and H. Tadmor, "Adad-nirari III in Syria: Another Stele Fragment and the Dates of his Campaigns," *Iraq* 35 (1973), 57–64
Miller	J. M. Miller, "Another Look at the Chronology of the Early Divided Monarchy," *JBL* 86 (1967), 276–288
Miller and Hayes	idem and J. A. Hayes, *A History of Ancient Israel and Judah*, Philadelphia 1986
Montgomery and Gehman	J. A. Montgomery and H. S. Gehman, *A Critical and Exegetical Commentary of the Books of Kings* (*ICC*), Edinburgh 1951
Mowinckel	S. Mowinckel, "Die Chronologie der israelitischen und jüdischen Könige," *AcOr* 10 (1932), 161–277
Murnane	W. J. Murnane, *Ancient Egyptian Coregencies*, Chicago 1977
Myers	J. M. Myers, *II Chronicles* (*AB*), Garden City, New York 1981
Na'aman 1974	N. Na'aman, "Sennacherib's 'Letter to God' on his Campaign to Judah," *BASOR* 214 (1974), 25–39
Na'aman 1977	idem, "Campaigns of the Assyrian kings to Judah in the Light of a New-Assyrian Document," *Shnaton: An Annual for Biblical and Ancient Near Eastern Studies* 2 (1977), 164–180 (Hebrew)
Na'aman 1985	idem, "The Historical Background of the Battle between Amaziah and Jehoash," *Shnaton: An Annual for Biblical and Ancient Near Eastern Studies* 9 (1985), 211–217 (Hebrew)
Na'aman 1986	idem, "Historical and Chronological Notes on the Kingdoms of Israel and Judah in the Eighth Century B.C.," *VT* 36 (1986), 71–92
Na'aman 1987	idem, "Pastoral Nomads in the Southwestern Periphery of the Kingdom of Judah in the 9th–8th Centuries B.C.E.," *Zion* 52 (1987), 261–278 (Hebrew)
Na'aman 1990	idem, "The Historical Background to the Conquest of Samaria (720 BC)," *Biblica* 71 (1990), 206–225
NCB	*New Century Bible*

Noth 1958	M. Noth, "Die Einnahme von Jerusalem im Jahre 597 v. Chr.," *ZDPV* 74 (1958), 133–157
Noth	idem, *The History of Israel*, New York and Evanston 1960 (2nd ed.)
Oded 1966	B. Oded, "When did the Kingdom of Judah become subjected to Babylonian Rule?," *Tarbiz* 35 (1966), 103–107 (Hebrew)
Oded 1972a	idem, "The Campaigns of Adad-nirari III into Syria and Palestine," *Studies in the History of the Jewish People and the Land of Israel*, 2 (1972), 25–37 (Hebrew)
Oded 1972b	idem, "The Historical Background of the Syro-Ephraimite War Reconsidered," *CBQ* 34 (1972), 153–165
Oded 1974	idem, "The Phoenician Cities and the Assyrian Empire in the Time of Tiglath-pileser III," *ZDPV*, 90 (1974), 38–49
Oded 1975	idem, "Assyria and the Phoenician City-States at the Time of the Assyrian Empire—II," *Shnaton: An Annual for Biblical and Ancient Near Eastern Studies* 1 (1975), 205–211 (Hebrew)
Oded 1979	idem, *Mass Deportations and Deportees in the Neo-Assyrian Empire*, Wiesbaden 1979
Olmstead, Assyria	A. T. Olmstead, *History of Assyria*, New York 1923
OLZ	*Orientalistische Literaturzeitung*
OTL	*Old Testament Library*
Parker and Dubberstein	R. A. Parker and W. H. Dubberstein, *Babylonian Chronology 626 B.C.—A.D. 75*, Providence 1956
PEQ	*Palestine Exploration Quarterly*
Pavlovsky and Vogt	V. Pavlovsky und E. Vogt, "Die Jahre der Könige von Juda und Israel," *Biblica* 45 (1964), 321–347
Pitard	W. T. Pitard, *Ancient Damascus: A Historical Study of the Syrian City-State from Earliest Times until its Fall to the Assyrians in 732 B.C.E.*, Winona Lake 1987
Pitard 1988	idem, "The Identity of the Bir-Hadad of the Melqart Stela," *BASOR* 272 (1988), 3–21
Rainey	A. F. Rainey, *A Handbook of Historical Geography*, Jerusalem 1984
Reade	J. Reade, "Mesopotamian Guidelines for Biblical Chronology," *Syro-Mesopotamian Studies* 4/1 (1981), 1–9
Reviv 1979	H. Reviv, *From Clan to Monarchy: Israel in The Biblical Period*, Jerusalem 1979 (Hebrew)
Rofe 1982	A. Rofé, *The Prophetical Stories*, Jerusalem 1982 (Hebrew)
Rost	P. Rost, *Die Keilschrifttexte Tiglath-Pilesers III*, Leipzig 1893
Rudolph	W. Rudolph, *Chronikbücher* (*HAT*), Tübingen 1955
SAAB	*State Archives of Assyria Bulletin*
Schedl 1962a	C. Schedl, "Textkritische Bemerkungen zu den Synchronismen der Könige von Israel und Juda," *VT* 12 (1962), 88–119
Schedl 1962b	idem, "Nochmals das Jahr der Zerstörung Jerusalems, 587 oder 586 v. Chr.," *ZAW* 74 (1962), 209–213
SHANE	*Studies in the History of the Ancient Near East*

Shea 1978a	W. H. Shea, "Adad-nirari III and Jehoash of Israel," *JCS* 30 (1978), 101–113
Shea 1978b	idem, "Menahem and Tiglath-pileser III," *JNES* 37 (1978), 43–49
Shea 1985	idem, "Israelite Chronology and the Samaria Ostraca," *ZDPV* 101 (1985), 9–20
Shenkel	J. D. Shenkel, *Chronology and Recensional Development in the Greek Text of Kings*, Cambridge, Massachusetts 1968
Snaith	N. H. Snaith, *The First and Second Books of Kings* (*IB*), New York and Nashville 1954
ST	*Studia theologica*
Tadmor, Jehu	H. Tadmor, "Jehu," *EB* 3 (1958), 473–478 (Hebrew)
Tadmor 1958	idem, "The Campaigns of Sargon II of Assur: A Chronological-Historical Study," *JCS* 12 (1958), 22–40, 77–100
Tadmor 1961	idem, "Azriyau of Yaudi," *Scripta Hierosolymitana* 8 (1961), 232–271
Tadmor 1962	idem, "Chronology," *EB* 4 (1962), 245–310 (Hebrew)
Tadmor 1967a	idem, "Introductory Remarks to a New Edition of the Annals of Tiglath-pileser III," *Proceedings of the Israel Academy of Sciences and Humanities* 2/9 (1967), 168–187 (Hebrew)
Tadmor 1967b	idem, "The Conquest of Galilee by Tiglath-pileser III, King of Assyria," in: H. Z. Hirschberg (ed.), *All the Land of Naphtali*, Jerusalem 1967, 62–67 (Hebrew)
Tadmor 1973	idem, "The Historical Inscriptions of Adad-nirari III," *Iraq* 35, (1973), 141–150
Tadmor 1979	idem, "The Chronology of the First Temple Period," in: A. Malamat (ed.), *The Age of the Monarchies: Political History. The World History of the Jewish People*, 4/1, Jerusalem 1979, 44–60, 318–320
Tadmor 1990	idem, "Tiglat-pileser III in Ancient Palestine," *Shnaton: An Annual for Biblical and Ancient Near Eastern Studies* 10 (1986–1989), 179–187 (Hebrew)
Tadmor, *ITP*	idem, *The Inscriptions of Tiglath-pileser III, King of Assyria*, Jerusalem 1994
Tadmor and Cogan	H. Tadmor and M. Cogan, "Hezekiah's Fourteenth Year: The King's Illness and the Babylonian Embassy," *Eretz-Israel* 16 (1982), 198–201 (Hebrew)
Talmon 1958	S. Talmon, "Divergences in Calendar-Reckoning in Ephraim and Judah," *VT* 8 (1958), 48–74
Thiele 1951	E. R. Thiele, *The Mysterious Numbers of the Hebrew Kings*, Chicago 1951
Thiele	idem, *The Mysterious Numbers of the Hebrew Kings*, Grand Rapids, Michigan 1965 (2nd ed.)
Thiele 1974	idem, "Coregencies and Overlapping Reigns among the Hebrew Kings," *JBL*, 93 (1974), 174–200
Thiele 1977	idem, *A Chronology of the Hebrew Kings*, Grand Rapids, Michigan 1977

Thiele 1983	idem, *The Mysterious Numbers of the Hebrew Kings*, Grand Rapids, Michigan 1983 (3rd ed.)
UF	*Ugarit-Forschungen*
Vogelstein	M. Vogelstein, *Biblical Chronology I: The Chronology of Hezekiah and his Successors*, Cincinnati 1944
Vogt 1975	E. Vogt, "Bemerkungen über das Jahr der Eroberung Jerusalems," *Biblica* 56 (1975), 223–230
Vries, de	S. J. de Vries, "Chronology of the Old Testament," *The Interpreter's Dictionary of the Bible*, New York and Nashville 1962, 580–599
VT	*Vetus Testamentum*
WBC	*Word Bible Commentary*
Weippert, Edom	M. H. E. Weippert, *Edom*, Tübingen 1971
Weippert 1973	idem, "Menahem von Israel und seine Zeitgenossen in einer Steleninschrift des assyrischen Königs Tiglathpileser III. aus dem Iran," *ZDPV* 89 (1973), 26–53
Wellhausen	J. Wellhausen, "Die Zeitrechnung des Buchs der Könige seit der Theilung des Reichs," *Jahrbücher für Deutsche Theologie* 20 (1875), 607–640
Welten	P. Welten, *Geschichte und Geschichtsdarstellung in den Chronikbüchern* (*WMANT* 42), Neukirchen-Vluyn 1973
Wifall	W. R. Wifall Jr., "The Chronology of the Divided Monarchy of Israel," *ZAW* 80 (1968), 319–337
Williamson	H. G. M. Williamson, *1 and 2 Chronicles* (*NCB*), Grand Rapids and London 1982
Whitley	C. F. Whitley, "The Deuteronomic Presentation of the House of Omri," *VT* 2 (1952), 137–152
WMAT	*Wissenschaftliche Monographien zum Alten und Neuen Testament*
WO	*Die Welt des Orients*
WZKM	*Wiener Zeitschrift für die Kunde des Morgenlandes*
Yeivin	S. Yeivin, "The Divided Monarchy: Rehoboam-Ahaz / Jeroboam-Pekah,"in: A. Malamat (ed.),*The Age of the Monarchies: Political History. The World History of the Jewish People*, 4/1, Jerusalem 1982, 82–120 (Hebrew)
ZAW	*Zeitschrift für die alttestamentlische Wissenschaft*
ZDPV	*Zeitschrift des deutschen Palästina-Vereins*
Zimmerli	W. Zimmerli, *Ezechiel* (*KAT*), Neukirchen-Vluyn 1969
ZWT	*Zeitschrift für wissenschaftliche Theologie*

Other abbreviations and symbols

A	Septuagint, Codex Alexandrinus
B	Septuagint, Codex Vaticanus
BCE	Before Common Era
diss.	dissertation
KR	Kaige recension
l(l).	line(s)
L	Septuagint, Lucianic recension
LXX	Septuagint
MS(S)	Manuscript(s)
MT	Masoretic Text
N	Septuagint, Codex Venetus
n. s.	new series
obv.	obvers
OGT	Old Greek Translation
par.	paragraph
rev.	reverse
supp.	supplement
s. t.	same title
v.	verse

CHAPTER ONE

INTRODUCTION

The chronology of the kings of Judah and Israel is one of the most complex issues in Biblical history. It has been discussed quite extensively in the scholarly literature, but no satisfactory solution has been offered to date, nor has the testimony of the Biblical and extra-Biblical sources received an exhaustive treatment. The determination of an absolute system of dates for the kings of Israel and Judah became possible only in the second half of the nineteenth century, following the deciphering of Assyrian royal inscriptions pertaining to the history of the two Israelite kingdoms. But the chronology of the kings of Israel and Judah was first discussed about two and a half millennia ago, in the sixth century BCE, with the writing of the Book of Kings (see below). Since then, countless efforts have been made to reconstruct the chronological framework of these monarchs, and to reconcile the many contradictions between the confusing data regarding the duration of the reigns of these thirty-nine kings. Some of these attempts have survived in the Septuagint and in the works of Josephus (see the discussion in Chapter Eight). A few proposals, mainly harmonious, appear in *Seder Olam Rabbah*, in the patristic literature, and in the works of the medieval commentators. Beginning in the midnineteenth century, researchers proposed a plethora of reconstructions of the chronological framework and of the principles underlying the chronology of Judaean and Israelite history in this period. Researchers deny the accuracy of the majority of the Biblical chronological data, arguing that these data are artificial and schematic, and cannot serve as a basis for the determination of the chronology the Israelite kings.[1]

The hypotheses of J. Wellhausen wield great influence.[2] Wellhausen, following in the footsteps of earlier Bible researchers, assumed that the chronology of the kings of Judah is based on a schematic framework spanning 430 years from the establishment of the Temple to the fall

---

[1] H. Ewald, *Geschichte des Volkes Israel*, Göttingen 1864, I (3rd ed.), 294–307; W. Robertson Smith, "The Chronology of the Books of Kings," *Journal of Philology* 10 (1882), 209–213; B. Stade, *Geschichte des Volkes Israel*, Berlin 1887, I, 558 ff.

[2] Wellhausen, 607–640.

of Jerusalem. He added to this count the 50 years from the destruction of the Temple to the Restoration, and supposed that the scribes reconstructed an artificial count of 480 years from the establishment of the Temple to the Restoration, closely resembling the count of 480 years from the Exodus from Egypt to the establishment of the Temple (I Kings 6:1).

This hypothesis, however, cannot be accepted. There is no mention in the Book of Kings or in any other Biblical or extra-Biblical source of the span of 50 years from the destruction of the Temple to the Restoration. Not only is this datum not accurate, it lies beyond the historical purview of the author of the Book of Kings. Furthermore, the arithmetic proximity of these numbers may be merely coincidental. This approach was prevalent mainly among German researchers at the end of the nineteenth century, and is currently regaining support among researchers.[3]

J. Begrich strenuously objected to Wellhausen's theory, and he proposed an alternative reconstruction of the time frame of Israelite history from the schism to the fall of Jerusalem.[4] In his view the Biblical chronological data derive from a multiplicity of sources, which reflect different counting systems. Begrich did not attempt to reconcile the different sources, preferring instead a single system which served as the basis for the chronology he reconstructed. He postulated that many Biblical data are not reflective of reality. Thus, e.g., for the period from the

[3] Mowinckel, 167 ff.; cf. Wifall, 333 ff., who surmised that the redactor of the Book of Kings arbitrarily attempted to reconstruct a framework of 480 years from the establishment of the monarchy to the fall of Jerusalem. Barnes has recently surmised that the data of the years of reign in the Book of Kings are based on a scheme of 480 years that elapsed from the coronation of David to the release of Jehoiachin from his prison (Barnes, 184 ff.). Barnes was compelled to deduct a year from the years of all the kings of the Davidic line, and to ignore the explicit coregency of David and Solomon, in order to maintain his theory. Wellhausen similarly amended the number of years of Baasha (22 instead of 24) to support another conjecture of his, also indicating the artificiality of the data in the Book of Kings: he found a strange ratio between the numbers of the years of the Israelite kings from Jeroboam to Joram: Jeroboam – 22 years; Nadab – 2; Baasha – 22; Elah – 2; Omri – 12; Ahab – 22; Ahaziah – 2; Joram – 12. These 8 kings ruled for a total of 96 years: the first four, for 48 years, and the last four, for 48 years. The average number is 12, and this is established for two kings; while the other kings are divided into three pairs: the father ruled for 22 (12 + 10) years, and the son ruled for 2 (12 – 10) years (J. Wellhausen, *Prolegomena zur Geschichte Israels*, Berlin 1899 [5th ed.], 276). If the number of years of Baasha (24) had fit this arithmetical scheme, it undoubtedly would have won many adherents. Wellhausen has recently been followed by Hughes (121 ff.)—see below.

[4] Begrich 14–16, 108 ff.; 132 ff.

schism to Jehu's revolt he cannot reconcile about two thirds of the approximately thirty chronological data relating to this period and his system of dating for this time span relies upon nineteen data which have no basis in the sources (see the discussion below, Chapters Two and Three). Furthermore, following Kleber, he assumed that in the years 882/1–879/8 no king ruled over Israel.[5] This unwarranted assumption compelled Begrich to decrease the reign of Omri from 12 to 8 years. In his opinion the new year in Israel began on 1 Tishri, while in Judah, the new year, which had initially started on this date, was changed in the reign of Ahaz to 1 Nisan. This assumption forced Begrich to propose a number of tenuous guesses, one of which asserts that Jeroboam counted his years of reign from the thirty-ninth year of Solomon.[6]

In 1944–45, two studies were published in the United States which greatly influenced the research of the chronology of the period of the divided monarchy: the works of E. R. Thiele and W. F. Albright.[7] Their proposals were accepted by many researchers, and to the present, almost half a century after their publication, most scholars are of the opinion that the system of Thiele or that of Albright is the most plausible for reconstructing the chronological frame of the period under discussion.[8] The two proposed systems differ from each other. Thiele assumed that the decisive majority of the synchronisms and the years of reign data in the Book of Kings are original and reliable. Thiele attempted to reconcile the contradictions inherent in these data and to prove their reliability in the following diverse ways:[9] (1) coregencies existed both in Judah and in Israel; (2) at times, the years of reign

[5] Idem, 155.

[6] In 1964 Jepsen aired a proposal which he defined as an attempt to correct Begrich's reconstruction (see Jepsen, 21 ff.). Jepsen was successful in refining Begrich's theory, but he was not capable of purging it of improbable elements, including the assumption regarding an interregnum in Israel, a conjecture concerning the coronation of Jeroboam before Rehoboam, etc. In some instances Jepsen resolved one discrepancy but at the price of creating another, as, e.g., a possible interregnum between Hezekiah and Manasseh (see op. cit., 39, 42).

[7] E. R. Thiele, "The Chronology of the Kings of Judah and Israel," *JNES* 3 (1944), 137–186; Albright, 17 ff.

[8] Thiele's view was accepted by many researchers, including K. A. Kitchen and T. C. Mitchell, "Chronology of the Old Testament," *The New Bible Dictionary*, London 1962, 212–223; Hallo, 34 ff.; H. S. Gehman, "Chronology," *The New Westminster Dictionary of the Bible*, Philadelphia 1970, 167–172; Rainey, 71; de Vries, 580 ff., and others. Albright's reconstruction was adopted by Bright, 230 ff.; Freedman, 208 ff.; R. J. Coggins, cited in Ackroyd, 345 ff., and others.

[9] Thiele 1983, 43–65.

were counted from the coronation of a king during his father's lifetime, while at other times, they were counted only from the beginning of his reign as an independent sovereign; (3) there was a gap of half a year between the new year in Judah and that in Israel—in the Northern Kingdom the new year began on 1 Nisan, while in the Southern Kingdom it was celebrated on 1 Tishri; (4) there were instances in which in Judah the years of the kings of Israel were counted in accordance with the Judahite calendar, and there were cases in which the Northern Kingdom enumerated the years of the kings of Judah in accordance with the calendar of the kings of Israel; (5) the system of counting in the two kingdoms was not constant, but rather was changed a number of times during this period—the Israelite kingdom initially employed the antedating system (until the time of Joash), and afterwards the postdating one; while in Judah postdating was used until the reign of Jehoram; antedating, from Jehoram to Amaziah; and once again postdating from Amaziah to the end of the First Temple period.

Thiele's view contains positive elements, but it also poses numerous difficulties. He incorrectly understood the annals of Tiglath-pileser III, and his determination that Menahem died in 742 contradicts the testimonies of the contemporaneous Assyrian inscriptions.[10] In his desire to resolve the discrepancies between the data in the Book of Kings, Thiele was forced to make improbable suppositions. He assumed that the system of counting the years of reign changed every few generations, or even after a few decades. This is improbable, and cannot be proved. Similarly, he presumes that the Northern and Southern Kingdoms numbered their years both by the local count and by that practiced by the other kingdom, also for short periods, while this practice ceased in other periods. Thiele even went so far as to assume that while this practice had fallen into disuse, there were scribes who continued to calculate the years in accordance with it. There is no basis for Thiele's statement that his conjectures are correct because he succeeded in reconciling most of the data in the Book of Kings, since his assumptions regarding Biblical chronological principles are derived from the chronological data themselves, whose reliability is unclear.

In contrast to Thiele, Albright assumed that many chronological

---

[10] For an analysis of the inscriptions of Tiglath-pileser III, see: Thiele 1983, 139–162; cf. Tadmor, *ITP*, 274–276 for criticism of Thiele's proposals.

data in the Book of Kings are unreliable, and that only the date of the fall of Samaria can be determined with certainty.[11] Although he proposed a table of dates, he emphasized that it was not certain, assuming a possible error of a year or two in some of the dates he established and up to five years in others. He gives preference to the Judahite synchronisms over other data, including those of the years of reign, while assuming that the author of the Book of Kings did not possess reliable Israelite synchronisms, and therefore this author or a later redactor calculated the Israelite synchronisms appearing in the Book of Kings. Albright instituted far-reaching changes in the chronological data of the kings of the two kingdoms: he arbitrarily shortened the count of Rehoboam's reign from 17 to 8; Uzziah ruled for 42 years, and not 52; Manasseh, 45 years, instead of 55; Amaziah, 18, and not 29, etc. In contrast to the free manner in which Albright changed the data he found in the Book of Kings, he regarded the chronological data in the Book of Chronicles as reliable. Thus he preferred, e.g., the account in II Chronicles 16:1 relating that the war of Baasha with Asa began in the thirty-sixth year of Asa, thereby rejecting all the Biblical synchronisms pertaining to the beginning of the divided kingdom.[12] In 1970, following the publication of the Tell al-Rimah stele, Albright suggested a number of insignificant changes to his original proposal, but did not essentially modify his view.[13]

In 1962 H. Tadmor published his reconstruction of the chronology of the monarchic period, which is accepted by many researchers, mainly in Israel, and which is based on a number of new principles.[14] Tadmor bases his reconstruction on the assumption that "the overwhelming majority of the chronological data in the Book of Kings are no longer original data accurately reflecting the official enumeration of years in effect during the lifetimes of the kings themselves."[15] He assumed that antedating was the system of counting in Israel and in Judah. In Judah it apparently was changed to postdating in the time of Amon or Manasseh (alternately, Tadmor assumed that it was not changed in practice, but that "the author of the chronological frame of the Book of Kings" counted the years according to this

---

[11] Albright, 17.

[12] Idem, 20. In Albright's opinion there was coregency only in the end of Uzziah's reign.

[13] Albright 1970, 33 ff.

[14] Tadmor 1962, 263 ff.

[15] Tadmor 1983, 42.

system). In Tadmor's opinion, the kings of Judah counted their years from 1 Nisan, and the kings of Israel from 1 Tishri or from 1 Nisan; and in both kingdoms there were periods of coregency. He assumed that the years of the coregents were counted at times from their coronation during their father's lifetimes, but in other instances their years were calculated only from the year of their father's death. Tadmor's major contribution lies in the study of the Assyrian synchronisms for this period, and his major innovation in the theoretical research of this period consists of his hypothesis that it is possible to resolve some of the discrepancies between the Biblical chronological data if we assume that the author of the Book of Kings (or the author of a portion of the sources integrated into the book) rounded off the counts of the years of the Judahite and Israelite kings.[16] This last conjecture is the weak point of Tadmor's system, because it is not applied in a consistent fashion. When it is convenient, the years had already been rounded off by an earlier redactor, and on other occasions when suitable, they were rounded off by the "author of the chronological system"; the latter adjusted the years downward, while the "early redactor" rounded the numbers upward; the years of most of the kings of Israel were adjusted upwards, but some were not changed at all; in contrast, the years of only a few Judahite kings were rounded off. It is not clear why the years were rounded off in some instances, but not in others, nor is the determination in which cases such adjusting took place. The starting point for Tadmor's deliberations also poses a methodological problem: if indeed the "decisive majority" of the data in the Book of Kings are derivative, what is the basis for his reconstruction of the chronological frame for the period? If this is the starting point, perhaps we should be satisfied merely with the dates clearly indicated by the extra-Biblical data?

J. Hughes has recently offered a new reconstruction of the chronology of the kings of Israel and Judah.[17] His proposal is based on Wellhausen's hypothesis that the chronological data in the Book of Kings are arranged in a schematic framework of 480 years from the establishment of the Temple to the Restoration. In his opinion, the author of this time frame was active after the composition of the Book of Kings, and he is responsible for the amending of a number of data regarding the duration of the reigns of a few Judahite kings. Most of

---

[16] Tadmor 1962, 271–274.
[17] Hughes, 121 ff.

the synchronisms are the product of later calculations and are not accurate; in contrast, most of the stated years of reign are firmly based in the reality. He rejects the prevalent assumption that there were periods of coregency in the two kingdoms, or that years were enumerated retroactively. He asserts that antedating was in force in both kingdoms, and that in both the year began on 1 Tishri. During the time of Josiah, the new year in Judah was changed to 1 Nisan.[18]

Hughes' proposals are neither likely nor systematic. He sought to provide support for Wellhausen's argument and to assume that a distinction must be made between the time of the writing of the Book of Kings and that of a redactor who changed some of the reigns of the Judahite kings in order to create a framework of 480 years from the establishment of the Temple to the Restoration.[19] No proof, however, has been given for this hypothesis. Furthermore, he asserts that six of the years of the kings of Judah given in the Book of Kings are not original; the later redactor was forced to add a number of years (28 in all) to the count of the years of the Judahite kings so that it would correspond to the schematic framework of 480 years. It is therefore surprising to find in Hughes' work four instances in which the datum in the extant Book of Kings is higher than what he presents as the original figure and, conversely, two cases in which the datum in the Book of Kings is lower than what he argues is the original datum. Hughes arbitrarily changed a portion of the data pertaining to the reigns of the kings of both realms. He established a reign of 25 years, instead of 22, for Jeroboam, arguing that this datum is based on the Septuagint.[20] In fact, however, there is no mention of this datum in any of the various manuscripts of the Septuagint, rather it is a mere assumption based on another assumption (see below, Chapter Eight). Hughes counts for Ahab 24 years, a figure which is not based on any source; and he allocates to Jehu 27, and not 28 years, based on a datum mentioned by Josephus.[21] Hughes' hypothesis that there were no coregencies in either of the two kingdoms, is unacceptable, for the Book of Kings provides unequivocal testimony of the coregency of David and Solomon; in essence, the duration of this coregency is unimportant, as is the possibility that David was on his deathbed when Solomon was installed.[22]

---

[18] Idem, 159 ff., 275–276.
[19] Idem, 121 ff.
[20] Idem, 132–134.
[21] Idem, 145, 275.
[22] Hayes and Hooker also negate the existence of coregencies (Hayes and Hooker,

All that can be established with certainty in the study of the chronology of the period from the Schism to the Exile is that a number of Biblical data are clearly erroneous, and only a limited number of dates can be determined with any degree of confidence (see appendix D). Notwithstanding this, most of the Biblical chronological data for this period can be reconciled with the extra-Biblical chronological data, without resorting to the tortuous and complicated hypotheses proposed by researchers. The many difficulties raised by the data in the Book of Kings most likely indicates that they are not an artificial and harmonious creation composed by an author who invented these details.

The sources do not contain explicit testimony regarding the system employed for counting the years of Israelite kings in the Biblical period. We cannot determine with certainty the new year; whether it was the same in the two kingdoms; whether they were counted by the antedating, the postdating or by another system. An answer to these questions is dependent upon the answer to yet another issue: the reliability of the Biblical chronological data. In other words, the chronological research of the history of Israel and Judah from the schism to the destruction of Jerusalem finds itself caught in a maze, with no certain exit. On the one hand, it is not possible to determine if the Biblical chronological data are reliable, and, on the other hand, we possess no explicit testimony regarding the system of counting the years of reign in the two kingdoms employed in the Biblical period. The researchers who attempt to reconstruct the systems of counting do so on the basis of data of questionable accuracy, and many proposals for the reconstruction of the chronological system of this period find

12 ff.). Along with this, however, they assumed that there were years which were counted for two kings, for there were a number of instances in which kings relinquished their role before their death, but the scribes nevertheless continued to count the years of their reign until they died. They not only cite as an example Uzziah, but also claim that this interesting phenomenon occurred in the time of Baasha, Asa, Joash and Amaziah as well (22 ff.). There is no proof, however, for this assumption. The chronological frame they propose is improbable and contains many dubious conjectures. Thus, e.g., in order to maintain as many Biblical data as possible, they assume that many events took place specifically in the month of Tishri: the death of Solomon, the death of Abijam, the coronation of Elah, etc. They also propose that the "Jehu" mentioned in the inscription of Shalmaneser III is in actuality Jehoram son of Ahab, and that "Jehoram the son of Ahab" is Jehoram son of Jehoshaphat (33; see below, Chapter Three).

themselves in a vicious circle: they determine the counting systems based on the chronological data and then test the reliability of these data in accordance with the counting systems established on the basis of these selfsame data.

We possess many data for the chronological reconstruction of the period of the divided kingdom, but their accuracy cannot be tested; therefore, it has been proposed to apply the following methodology: to accept as an initial working hypothesis the reliability and accuracy of the Biblical data, and to attempt to construct a set of principles that corresponds to as many Biblical and external data as possible. We do not claim that such a set of principles testifies that the data are reliable, it rather reflects our *ab initio* agreement that at the present we do not possess a certain resolution of the chronology of the period of the divided kingdom; this therefore merely constitutes a system for fully developing the testimony of the Biblical and external sources relating to this period.

Accordingly, the research of this topic is governed by the laws of uncertainty, and the limits they impose cannot be exceeded on the basis of the information we possess. At the same time, however, it is possible, and even desirable, to propose a system which will not, on the one hand, be influenced by the unjustifiable, nihilistic approach, nor, on the other hand, seek forced solutions whose sole merit lies in their resolution of all the extant data. It is difficult to believe that no errors crept into these data over the course of centuries of transmission and copying.

The following system is successful in reconciling approximate 90% of the Biblical and external data, making use of a relatively simple set of principles. Hopefully, in the future we will possess additional information which shall enable us to test the proposed system.

The following are the presumed principles of the chronology of the period of the divided monarchy of Israel:

1. The new year in the kingdom of Judah fell on 1 Nisan, and in Israel, on 1 Tishri. It cannot be determined whether the two kingdoms maintained different calendars that began on different dates. The text in Jeremiah 36:22 attests that King Jehoiakim "was sitting in the winter-house in the ninth month; and the brazier was burning before him," thereby decisively demonstrating that in the last years of the Judahite kingdom the new year began on 1 Nisan. At the same time, however, it cannot be established with certainty that this was

the practice during the entire period of the monarchy, or if the intent of the Biblical text is to the beginning of the year of reign. It is quite likely that the answer to both questions is affirmative, but this is not certain.[23]

2. Postdating was the system used in Judah, while in the Northern Kingdom antedating was the system until the end of the ninth century BCE, and postdating from the beginning of the eighth century onward.

3. Some of the kings of Israel and Judah crowned their sons in their lifetime (coregencies). Certain testimony for a coregency in Israel appears in I Kings 1–2.

4. The years of all the kings of the two kingdoms were counted from their coronation, whether they were invested during the lifetime of their predecessor, or only after his death.

5. The years of two kings, Pekah of Israel and Jehoash of Judah, apparently were counted retroactively. Jehoiada the priest, who was the *de facto* ruler of Judah in the beginning of Jehoash's reign, apparently did not recognize the validity of Athaliah's rule, and he counted Jehoash's years from the murder of his father Ahaziah (for the reign of Pekah, see below, Chapter Four).

6. The Judahite calendar did not necessarily correspond to the Assyrian or Babylonian calendars.

The years of the kings of Israel probably were not counted in Judah in accordance with the Judahite calendar, and the years of the kings of Judah probably were not enumerated in the Northern Kingdom according to the Israelite calendar. Nor may it be assumed that the data in the Bible regarding the years of reign were rounded off, or that there was an interregnum in either of the two kingdoms.

Most of the chronological information pertaining to this period is preserved in the Book of Kings, which was composed in the midsixth century BCE. It is most likely that the author of the Book of Kings compiled tens of chronological data from his two main sources: the

[23] All the testimonies discovered by researchers attesting that the new year began in Israel or in Judah in the spring or in the fall are unconvincing, and cannot provide a decisive answer to this question. For an excellent discussion of the new year in the two kingdoms, see: Clines 1974, 22–40; cf. Hughes, 159 ff.

"Book of the Chronicles of the Kings of Judah" and the "Book of the Chronicles of the Kings of Israel." From the first book he apparently cited the data regarding the reigns of the kings of Judah, testimonies about the ages of the Judahite kings at the time of their coronation, "Judahite" synchronisms, and additional information pertaining to the history of the Southern Kingdom; and from the latter work he took the data concerning the years of the kings of Israel, and perhaps some of the "Israelite" synchronisms as well. The author of the Book of Kings undoubtedly attributed great importance to these data. He included in his composition the data concerning the reigns of all the kings of Israel and Judah, without exception, including the kings who ruled only a few days or weeks. He also took pains to mention the synchronisms of all the kings of the Northern and Southern Kingdoms from the schism to the fall of Samaria, and even arranged his composition in chronological-synchronistic order. The Book of Kings includes a total of approximately 115 numerical chronological data (see appendix A). There are blatant inconsistencies between these data. They have been discussed extensively in the research, and they will be examined below. There are at least twenty such inconsistencies, and it is difficult to imagine that they were hidden from the author of the Book of Kings; it is clear, however, that at least a portion of them are not the consequence of intervention by a redactor who was active after the stage of the composition of the book. It therefore may reasonably be assumed that the author of the book cited from his sources data which he himself regarded as inconsistent, and he did not make a comprehensive effort to resolve these inconsistencies.[24] Once this is said, however, it is possible that he calculated a number of data, possibly because he did not find data in his sources, and it is likely that other data were calculated by a redactor (see the discussion in the following chapters).[25]

---

[24] For the contradictions between the chronological data in the Book of Kings, see: Thiele 1983, 33 ff.; Hughes, 97 ff.; also see the discussion below.

[25] For the sources and process of composition of the Book of Kings, see the introductions to the commentaries on the Book of Kings; also see: Thiele 1983, 193–204; Halpern and Vanderhooft, 179 ff.; Hughes, 77 ff., 97 ff., and loc. cit. for additional literature.

CHAPTER TWO

THE CHRONOLOGY OF THE KINGS OF ISRAEL AND JUDAH FROM THE SCHISM TO THE DEATH OF AHAB

Thirty chronological data regarding this period are preserved in the Biblical and Assyrian sources.[1] The Biblical data for this period appear to be erroneous and contradictory. The following are a few examples:

1. Since Rehoboam and Jeroboam apparently began to rule at the same time (I Kings 12), and since both King Joram of Israel and King Ahaziah of Judah were killed during the revolt of Jehu (II Kings 9:24, 27), it therefore follows that the count of the years of the kings of Israel from the coronation of Jeroboam to the death of Joram would coincide with that of the years of the kings of Judah from the installation of Rehoboam to the death of Ahaziah. But the count of the years of the Israelite kings in this period is 98, while there are only 95 years of reign in Judah. There is a similar incongruity between the count of the royal years from the schism to the death of Ahab. The count for the kings of Israel in this period is 84, while that of the kings of Judah (until year 17 of Jehoshaphat, the year of the coronation of Ahaziah son of Ahab) totals only 78.

2. There appear to be discrepancies in the Judahite synchronisms connected with the year of the coronation of Omri. One verse attests that King Omri ascended the throne of Israel in year 31 of Asa (I Kings 16:22–23), while another passage relates that Omri was invested in the encampment against Gibbethon, during the short-lived reign of Zimri, in year 27 of Asa (ibid., v. 15). If it is assumed that Omri was enthroned in year 31 of Asa, and that after his death his son Ahab succeeded him in year 38 of Asa (ibid., v. 29), it is presumably impossible to accept the datum stating that Omri ruled for twelve years (ibid., v. 23).

3. A comparison of the chronological data in the Book of Kings with those in Chronicles raises additional difficulties: if Asa was crowned after the death of his father Abijam, in year 20 of Jeroboam

[1] See appendix A, data nos. 1–7, 20–22, 39–41, 51–57, 74, 123–128, 134–135,

(I Kings 15:9), how could Jeroboam have died in the time of Abijam (II Chronicles 13:20)? Furthermore, if Baasha died in year 26 of Asa (I Kings 16:8), how could he have fought Judah in year 36 of Asa (II Chronicles 16:1)?

We shall now examine the opinions of the researchers regarding these issues, and reconstruct the time framework of the history of Judah and Israel in this period. We shall demonstrate that it is possible to reconcile all the chronological data cited in the Book of Kings regarding Israelite history from the schism to the death of Ahab (23 data), while assuming that the majority of the data in the Book of Chronicles served the purposes of the author of Chronicles, who, for reasons to be clarified below, fabricated chronological data, preferring his own inventions to the data he found in the Book of Kings. Regarding the presumed internal inconsistencies in the Book of Kings, they apparently are illusory, as was suggested above, and cannot indicate the unreliability of the data in the Book of Kings, because the Bible does not count calendar years, but rather years of reign, and there is no system of counting in which the duration of each of the years of a certain king's reign, including his first and last years, is identical with the duration of a complete calendar year. Consequently, the counts of the years of a number of kings who ruled in each kingdom during the identical period will correspond only if the systems of counting are identical (and this will be so only if kings were not installed during the time of their predecessors). Many more kings ruled in Israel from the schism to the death of Ahab than in Judah (six as opposed to four); nor was the system of counting employed in Israel identical to that practiced in Judah; it will be argued below that these are the causes of the above-mentioned inconsistencies.

The time of the schism is the subject of controversy. Those postulating an early date hypothesize that it occurred in 937, while those favoring a later time are of the opinion that it took place in 922 or 921/20.[2] Many researchers have also proposed dates falling between these two years.[3] The advocates of the earlier date hypothesized that

151. Twenty-three data are preserved in the Book of Kings; six in Chronicles; and one in the Assyrian sources.

[2] For the conjecture that the schism occurred in 937, see: Curtis, 401; and recently, Hughes, 191. For the assumption that the schism took place in 922, see: Albright 1963, 116–117. Lewy, 32, is of the opinion that the schism occurred in 921/20.

[3] See Tadmor 1962, 261–262, and the comparative table.

the majority of the data regarding the years of reign are accurate (but not the synchronisms); while those championing the later date based their assumption on the Egyptian or Tyrean chronology and amended many Biblical data. The time of the schism cannot, however, be based on either of these external chronologies (see below), rather the year of the schism is to be calculated retroactively from 853 (the battle of Qarqar, in which Ahab was a participant), or from 841 (the offering of tribute to Assyria by Jehu). If all the chronological data for this period appearing in the Book of Kings are accurate, then it follows that the schism occurred in 931/30 BCE (on the assumption that the system of counting in Israel was antedating, while postdating was in use in Judah; and also, that there was an interval of six months between the beginning of the year in Israel and that of the year in Judah).

It is likely that the death of Solomon was soon followed by the coronation in Jerusalem of his son Rehoboam, and the coronation of Jeroboam as king of Israel by the congregation ("עדה").[4] The Biblical testimonies indicate that Jeroboam returned to the land of Israel after the death of Solomon ("and he was in Egypt until the death of Solomon"—I Kings 11:40), and other passages report that he returned to the land for the events in Shechem (I Kings 12:2–3; II Chronicles 10:2–3; 12); while I Kings 12:20 indicates that Jeroboam was called to assume the kingship only after the schism was a *fait accompli*. Nevertheless, some researchers are of the opinion that the years of the reign of Jeroboam were counted from year 39 of Solomon, about one year before the coronation of Rehoboam.[5] This hypothesis, however, is baseless, and is merely a forced attempt to resolve a presumed

[4] For the term "עדה" (congregation) in I Kings 12:20, see: H. Reviv, "History and Historiography during the time of the Kingdom: Toward an Understanding of the term ʿEdah in I Kings 12:20," *Zion* 50 (1985), 59–63 (Hebrew).

[5] The hypothesis was first put forth by Thilo in his dissertation (M. Thilo, *Die Chronologie des Alten Testaments*, Bremen 1917, 20), and was accepted by a number of researchers, including Lewy (32), Begrich (138), Mowinckel (266–267, 271), and Jepsen (39). These researchers argue that in both kingdoms the years were counted by the antedating system, and that the new year began, both in Israel and in Judah, on 1 Tishri. In their view, if Rehoboam and Jeroboam were invested at the same time, then year 17 of Rehoboam (= year 1 of Abijam) would be year 17 of Jeroboam. Since, however, they sought to maintain that Abijam was crowned in year 18 of Jeroboam (I Kings 15:1), they were forced to admit that year 17 of Rehoboam was year 18 of Jeroboam, and consequently year 1 of Rehoboam was year 2 of Jeroboam. This led to the conclusion that Jeroboam counted the years of his reign from the last year of Solomon, i.e., ca. one year before the coronation of Rehoboam. Cf. Gray 1964, 70. For criticism of this proposal, see: H. Tadmor, "Jeroboam Son of Nabat," *EB* 3 (1958), 775 (Hebrew).

discrepancy. It may be assumed that the year of the schism was that of the coronation of Jeroboam, which corresponds well with all the Biblical data, if the year in Israel began six months before that of Judah.

It is likely that in the beginning of his reign Jeroboam established 1 Tishri as the beginning of the year in his realm (instead of 1 Nisan, which apparently marked the new year in Judah). At that time he apparently also changed the system of counting in Israel, preferring antedating, which was in practice in Egypt, to postdating, which was in use in Judah. The purpose of these changes, like the other changes which he instituted, was to emphasize the independent status of the kingdom of Israel; and to deepen the division between Israel and Judah, to enable the creation of two distinct entities with different cultic centers and ritual symbols which would develop disparate primal traditions, celebrate their festivals at different times, and live their daily lives in accordance with different calendars.[6] If these changes did in fact take place at the beginning of the reign of Jeroboam, then his second year began in the autumn of 930, while the second year of Rehoboam began only half a year later (see table 1 – p. 24).

The campaign of Shishak began in the fifth year of Rehoboam (I Kings 14:25; II Chronicles 12:2), which probably was the calendar year 926/5 BCE.[7] Albright, relying upon the Egyptian chronology, established the time of the campaign in 918.[8] Kitchen, however, had

---

[6] For the change of the new year by Jeroboam, see: Talmon 1958, 54 ff.; Yeivin, 86.

[7] For the time of the campaign of Shishak, see: Thiele, 55; Miller, 276; Kitchen, 295; Donner, 389; Barnes, 70–89 idem, *Studies in the Chronology of the Divided Monarchy of Israel*, Atlanta 1991, 57–71.

[8] Albright 1953, 4 ff.; idem 1956, 23 ff.; Bright, 233. Rowton attempted to base Albright's Biblical chronology on the Tyrean chronology (M. B. Rowton, "The Date of the Founding of Solomon's Temple," *BASOR* 119 [1950], 20–22), but his approach is basically flawed. The Tyrean chronology is mainly based on the data cited by Josephus in the name of Menander of Ephesus (see Liver, 190 and n. 5). Josephus provides two Tyrean-Israelite synchronisms: (1) the founding of the Temple of Solomon in the eleventh year (*Antiquities* 8:62) or in the twelfth year of Hyram I king of Tyre (*Against Apion*, 1:126); (2) the establishment of the Temple of Solomon 143 years and 8 months before the establishment of Carthage (*Against Apion*, loc. cit.). These two synchronisms are actually one and the same, for the second datum is merely a calculation made by Josephus, who subtracted from the sum total of the years of reign that passed from the crowning of Hiram to the establishment of Carthage (155 years, 8 months) the first datum, that Solomon's Temple was founded in year 11 or 12 of Hiram. The question arises of the reliability of these data. Can they serve as the basis for the time of the schism and the chronology of the kings of Tyre? The data cited by Josephus were undoubtedly deficient and erroneous. Among the various proposals concerning this issue, that of F. M. Cross, Jr. is to be preferred (see the recent work by Barnes, 40–69 and loc. cit. the list of additional

already demonstrated that Albright's arguments were insubstantial,[9] and that the Biblical chronology could not be based on Egyptian chronological data. To the contrary, the Biblical synchronism placing the campaign of Shishak in year 5 of Rehoboam may aid in determining the times of the Egyptian rulers during this period. Consequently, if the campaign was conducted in the penultimate year of Shishak,[10] then his coronation may be determined ca. 945, and his death ca. 924.[11]

Rehoboam probably died in 914, the seventeenth year of his reign and year 18 of Jeroboam (I Kings 14:21; 15:1; II Chronicles 12:13; 13:1).[12] Abijam ruled ca. three years (914–911) and died in year 20 of Jeroboam (I Kings 15:9).[13] In year 2 of Asa (909), Jeroboam died, in his twenty-second year (I Kings 14:20), and his son Nadab ascended

---

literature). Cross' proposal may serve as the basis for a tentative reconstruction of the Tyrean chronology, which in turn is likely to correspond to the Biblical chronology. Under no circumstances, however, is this to be regarded as indisputable testimony regarding the time of the schism, for any reconstruction of the original text is merely an assumption; and any reconstruction of the time framework of the kings of Tyre based on an estimated reconstruction of the text will be merely an assumption based on an assumption. Accordingly, there is no basis for the claim by Albright and his school that the Tyrean chronology constitutes proof establishing the schism in 922. Josephus apparently copied from reliable sources, but as time passed the data were corrupted, and can no longer serve as unquestionable testimony (in contrast with the Assyrian synchronisms, which are based on Assyrian sources). A proposed reconstruction of the original Tyrean kings' list and the chronological table of the kings of Tyre appear below in appendix F.

[9] Kitchen, 181.

[10] For the determination of the campaign in the last year or in the penultimate year of Shishak, see: Kitchen, 73–75 and loc. cit. for additional literature. But cf. D. B. Redford, *Egypt, Canaan and Israel*, Princeton, NJ 1992, 312.

[11] The chronology of the XXIInd Dynasty in Egypt proposed by Kitchen (85 ff., 467) is the best suggested to the present. See also: M. L. Bierbrier, *The Late New Kingdom in Egypt (1300–664)*, Warminster 1975, 54 ff.

[12] In contrast to the opinion of a majority of the researchers, Tadmor argues that the reign of Rehoboam spanned eighteen years (see Tadmor 1962, 298). This assumption is based on the hypothesis that the author of the Book of Kings rounded off the exact data he possessed, but there is no proof for this hypothesis. Also to be rejected is the conjecture restricting the reign of Rehoboam to only eight years (see: Albright 20, n. 14; idem 1963, 116).

[13] Most scholars are of the opinion that Abijam ruled for three years. According, however, to Tadmor's calculations, Abijam is to be allocated four years (Tadmor 1962, 299); Vogelstein suggests that Abijam's reign extended for nine years, six years as coregent and three years as an independent monarch (Vogelstein, 20–21 and n. 71). This claim is based on a manuscript of the Septuagint (i), which maintains in its translation of I Kings 15:2 that Abijam ruled "six and three years." This strange formulation apparently is nothing more than a corrupted conglomeration of MT (three) and a version from some of the Lucianic manuscripts (six). Similarly corrupted is version A which counts sixteen years to Abijam (see below, Chapter Eight). For the assumption that Abijam ruled six years, see: Hughes, 189–190, 275–276.

the throne in his stead.[14] During the short reign of Nadab, which lasted ca. a single year (909–908), siege was laid to the Philistine city of Gibbethon, during the course of which Nadab was murdered by Baasha, in the third year of Asa (I Kings 15:27–28, 33; see table 3).

The chronology of the time of Asa is a complicated and controversial subject. The difficulties in the creation of a chronological framework for this period ensue mainly from the discrepancies between the testimony of the Book of Kings and the chronological data included in Chronicles. The information in the Book of Kings regarding the kingdom of Asa is sparse, and is not connected with any specific period within the time of his reign (I Kings 15:9–24). It is unclear when the ritual purification was conducted, or when the mother of the king was removed. Similarly, there is no mention of the time of the Asa-Baasha war, in the wake of which Aram invaded Israel. The only two chronological markers in the Book of Kings relating to Judaean history during the time of Asa are of a general nature: the first indicates that there was war between Asa and Baasha "all their days" (I Kings 15:16, 32), and the other, that Asa was diseased in his feet "in the time of his old age" (ibid., v. 23). The Book of Kings, in contrast, contains eight precise chronological indicators enabling us to determine the time of seven events central to the history of the kingdom of Israel that took place during the reign of Asa (the date of the coronation of six of the seven Israelite kings who ruled during the time of Asa, along with the year of the death of Tibni—I Kings 15:25, 28, 33; 16:8, 10, 15, 22–23, 29).

Three chapters are required for the extremely detailed description in Chronicles of Asa's reign (II Chronicles 14–16). The Chronicler

---

[14] II Chronicles 13:20 states that Jeroboam died of an illness during the time of Abijam. This report contradicts the chronological datum in I Kings 14:20, which is not cited in Chronicles, that Jeroboam ruled for twenty-two years. The chronological data in the Book of Kings indicate that the version of the Chronicler is not to be preferred. Advancing the death of Jeroboam before that of Abijam may possibly ensue from the difficulty of the Chronicler in explaining the death of Abijam, the young and righteous king, a relatively short time after his coronation, for no sin of his own, close to his victory over the wicked Jeroboam, and two years before the death of the latter (Abijam and his grandfather Solomon are the only two kings to whom the Chronicler does not attribute any sin). Jeroboam's defeat and his death could easily be interpreted as punishment for the sin of the schism, but this example is not to be presented as an example of immediate divine action against the sinner (so Japhet, 120), for even in the Chronicler's view more than eighteen years elapsed between the schism and Jeroboam's defeat and death (the synchronistic datum brought in I Kings 15:1—the coronation of Abijam in year 18 of Jeroboam—is cited by the Chronicler in II Chronicles 13:1. This is the only quoted synchronism appearing in

omitted all the chronological details provided by the Book of Kings (except for the count of the years of Asa), proposing instead an alternative system of data of which no mention is made in the Book of Kings. The following is the order of events during the reign of Asa suggested by Chronicles: (1) until the tenth year of Asa "the land was quiet" (ibid, 13:23; 14:4–5); (2) in year 15 of Asa (in the third month) the people gathered together in Jerusalem and renewed the covenant with the Lord (15:10); (3) between these two events (but near to the second event),[15] the author includes a description of the war of Zerah (14:8–14), in the wake of which Asa conducted a ritual purification of broad scope (15:8 ff.); (4) this is followed by a period of peace which continues until year 35 of Asa (15:19); (5) the Asa-Baasha war erupts in year 36 of Asa (16:1); (6) in his thirty-ninth year, Asa becomes ill in his feet (16:12); (7) ca. two years later, in the forty-first year of his reign, Asa dies (16:13).

It is possible that some of the events which are mentioned in Chronicles but which do not appear in the Book of Kings, such as: the campaign of Zerah, or the internal opposition to Jehoshaphat's policy and the response of the king of Judah to this dissent, are not fictions invented by the author of Chronicles.[16] On the other hand, the chronological framework he proposes is an artificial and insubstantial construction.[17] This is especially true regarding his determining of

Chronicles). For the preference of the testimonies in the Book of Kings regarding the deaths of Jeroboam and of Abijam to the testimony of the Chronicler, see: Curtis and Madsen, 377; Rudolph, 239; Myers, 81; Japhet, loc. cit.; Williamson, 255.

[15] The proximity of the two events is obviously artificial, and does not reflect any historical reality. This closeness is attained by mentioning the offering of the plunder presumably taken from Zerah during the gala assembly in Jerusalem. But the Chronicler does not show any finesse on this subject, and he makes no attempt to match the list of spoils he copied from his early source to the booty which was offered (cf. 14:14–15:11).

[16] For the campaign of Zerah, see: Bright, 234–235; Yeivin, 90–91, 234, n. 42; Kitchen, 309; Welten, 129–140; Myers, 85; Williamson, 263–266; and lately, Na'aman 1987, 263 ff., 270 ff.

[17] See the extensive treatment of this in: W. Rudolph, "Der Aufbau der Asa-Geschichte (2 Chr. XIV–XVI)," *VT* 2 (1952), 367–371; and his commentary on Chronicles, 239 ff. See also: S. Japhet, *I and II Chronicles: A Commentary* (*OTL*), London 1993, 702 ff. The description of the last five years of Asa constitutes an instructive example of the adaptation of history according to the principles of reward and punishment. The Chronicler lists a series of sins and punishments, each sin with its punishment, appearing three times in the pattern of one sin leading to another. It is this system which apparently dictates the chronological framework. The proximity of events is of great importance to the Chronicler. Until his thirty-fifth year, Asa is presented as a perfectly righteous king. He removes the foreign altars and the high

the Asa-Baasha war in year 36 of Asa, which is an impossibility. This datum is not supported by the Bible or by the extra-Biblical sources. To the contrary, it contradicts all the Biblical synchronisms for this period, and it may be assumed to be erroneous.[18] It is similarly doubtful whether the datum in Chronicles establishing the war in year 36 of Asa should not in fact read 26.[19]

The order of the events in the time of Asa and Baasha may be reconstructed as follows: the war between Israel and Judah during the time of Baasha apparently continued for many years. It took the form of border incidents accompanied by territorial changes, to the advantage of one or the other sides, in the contested territory between the two kingdoms. Support for this conjecture is provided by I Kings 15:16, 32: "And there was war between Asa and Baasha king of Israel

---

places, seeks the Lord, and commands his people to observe the Torah and its commandments (II Chronicles 14:1–4). In response, he is granted peace, prosperity, and victories over his enemies. A change takes place in his thirty-sixth year. Baasha attacks Judah, but this time Asa does not call upon his God as he had previously when Zerah marched against him, he rather turns to the king of Aram for help. For this sin a double punishment is inflicted upon Asa: "Because you have relied upon the king of Aram, and have not relied upon the Lord your God, therefore is the host of the king of Aram escaped out of your hand" (II Chronicles 16:7). Furthermore: "Herein you have done foolishly; for from henceforth you shall have wars" (ibid., v. 9). The first transgression leads to an additional sin: not only does Asa not admit his error and repent, he imprisons Hanani the seer and persecutes the people: "And Asa oppressed some of the people the same time" (ibid., v. 10). As punishment for his sins Asa is stricken with an illness in his feet in proximity to his wrongdoing, less than three years after his first transgressions (year 39 of his reign—ibid., v. 12). Once again Asa sins. This time, by seeking the physicians, and not the Lord. He is severely punished this time: he does not recover from his illness, which proves to be fatal. For these events, see: R. B. Dillard, *2 Chronicles* (*WBC*), Waco 1987, 112–128; cf. Halpern, Chronology, 132 ff. D. A. Glatt, *Chronological Displacements in Biblical and Related Literatures*, Atlanta 1993, 55–74.

[18] Albright, assuming that this datum is accurate, conjectured that all the Biblical synchronisms for this period are erroneous (Albright, 20 ff.). For criticism of this view, see the extended discussion in Thiele, 60 ff.

[19] For the hypothesis that the number 36 is a corruption of 26, see: H. Tadmor, "Asa son of Abijah," *EB* 1 (1950), 469–470 (Hebrew); Mazar, Canaan and Israel, 251; Schedl 1962a, 112. For a discussion of this issue, see also: Curtis and Madsen, 387–388; Williamson, 255–258. Some researchers determine this war in year 16 of Asa. See: C. F. Keil, *The Books of Chronicles*, Edinburgh 1872, 367; E. Bertheau, *Die Bücher der Chronik*, Leipzig 1873 (2nd ed.), 315–316; Kleber, 173, and others. They maintain that the number 36 refers to the schism. This hypothesis is difficult and should not be accepted, for it is stated explicitly that this count is "of the reign of Asa," and there is no support for the assumption that there was a count from the schism.

all their days," and possibly also in two testimonies in Chronicles, which indicate that Asa (and not Abijam) conquered cities in the hill country of Ephraim (15:8; 17:2).[20] The war apparently took a decisive turn after Baasha succeeded in forming an alliance with Aram of Damascus; following this agreement, a portion of the Israelite standing army, which was encamped in the north to forestall an Aramean attack, was transferred to the south, where this shift brought about a significant change in the war against Judah. Baasha restored to Israel all its territories held by the Southern Kingdom, and even posed a threat to Jerusalem. The Israelite army was now encamped at Ramah (the present-day er-Ram), two hours' march from the Judaean capital (I Kings 15:17). The Israelite advances and the threat to Jerusalem impelled Asa to seek the aid of Ben-hadad I, king of Aram of Damascus. The latter seized this opportunity to attack Israel, and he smote the cities of northeast Galilee (ibid., 15:20). Asa's appeal to the Aramean king was granted only because it coincided with Aramean interests. Baasha, who miscalculated regarding his relations with Aram (or who had violated the terms of his agreement with his neighbor to the northeast?) was forced to stop his war against Judah and move most of his army northward to halt the Aramean advance. The withdrawal of the Israelite army in turn enabled Judah to improve its positions and set the border along the Mizpah-Geba line (ibid., 15:22). The exact time of this war cannot be determined, nor is it clear if this was the last clash between the two kingdoms, and if Israel was reconciled to the new reality that had come into being.

Baasha apparently died in 885, the twenty-fourth year of his reign, and was succeeded by his son Elah.[21] In the latter's reign the siege

---

[20] Curtis and Madsen (385), following other commentators, assumed that this was a simple mistake by the Chronicler, who exchanged Asa for Abijam. This hypothesis, however, is not necessarily the only possibility. To the contrary, it must be stressed that these testimonies are not part of the chronological scheme proposed by the Chronicler for the time of Asa, nor do they serve his purposes. Accordingly, it is more likely that they are not a figment of his imagination; indeed, they may possibly indicate the ongoing border clashes between Israel and Judah. For a view emphasizing the historical reliability of these reports, see: Bright, 235; Myers, 88–89; Williamson, 269–270.

[21] Scholarly opinion is unanimous that Baasha's reign extended for twenty-four years. In contrast, Miller (280–288; and recently Miller and Hayes, 251) conjectured that Baasha ruled only seventeen years, and accordingly, he proposed shortening the reign of Asa to thirty years. These hypotheses are based partly on the data of the Septuagint that maintain, e.g., that Elah son of Baasha was invested in the twentieth year of Asa, and not in his twenty-sixth year. Hayes and Miller supposed that it is preferable to amend the Biblical data than to assume their accuracy and

of Gibbethon was renewed (probably in the spring of 884, year 27 of Asa), in the course of which Zimri murdered Elah in Tirzah, only about a year after he ascended the throne (see table 5 – p. 28).

There is a marked similarity between these events and the circumstances leading to the end of the dynasty of Jeroboam.

The short reign of Zimri indicates the speed of the response by Omri, the commander of the army. As soon as the report of Elah's murder arrived, Omri was crowned in the camp at Gibbethon (I Kings 16:15 ff.). The siege of the Philistine city was lifted, and the army marched against Tirzah, Zimri's capital, and besieged it (ibid., v. 17). The military detachments which were garrisoned in the city and which were loyal to Zimri apparently surrendered, and Zimri took his own life in the royal palace, about seven days after he was crowned there (ibid., v. 18). A movement opposing Omri's rule came into existence after the death of Zimri, and many ("half of the people"—ibid., v. 21) preferred Tibni the son of Ginath, "to make him king." Nothing is known about Tibni, or whether he was crowned and ruled parts of the Israelite kingdom at the beginning of the reign of Omri. The Biblical text indicates that this was the intent of his followers, and that "half of the people" did not recognize Omri's authority, possibly even engaging in armed resistance for a number of years.[22]

The year of Omri's coronation and the number of years he reigned are the subject of debate. It is related, on the one hand, that Omri ascended the throne in year 27 of Asa, and that he ruled until year 38 of Asa, the year in which Ahab was crowned (ibid., 16:29), therefore ruling for twelve years, as is stated explicitly in v. 23. On the other hand, however, this and the preceding verse seemingly indicate that Omri was invested in year 31 of Asa: ". . . so Tibni died, and Omri reigned. In the thirty and first year of Asa king of Judah began Omri to reign over Israel, and reigned twelve years." This report presumably contradicts the passage in vv. 15–16, which indicates that Omri was enthroned in the camp at Gibbethon as soon as word was received of Zimri's rebellion: "And the people that were encamped heard say:

---

attempt to strengthen them by assuming the existence of coregencies (228). Their hypotheses also rely upon the conjecture of Albright, based upon the Egyptian chronology, that the schism occurred after 925. But the Biblical chronology is not to be based upon the Egyptian; nor are the Septuagint versions to be used as support (see Chapter Eight).

[22] For Tibni and his struggle with Omri, see: H. Tadmor, "Tibni," *EB* 8 (1982), 413 (Hebrew) and loc. cit. for additional literature.

'Zimri has conspired' . . . wherefore all Israel made Omri, the captain of the host, king over Israel that day in the camp." These conflicting testimonies raise the question: in which year was Omri invested, in year 27 or in year 31 of Asa? Also, did he reign for twelve years, or less? Among the different views expressed on this point, to be preferred is the assumption that Omri ascended the throne in year 27 of Asa, and ruled for twelve years, until year 38 of Asa.[23] The chronological statement: "In the thirty and first year of Asa king of Judah" refers to the death of Tibni and not to the installation of Omri, and the words "Omri began to reign" in this passage emphasize Omri's victory and his continued rule over Israel after the defeat of Tibni. Some error apparently was introduced into vv. 22–23; the original version may possibly have read: "So Tibni died, and Omri reigned in the thirty and first year of Asa king of Judah. [In the twenty and seventh year of Asa king of Judah] began Omri to reign over Israel for twelve years in Tirzah. . . ."[24]

In the seventh year of Omri (879/8), the seat of the government was moved from Tirzah to Samaria (I Kings 16:23). Under Omri, Israel conquered the plain of Madaba (Mesha inscription, ll. 7–9), but the time of this event cannot be determined with certainty.[25]

Omri ruled for twelve years, until 873, when he died in the spring/summer of this year, in the first half of year 38 of Asa. The few months

---

[23] This is the opinion of the majority of the researchers. See: Lewy, 22 ff., 32; Mowinckel, 249; Tadmor 1962, 294–297, 302; Schedl 1962a, 100 ff. According to Septuagint L, Omri ruled from year 31 of Asa to year 2 of Jehoshaphat. Tibni ruled before Omri, from years 27 to 31 of Asa (and therefore it is stated in Septuagint L: "And Tibni died, and Omri reigned *instead of Tibni*"), with the consequent change of all the chronological data pertaining to this period (see the detailed discussion of this subject below, Chapter Eight). Kleber (21–22, 173–174) followed the Septuagint and counted the years of Omri beginning from year 31 of Asa, assuming an interregnum between years 27 and 31 of Asa. Begrich (155), who adopted the concept of the interregnum, was forced to shorten Omri's reign to eight years. For a similar view, see: Donner, 399. Tadmor has recently raised once again the possibility of the interregnum in this period (Tadmor, above, n. 22, 413); also see: Andersen, 81–82; idem 1989, 37–38.

[24] Alternatively, the following emendation may be proposed: "So Tibni died, and Omri reigned in the thirty and first year of Asa king of Judah. [And the time that] Omri reigned over Israel, twelve years in Tirzah . . ."; cf.: "And the time that Jehu reigned over Israel in Samaria was twenty and eight years" (II Kings 10:36); and "And the days which Jeroboam reigned over Israel were two and twenty years" (I Kings 14:20).

[25] For the time of the conquests of Omri in the plain of Madaba, see: G. Wallis, "Die virzig Jahre der achten Zeile der Mesa-Inschrift," *ZDPV* 81 (1965), 180–186 and loc. cit. for additional literature; A. Lemaire, "Notes d'épigraphie nord-ouest sémitique," *Syria* 64 (1987), 210–214.

remaining until 1 Tishri 873 were regarded as the first year of Ahab (I Kings 16:29; see table 6 – p. 29). If Ahab was crowned in year 38 of Asa, i.e., ca. four years before the death of Asa, and Jehoshaphat began to rule in year 4 of Ahab (I Kings 22:41), then Jehoshaphat was not crowned during his father's lifetime, but only after the latter's death, in 870, in the second half of year 4 of Ahab (see table 7).[26]

The alliance between the line of Omri and the Davidic dynasty was made (at the very latest) at the beginning of the reign of Jehoshaphat, for II Kings 8:26 indicates that Ahaziah, the son of Jehoram and Athaliah, was twenty-two years old when he ascended the throne (843/2),[27] i.e., he was born ca. 865, and consequently Jehoram and Athaliah were wed no later than 866, which was year 3 or 4 of Jehoshaphat (= year 8 or 9 of Ahab). This date cannot be advanced excessively, for Jehoram was 32 when he ascended the throne; consequently, he was born ca. 883 and was approximately 17 years old when he married (if the wedding was held in 866). The nuptial alliance between the two dynasties may possibly have constituted an additional step in the process of rapprochement between Israel and Judah that had begun during the time of Omri and Asa.[28]

---

[26] Many researchers are of the opinion that Jehoshaphat was crowned during the time of his father Asa, thus Lewy, 32; Begrich, 155; Vogelstein, 21 and Table II; Tadmor 1962, 296, 301; Pavlovsky and Vogt, 347; Thiele 1983, 96, etc. A majority of these scholars supposed that Jehoshaphat was crowned in consequence of his father's illness, and the coregency continued for two to three years.

[27] II Chronicles 22:2 indicates that Ahaziah was 42 years old when he ascended the throne. This number, however, is patently baseless, for his father Jehoram was ca. 39 when he died. For this issue, see: Myers, 125; Williamson, 310.

[28] For the conjectured alliance between Israel and Judah during the time of Asa and Omri, see: B. Mazar, "Omri," *EB* 6 (1972), 303 ff. (Hebrew).

Table 1

Judah 1 Nissan (postdating)	*Year* BCE	*Israel* 1 Tishri (antedating)
THE SCHISM		
Rehoboam Accession year	930	*Jeroboam* 1
1	929	2
2	928	3
3	927	4
4	926	5
5	925	6
6	924	7
7	923	8
8	922	9
9	921	10
10		

Table 2

Judah	*Year BCE*	*Israel*
Rehoboam 10	921	*Jeroboam*
11	920	11
12	919	12
13	918	13
14	917	14
15	916	15
16	915	16
17 *Abijam* Accession year	914	17
1	913	18
2	912	19

Table 3

Judah	*Year BCE*	*Israel*
Abijam 2	912	*Jeroboam* 20
3 *Asa* Accession year	911	
1	910	21
2	909	22 *Nadab* 1
3	908	2 *Baasha* 1
4	907	2
5	906	3
6	905	4
7	904	5
8	903	6
9	902	7

Table 4

Judah	*Year BCE*	*Israel*
Asa 9	902	*Baasha* 8
10	901	
11	900	9
12	899	10
13	898	11
14	897	12
15	896	13
16	895	14
17	894	15
18	893	16
19	892	17

Table 5

Judah	*Year BCE*	*Israel*
Asa 19	892	*Baasha* 18
20	891	19
21	890	20
22	889	21
23	888	22
24	887	23
25	886	24 *Elah* 1
26	885	2 *Zimri* *Omri* Tibni 1
27	884	2 Tibni
28	883	3 Tibni
29	882	

Table 6

Judah	*Year BCE*	*Israel*
Asa 29	882	*Omri*
30	881	4 Tibni
31	880	5 Tibni
32	879	6
33	878	7
34	877	8
35	876	9
36	875	10
37	874	11 12
38	873	*Ahab* 1
39	872	2

Table 7

Judah	*Year BCE*	*Israel*
Asa 39	872	*Ahab* 3
40	871	
41 *Jehoshaphat* Accession year	870	4
1	869	5
2	868	6
3	867	7
4	866	8
5	865	9
6	864	10
7	863	11
8	862	12

Table 8

Judah	*Year BCE*	*Israel*
Jehoshaphat 8	862	*Ahab* 13
9	861	14
10	860	15
11	859	16
12	858	17
13	857	18
14	856	19
15	855	20
16	854	21

CHAPTER THREE

ISRAEL AND JUDAH FROM THE DEATH OF AHAB TO THE REVOLT OF JEHU

The time frame of the short period from the death of King Ahab of Israel to the revolt of Jehu is one of the most difficult and complicated subjects in Biblical chronology. The Biblical data are contradictory and appear to be erroneous. II Kings 3:1 indicates that Joram son of Ahab (henceforth: Joram) was crowned in year 18 of Jehoshaphat while II Kings 1:17 states that he ascended the throne in year 2 of Jehoram son of Jehoshaphat (henceforth: Jehoram). This datum can presumably be reconciled if it is assumed that year 2 of Jehoram = year 18 of his father Jehoshaphat, i.e., that Jehoram was crowned in the seventeenth year of his father, and Joram in the eighteenth year of Jehoshaphat (= year 2 of Jehoram). The count of the years of reign, however, contradicts this possibility, for Jehoram and his son Ahaziah reigned only a total of nine years, while Joram's reign spanned twelve years. II Kings 9:24–27 attests that Joram and Ahaziah were murdered at the same time, and thus the years of reign of Jehoram and his son Ahaziah had to total thirteen, if Joram was in fact crowned in year 2 of Jehoram. The coronation of Joram in the second year of Jehoram also contradicts (a) the datum stating that the latter was crowned in year 5 of Joram (II Kings 8:16); and (b) the contradictory testimonies indicating that Ahaziah was crowned in year 11 or year 12 of Joram (II Kings 8:25; 9:29).

The confrontation of the Biblical data with the external synchronisms apparently raises additional difficulties. The Assyrian sources indicate that Ahab was one of the leaders of the alliance of kings that fought against Assyria in Qarqar in year 6 of Shalmaneser III (= 853; the battle was waged no earlier than the month of Tammuz in this year).[1] Less than thirteen years later, in year 18 of Shalmaneser III

[1] For the inscriptions of Shalmaneser III, see: D. D. Luckenbill, *Ancient Records of Assyria and Babylonia*, I, New York 1926, par. 611, 646–647, 686, 691; E. Michel, "Die Assur-Texte Shalmanassars III (858–824)," *WO* 1/2 (1947), 57–71; idem, s. t., *WO* 1/4 (1949), 255–271; Michel, 27 ff., 137 ff., 221 ff.; Cameron, 6–26; F. Safar, "A Further Text of Shalmaneser III from Assur," *Sumer* 7 (1951), 3–21; P. Hulin, "The Inscriptions on the Carved-Throne-Base of Shalmaneser III," *Iraq* 25 (1963),

(841/40), Jehu offered tribute to the Assyrian king.[2] According to the Biblical testimony, the interval between 853 and 841/40 comprises four secondary periods: the last part of Ahab's reign, from the battle of Qarqar to his death (henceforth: A); the two years of the reign of Ahaziah; the twelve years of Joram; the beginning of the reign of Jehu, from his coronation to the presentation of the tribute to Assyria (henceforth: B). The count of these years of reign totals more than 14 (A + 2 + 12 + B), while less than 13 years elapsed from the battle of Qarqar and the submission of Jehu.

An examination of all the theories which have attempted to reconstruct the time frame of this period (more than twenty main proposals) reveals the impossibility of reconciling all the Biblical and external data; nevertheless, as will be demonstrated below, the majority can be confirmed, and they may possibly be based on a reliable tradition reflective of the reality.

48–69; H. Tadmor, "Assyria and the West: the Ninth Century and its Aftermath," in: H. Goedicke and J. J. M. Roberts (eds.), *Unity and Diversity*, Baltimore and London 1975, 36 ff.; T. J. Schneider, *A New Analysis of the Royal Annals of Shalmaneser III* (diss.) University of Pennsylvania 1991.

[2] It has been conjectured that the Israelite king mentioned in the inscriptions of Shalmaneser III, in the eighteenth year of his reign, is not Jehu, but rather a descendent of Omri: P. Kyle-McCarter, "'Yaw, son of Omri,' A Philological note on Israelite Chronology," *BASOR* 216 (1974), 5–7. The following are the arguments raised against the reading "Jehu son of Omri": (1) it is difficult to read ia-u-a as "Jehu"; (2) Jehu is not the son of Omri; (3) the chronological difficulty is created by this identification (see the discussion, below). In Kyle-McCarter's opinion, the word "YHW" appearing in the Assyrian inscriptions is merely a hypocoristicon of "Jehoram," the son of Ahab and grandson of Omri; consequently, the rebellion of Jehu does not have to be pushed back to 841, but rather can be dated two years later, thereby reconciling all the Biblical and external chronological data for the period between the death of Ahab and the revolt of Jehu. This hypothesis is not to be accepted, for the following reasons: (1) the reading of ia-u-a as Jehu is precise, and apparently indicates a consonantal *alef*. The transliteration of Jehu is ia-u, thus the name of King Jehoahaz (Ahaz) of Judah is Ia-u-ha-zi, and similarly the name of the land of Judah in the Assyrian inscriptions: Ia-u-di; (2) Jehu is referred to in this inscription as "son of Omri," because this was the name of the kingdom of Israel for the Assyrians; similarly, the city of Abel is mentioned in the inscriptions of Tiglath-pileser III as a city "on the border of the land of the House of Omri," and the districts of the kingdom of Israel which were conquered by the Assyrians are called in these inscriptions: "districts of the land of the House of Omri," more than a century after the rebellion of Jehu. See: Tadmor, Jehu, 477; M. Weippert, "Jau(a) mar Ḫumrî—Joram oder Jehu von Israel?," *VT* 28 (1978), 113–118; (3) regarding the chronological problems which seemingly are resolved by the reading of Jehoram in place of Jehu, it should be noted that this difficulty is only a seeming one, and the Biblical and external data for this period can be reconciled even with the reading of Jehu. For this issue, see the discussion below; cf.: E. Thiele, "An Additional Chronological Note on 'Yaw, Son of 'Omri,'" *BASOR* 222 (1976), 19–23; idem 1977, 29–30; Halpern, Yaua, son of Omri, 81–85.

The circumstances surrounding the death of Ahab are unclear. According to the Bible, he fell in battle at Ramoth-gilead (I Kings 22:34–37). An analysis of the Biblical and external chronological data for this period indicates that Ahab's last battle apparently took place in the winter of 853/2, ca. 11 years before the revolt of Jehu. A few researchers have argued that Ahab died a natural death, and that the battle of Ramoth-gilead took place in the time of his son Joram, in the time of Jehoahaz the son of Jehu, or in the time of Joash son of Jehoahaz; at any rate, not in the time of Ahab.[3] Their hypothesis is based on the following arguments: (1) during the years 853–845 Israel was joined to Aram by an alliance, and it is unlikely that they fought each other during this period; (2) the description in the Book of Kings of Ahab's reign ends with the formula: "So Ahab lay with his fathers" (I Kings 22:40). This conclusion indicates that Ahab died a natural death, for this formula is not used if a king died in another fashion; (3) it cannot be assumed that Ahab sought to conquer a single city in Gilead when most of this region was in Israelite hands; (4) the similarity between the description of the death of Ahab and that of the death of his son Joram (cf.: I Kings 22:34–38 with II Kings 8:28–29; 9:24–26) indicates that the narrative of the death of Ahab is merely a corrupted version of the narrative of the death of his son Joram; (5) the description of the death of Ahab in I Kings 22 contradicts the divine message to Elijah in I Kings 21:29, which indicates that the Lord forgave Ahab because he repented.

These arguments are not compelling, and it may be assumed that Ahab did in fact fall in the battle of Ramoth-gilead. The reasons for the war were the "historical rights" of Israel to northern Gilead and the economic and military advantages possessed by this region. The formula "So Ahab lay with his fathers" itself is not decisive, because there

---

[3] Jepsen conjectured that the war was waged during the time of King Joash of Israel (A. Jepsen, "Israel und Damaskus," *AfO* 14 [1942], 155–157). Miller, in contrast, argues that an echo of two battles is preserved in I Kings 22: one from the time of Joram son of Ahab, and the other from the time of Jehoahaz son of Jehu. In his opinion, the battles described in I Kings 20 also are from the time of Jehoahaz son of Jehu (J. M. Miller, "The Rest of the Acts of Jehoahaz (I Kings 20; 22:1–38)," *ZAW* 80 [1982], 337–342). For a similar opinion, see: E. Würthwein, "Zur Komposition von I Reg 22 1–38," *Das ferne und nahe Wort: Festschrift L. Rost*, Berlin 1967, 245–254; H. C. Schmitt, *Elisa: traditionsgeschichtliche Untersuchungen zur vorklassischen nordisraelitischen Prophetei*, Gütersloh 1972, 42–45; Weippert, op. cit., 118, n. 23; Herrmann, 215. See also: Noth, 236; Whitley, 137–152, esp. 148; M. F. Unger, *Israel and the Aramaeans of Damascus*, London 1957, 69–74, 154 ff.; Halpern and Vanderhoft, 230 ff.

are exceptions to every rule.[4] The similarity between the descriptions of the death of each king is not as great as these researchers presumed. The narrative of the wounding of Joram is not related. Ahab was wounded on the battlefield and died of this injury, while Joram was wounded twice: the first time in the fighting at Ramoth-gilead (but

[4] The formula: "RN lay with his fathers" appears in the book of Kings in the death and burial formulae of 22 of the 39 kings of Israel and Judah. It is accepted that these kings, with the exception of Ahab (and possibly also of Jehoiakim—see below) died a natural death, i.e., they were not assassinated, did not fall in battle, did not fall prey to illness or accident, nor were exiled (and died in exile). Seventeen of the remaining kings died unnatural deaths (the majority were murdered), and consequently the passage summing up their reign does not employ this formula (if they were assassinated by a conspirator, the following complex model is usually used: "And X conspired against him . . . and X smote him. . . . and X slew him . . . and X reigned in his stead"—I Kings 15:27–29; II Kings 12:21–22; 15:25, etc.). There are a number of exceptions to this rule. Uzziah was a leper "until the day of his death" (II Kings 15:5), but, nevertheless, it is said of him that he lay with his fathers (ibid., v. 7). It is related in II Chronicles 21:18–20 that King Jehoram of Judah was stricken with an incurable illness at the end of his days "and he died of sore diseases." Jehoram's relatively young age at his death (ca. 39) is likely to support the version of the Chronicler (see appendix C). In the Book of Kings, it is written that he lay with his fathers (II Kings 8:24). King Amaziah of Judah was murdered by his servants in Lachish (II Kings 14:19–21); although the passage concluding his reign does not state that he lay with his fathers, v. 22 (= II Chronicles 26:2) relates that Uzziah, who succeeded his father Amaziah, built Elath and restored it to Judah, "after that the king (= Amaziah) lay with his fathers." Although it is stated that Jehoiakim lay with his fathers, it is possible that he did not die a natural death: he was only 36 at the time of his death; Jeremiah prophesied about him that he would receive the burial of an ass, "drawn and cast forth beyond the gates of Jerusalem" (Jeremiah 22:19), and that his carcass "shall be cast out in the day to the heat, and in the night to the frost" (ibid., 36:30). MT of II Kings 24:6 makes no mention of the burial of Jehoiakim, in contrast with the fixed death and burial formulae of the kings of Israel and Judah who died a natural death, which usually contained three components: (1) "RN lay with his fathers"; (2) "and was buried in . . ." ("with his fathers" or "with the kings of Israel"); (3) "and X reigned in his stead." The passage concluding the reign of Jehoiakim lacks the second element of the model (Septuagint L, however, states that he was buried in the garden of Uzzah). This omission is especially conspicuous in light of the fact that the model concluding the history of the kings of Judah always mentions their burial, without distinguishing between kings who died a natural death and those who were assassinated or who fell in battle (with two exceptions: Athaliah, who apparently was not recognized as a queen, and Hezekiah. Septuagint L states regarding the latter: "And he was buried with his fathers in the City of David," and II Chronicles 32:33 contains the complete version, which may have been erroneously omitted from the Book of Kings: "and they buried him in the ascent of the sepulchres of the sons of David"). To these we must add the description in II Chronicles 36:6–7 of the conveyance to Babylon of Jehoiakim (for the description of the unnatural death of Jehoiakim, see: Josephus, *Antiquities* 10:97; see also: Genesis Rabbah 94:9; Leviticus Rabbah 19:6). For the death of Jehoiakim, see also: Malamat, 262. To the above-mentioned examples must be added the case of Ahab, of whom the Bible states that he lay with his fathers, despite his having fallen in battle. It is instructive that only in the case of Ahab does the Bible

did not die from this wound), and the second time, when Jehu smote Joram in his chariot and killed him. The partial resemblance is reflective of the reality. In northern Gilead there were protracted border incidents, which at times developed into battles which ended indecisively and which did not lead to significant territorial changes. This was the case in the battle at Ramoth-gilead in the time of Ahab, as in the battle in the time of his son Joram. Furthermore, there is no discrepancy between the description of the death of Ahab in I Kings 22 and the word of the Lord to Elijah in I Kings 21:28–29 and the prophecy of Elijah, ibid., vv. 19–22. Verse 29 states: "I will not bring the evil in his days; but in his son's days will I bring the evil *upon his house.*" This refers to the prophecy of Elijah, ibid., vv. 21–22: "Behold, I will bring evil upon you, and will utterly sweep you away, and will cut off from Ahab every man-child, and he that is shut up and he that is left at large in Israel. And I will make *your house* like the house of Jeroboam the son of Nabat, and like the house of Baasha the son of Ahijah". This decree against the line of Ahab is postponed, thanks to Ahab's repentance. Not so the prophecy regarding the personal fate of Ahab, which is fulfilled in its entirety; the author takes pains to emphasize this fact and to compare the two: the word of the Lord to Elijah, on the one hand, and, on the other hand, the realization of the prophecy and the punishment of Ahab, as an instance of measure for measure: "And the word of the Lord came to Elijah the Tishbite, saying: 'Arise, go down to meet Ahab . . . And you shall speak to him, saying: Thus says the Lord: In the place where dogs licked the blood of Naboth shall dogs lick your blood, even yours'" (I Kings 21:17–19)—"And the king was stayed up in his chariot against the Arameans, and died at even; and the blood ran out of the wound into the bottom of the chariot. . . . And they washed the chariot by the pool of Samaria; and the dogs licked his blood; the harlots also washed themselves there; according unto the word of the Lord which He spoke" (ibid., 22:35, 38).

use the verb "and he died," in addition to the formula "And he lay with his fathers." In practice, the Bible contains two versions of the death of Ahab: in I Kings 22:40 it is stated, "So Ahab lay with his fathers; and Ahaziah his son reigned in his stead," while v. 37 declares: "So the king died, and was brought to Samaria; and they buried the king in Samaria." In conclusion, it may be established that the statement that Ahab lay with his fathers is not the only exception to the above-mentioned rule, and certainly does not constitute proof that he did not fall in battle. For this topic see also: Begrich, 190 ff.; B. Alfring, "L'Expression שכב עם אבותיו" *Oudtestamentlische Studien* 2 (1943), 106–118; Halpern and Vanderhooft, 183 ff., 230 ff.

Nor is the sole mention of Ahab in chap. 22 of significance. It does not indicate that this was a later addition, just as nothing is to be learned from the only mention of Joram in II Kings 3.[5] I.e., Ahab did in fact lead his army to Ramoth-gilead, where he died in battle.

It is unclear when Ahaziah son of Ahab was crowned. There are two possibilities, neither of which is to be preferred (see table 9 – p. 44): (1) it may be surmised that Ahaziah was crowned after Ahab's death, at the end of year 17 of Jehoshaphat, and was king for two years of reign, which comprised approximately one calendar year. Joram was installed after Tishri 852, and his reign extended for 11 years (see table 9, possibility A; it is also possible that Joram was crowned by Ahaziah soon after the Latter's accident); (2) alternatively, it may be conjectured that Ahaziah was crowned in the spring of 853, in the beginning of the seventeenth year of Jehoshaphat, as the Israelites prepared to set out for the battle of Qarqar. The installation was meant to ensure the continuity of the dynasty and to maintain stability in the kingdom and in the province of Moab when the Israelite army marched northward, far from the boundaries of the kingdom, for the decisive war against Assyria. Ahaziah was fatally injured at the beginning of his short reign (as a sole sovereign), close to the death of his father Ahab in the battle of Ramoth-gilead (II Kings 1:2 ff.). Ahaziah's reign as sole monarch was short-lived, and began at the end of the seventeenth year of Jehoshaphat. Ahaziah died, and his brother Joram succeeded him in 852, at the beginning of the eighteenth year of Jehoshaphat (II Kings 3:1; see table 9, possibility B).[6]

Joram consequently was crowned in the autumn of 852 or the winter of 851, and he ruled until the winter of 842/1. It may reasonably be assumed that in his second year Jehoram son of Jehoshaphat was crowned (see the discussion, below). In the following six years two

[5] For the death of Ahab, see also: B. D. Napier, "The Omrides of Jesreel," *VT* 9 (1959), 374 ff. and loc. cit. for additional literature.

[6] II Chronicles 20:35–37 contains a description of Ahaziah and Jehoshaphat joining together to make ships to go to Tarshish. The description in the Book of Kings, which relates that the entire enterprise, from the outset, was a Judahite initiative, is to be preferred. There is no clear information as to when Jehoshaphat began this undertaking, undoubtedly a few years before his failure, and before the short reign of Ahaziah. Only after the ships were broken, possibly during their launching or their departure from the harbor of Ezion-geber—apparently due to a lack of technical skills in the construction or navigation of the ships—did Ahaziah offer to aid Jehoshaphat by sending (Phoenician?) advisors and sailors, but Jehoshaphat turned down this offer. This was not a project that began in the time of Ahaziah, but rather an Israelite response following the failure of Judah. This reaction is to be

kings reigned in Judah: Jehoshaphat and his son Jehoram. After the death of the former, for ca. two years the kings of Israel and of Judah bore the same name.[7] During the last months of Joram's reign, Judah was ruled by Ahaziah, the grandson of Jehoshaphat (see table 10 – p. 45).

It cannot be determined if Ahaziah was installed in the eleventh year of Joram (II Kings 9:29) or in his twelfth year (ibid., 8:25). This difficulty cannot be resolved by assuming that in Israel the years of reign of the kings of Judah were enumerated by the Israelite system, and that in Judah the years of the kings of Israel were counted by the Judahite system, as Thiele argued.[8] His hypothesis is too complicated and is improbable. It is difficult to assume that in each kingdom the years of reign of the other kingdom were counted in accordance with the local system. If this is the only way to reconcile all the contradictions between the Biblical data, it is preferable to assume that some of them are erroneous.

One scholarly opinion argues that Ahaziah was crowned in the twelfth year of Joram,[9] but the majority of researchers maintain that Ahaziah did not rule in year 11, and certainly not in year 12, since, in their opinion, Joram's rule did not extend for more than ten years.[10]

The chronological datum stating that Joram was crowned in the second year of Jehoram is at variance with the following Biblical testimonies: (1) the crowning of Joram in the eighteenth year of Jehoshaphat; (2) the installation of Jehoram in the fifth year of Joram; (3) Joram and Jehoshaphat setting out to war with Moab; (4) the count

---

understood on the background of the close alliance between the two kingdoms in this period. The assumptions that Ahaziah sought to take advantage of this opportunity to attain some economic privileges at the expense of Judah are baseless, as are the conjectures that this attests to a worsening of relations between the two kingdoms following the death of Ahab. Jehoshaphat's refusal did not ensue from his desire to maintain these privileges for himself, but rather reflected his intention not to continue with this undertaking in the light of his failure. See: Rudolph, 263; Reviv 1979, 180; cf. Yeivin, 99, 236, n. 88; Bright, 242 and loc. cit., n. 40; Na'aman 1985, 215.

[7] This similarity led to the improbable hypothesis that there were not two kings, but only one. See: J. Strange, "Joram, King of Israel and Judah," *VT* 25 (1975), 191–201. In Strange's opinion, Ahab did not have a son named Joram; Joram the son of Jehoshaphat succeeded Ahaziah the son of Ahab, because Ahaziah did not have a son. See also: Miller and Hayes, 281–282.

[8] Thiele, 67 ff.; idem 1977, 19–20.

[9] See: Hughes, 190, 277.

[10] See: Lewy, 32; Begrich, 155; Jepsen, 42; Mowinckel, 271; Albright, 21; Tadmor 1962, 292–294.

of the years of Jehoram (eight) or of Ahaziah (one), or, alternatively, the number of years of Joram (twelve), for the total of the years of Jehoram and Ahaziah must exceed the number of years of Joram, if the latter was indeed installed in year 2 of Jehoram, for it is known that Joram and Ahaziah were murdered at the same time. The first contradiction presumably may be resolved if it is assumed that year 1 of Joram = year 2 of Jehoram = year 18 of Jehoshaphat. The significance of this, however, is that Jehoshaphat died ca. one year after the death of his son Jehoram, and possibly also some months after the death of his grandson Ahaziah, unless it is assumed that Jehoshaphat ruled less than 25 years; consequently, this would resolve one contradiction while creating another, in addition to the three contradictions listed above.

Additional proposals for the resolution of the above-mentioned contradictions may be offered, but all of them suggest that a number of Biblical and external data are inaccurate. One of the less objectionable proposals was raised by Thiele, who assumed that Jehoram was crowned during the lifetime of Jehoshaphat on the eve of the battle of Qarqar.[11] In his opinion, Jehoram ruled as coregent and as a sole monarch for 13, and not 8, years. It is difficult to accept this proposal, however, for it cannot be assumed that his years as coregent with his father were counted by one method, and his years as sole king by the other system. It therefore is preferable to assume that it is not possible to reconcile the datum that Joram was crowned in the second year of Jehoram with the datum that Joram began to rule in year 5 of Jehoram. In this instance as well, Thiele attempts to take on more than he can handle.

In the opinion of Tadmor as well, Joram was crowned in year 2 of Jehoram = year 18 of Jehoshaphat.[12] He too counts in one instance from the coronation of the king as coregent, and at other time from the death of his father. There is no evidence of this double count. The coregent was regarded as a king in all matters, and consequently the years of his reign were counted from his coronation. It also must be assumed that his title was "king," and therefore it is not surprising that no special title for coregent is preserved in the Bible.[13] Furthermore, there is no report in the Bible of the coronation of a king after the death of his father. Solomon was crowned twice (I Chronicles 29:22), but the second installation also was during the lifetime of

[11] Thiele, 67 ff.; cf. Hallo, 40; de Vries, 588.
[12] Tadmor 1962, 291 ff.
[13] Contrast: Na'aman 1986, 91; see also the discussion below, Chapter Six.

David.[14] Tadmor was forced to shorten the reign of Joram from 12 to 10 years, and to lengthen the reign of Jehoram from 8 to 9 years, and the rule of Ahaziah from 1 to 2 years.

In the opinion of Begrich as well, Joram began to rule in year 2 of Jehoram, but he argues that this was year 22 of Jehoshaphat.[15] He was also compelled to shorten the reign of Joram to seven years, and to claim that a majority of the Biblical data are incorrect. Of the 12 numerical data in the Bible relating to this period, Begrich and Tadmor, each following his own system, amended 8. Following the Septuagint, Begrich proposed to change the name of the king of Judah in II Kings 3 and to read Ahaziah instead of Jehoshaphat.[16]

In other words, if it is assumed that Joram was crowned in the second year of Jehoram, we are forced to amend most of the Biblical data relating to this period, or to make difficult and improbable assumptions, as did Thiele. It is preferable to assume that this datum is erroneous, and that it is one of the very few data in the Bible which were corrupted for some reason.

Jehoram son of Jehoshaphat was probably crowned in year 2 of Joram of Israel; it is possible that the author of the Book of Kings found in his sources a synchronism establishing the coronation of Joram in year 2 of Joram, and erroneously presumed that it referred to King Joram of Israel, and therefore assumed that he was crowned in year 2 of King Jehoram of Judah.

The unique synchronism included in II Kings 8:16 ("And in the fifth year of Joram the son of Ahab king of Israel, Jehoshaphat being then king of Judah, Jehoram the son of Jehoshaphat king of Judah began to reign"), probably was calculated by the redactor, who assumed that year 8 of Jehoram, in which Ahaziah was crowned, was year 12 of Joram; counting back, year 7 of Jehoram = year 11 of Joram, and, consequently, year 1 of Jehoram (his installation) = year 5 of Joram. The words "Jehoshaphat being then king of Judah" apparently do not constitute proof of the coronation of Jehoram in the lifetime of his father.[17]

---

[14] For the coregency of David and Solomon, see: E. Ball, "The Co-Regency of David and Solomon (I Kings 1)," *VT* 27 (1977), 268–279.

[15] Begrich, 105 ff., 121; cf. A. Laato, "New Viewpoints on the Chronology of the Kings of Judah and Israel," *ZAW* 98 (1986), 210–221, esp. 219–221.

[16] For the Septuagint versions, see: Shenkel; cf. Thiele 1951, 167–203; idem 1974, 181–190; Miller, 284 ff.; below, Chapter Eight.

[17] Many researchers assume that the words "Jehoshaphat then being king of Judah"

The campaign of Joram and Jehoshaphat against Moab probably occurred at the beginning of the former's reign. This assumption is based, *inter alia*, on the formulation in II Kings 3:5–6. The campaign came in the wake of the Moabite rebellion and the conquests of Mesha in the Mishor described in the Mesha inscription. The Moabite king conquered the Mishor after the death of Ahab (II Kings 1:1; 3:5), probably during the short reign of Ahaziah.[18]

It is quite likely that Israel and Judah participated in the wars between Assyria and the coalition of "the twelve kings of the sea coast" in 849, 848, and 845.[19] Jehoram was installed probably in 851, during the lifetime of his father Jehoshaphat.[20] There may possibly be an allusion to the crowning of Jehoram in his father's time in II Chronicles 21:3: "but the kingdom gave he to Jehoram, because he was the first-born."[21]

Following the death of Jehoshaphat (between Nisan 845 and Adar 844), the kingdom of Judah underwent severe crises and was subject to both internal and external rebellions. These events probably began during the reign of Jehoram as sole king (845/4–843/2). This period commenced with an additional war between the coalition of "the

are merely a copyist's error. See: R. Kittel, *Die Bücher der Könige* (*HAT*), Göttingen 1900, 223; Begrich, 169–170; Montgomery and Gehman, 395, 397; Snaith, 228; for a different opinion, see: Gray 1964, 66.

[18] One opinion, based on the Mesha inscription, establishes the time of the conquests of Mesha at the end of Ahab's reign (Liver, 206 ff.), but this cannot be accepted. It is not clear from the Mesha inscription whether the revolt took place during the time of the son of Omri, or during the time of one of his descendants. The Biblical sources, in contrast, clearly indicate that Mesha rebelled "after the death of Ahab" (II Kings 1:1; 3:5). For the time of the Moabite rebellion, see: Wallis, (above, 22, n. 25), 180 ff.

[19] Thus Elat, 30–31, and many additional researchers. For a different view, see: Noth, 246.

[20] For the coregency of Jehoram and Jehoshaphat, see: Kleber, 174, Lewy, 25 26, 32; Begrich, 155; Aharoni, 98–100; Thiele, 64 ff.; Tadmor 1962, 291 ff.; Schedl 1962a, 100, 110–111. Coucke supposed that Jehoshaphat and Jehoram ruled jointly for seven years (854–848—V. Coucke, "Chronologie Biblique," *Dictionnaire de la Bible*, Supp. 1, Paris 1928, 1252–1254). He also suggested that Jehoram ruled as an independent king only one year. See also Gray 1964, 66, 74.

[21] This verse is not to be regarded as proof of the coronation of Jehoram during the lifetime of Jehoshaphat, for it may possibly indicate only Jehoram's designation for kingship as the firstborn (and perhaps in the face of opposition to his selection). Also noteworthy, however, is the emphasis that Jehoshaphat "gave" the kingdom to Jehoram, as he had given, in his lifetime, gifts and fortified cities to his other sons. If he had been designated as king but had not been actually installed, a different definition could have been expected, perhaps terminology like that in II Chronicles 11:22: "And Rehoboam appointed Abijah . . . to be chief, even the prince among his brethren, for he was minded to make him king."

twelve kings of the sea coast" and Assyria (845). It may reasonably be assumed that at this time Edom rebelled against Judah and established an independent monarchy (II Kings 8:20; II Chronicles 21:8). Jehoram's campaign against Edom was not successful; although we possess no details regarding the progress of this offensive, it undoubtedly ended in failure and in the retreat of the Judahite army from Edom (II Kings 8:21).[22] If we are to accept the report of the serious illness from which Jehoram suffered in the last two years of his reign (II Chronicles 21:19)—which is consistent with his death at a relatively young age (approximately 39)—then it may be assumed that he waged war against Edom in 844, the seventh year of his reign, and that the Edomite revolt had taken place ca. 845, i.e., close to the death of Jehoshaphat. It is likely that the failure of the campaign against Edom led to an increase in the internal opposition to Jehoram, which was expressed in a revolt in the Shephelah.[23] Perhaps there is a connection between this rebellion and the struggle between Jehoram and his brothers for control of Judah after the death of Jehoshaphat? Jehoshaphat divided governmental powers among his sons: the kingship was intended for Jehoram, and to his other sons he gave "fortified cities in Judah" (II Chronicles 21:3), i.e., he appointed them over administrative districts.[24] Chronicles does not establish the time when Jehoram killed his brothers and the ministers who supported them. The placement of this passage in the text may indicate that, in the Chronicler's opinion, it occurred at the beginning of his reign; but it possibly should be dated to the last years of his reign, after his authority had been undermined as a result of his illness and his military debacles against Edom and on the southwestern front of the kingdom (II Chronicles

---

[22] For the campaign of Jehoram against Edom, see: H. Tadmor, "Jehoram, Joram Son of Jehoshaphat," *EB* 3 (1958), 539 ff. (Hebrew); Reviv 1979, 187. The formula "and he rose up by night, and smote the Edomites that compassed him about, and the captains of the chariots" (II Kings 8:21; and with a minor change also in II Chronicles 21:9) is undoubtedly corrupted; it possibly should be read "and the Edomites smote those that compassed them about..." For other proposals, see: Curtis and Madsen, 415.

[23] The term "Libnah" may possibly refer not only to the city of Libnah, but also to the district by this name, which comprised extensive regions in the Shephelah (the fourth district in Joshua 15:42–44). For the identification of Libnah with Tell 'Aiṭun, see: G. Galil, "The Administrative Division of the Shephelah," *Shnaton: An Annual for Biblical and Ancient Near Eastern Studies* 9 (1985), 67–71 (Hebrew).

[24] For the administrative division of the kingdom of Judah, see: Galil, loc. cit.; idem, "The Administrative Districts of the Judaean Hill Area," *Zion* 49 (1984), 205–224 (Hebrew).

21:16–17).[25] It is possible that at this time Jehoram's brothers unsuccessfully attempted to depose him and rule in his stead.

Ahaziah, Jehoram's son, was crowned in Jerusalem, apparently in the winter of 843/2, and ruled for ca. one year. During his short-lived reign, Israel and Judah failed in their second attempt to achieve a decisive victory against the Arameans at Ramoth-gilead. The revolt of Jehu apparently took place close to the defeat at Ramoth-gilead, between Tishri 842 and Nisan 841 (see below, chapter four).[26] In contrast to the majority of scholarly opinion, Pavlovsky and Vogt argue that the rebellion occurred in the winter of 841, close to the end of year 18 of Shalmaneser III.[27] This conjecture, however, is unlikely. Also difficult is the proposal by Begrich and Jepsen to move the revolt back to 845/4 (after 1 Tishri 845 and before 1 Tishri 844).[28] King Ben-hadad II (Hadadezer) of Aram is mentioned in the Assyrian inscriptions as the head of the coalition of the twelve kings of the sea coast in 845. Since Ben-hadad was murdered by Hazael, and Joram fought Hazael at Ramoth-gilead, consequently Hazael seized power between 845 and 842.[29]

---

[25] For the invasion of Judah by the "Arabs and Philistines" in the time of Jehoram, see: B. Mazar, "A New Assyrian-Israelite synchronism?," *Tarbiz* 19 (1948), 123–124 (Hebrew); Na'aman 1987, 272 ff.

[26] Thus also Vogelstein, 18 ff.; Thiele, 69; Schedl 1962a, 110–111; Tadmor 1962, 292. These researchers took note of the fact that Joram recuperated from his wounds in the royal winter palace in Jezreel, and not in Samaria.

[27] Pavlovsky and Vogt, 327.

[28] Begrich, 113 ff., 155; Jepsen, 39–42. For the time of the rebellion of Jehu, also see: Miller, 288; Andersen, 86; idem 1989, 26–28.

[29] The names of Joram and Ahaziah, and their war with Hazael, are probably mentioned in the Dan stele; see: A. Biran and J. Naveh, "The Tel Dan Inscription: A New Fragment," *IEJ* 45 (1995), 1–18.

Table 9

<table>
<tr><th>Assyria</th><th>Judah</th><th>Year BCE</th><th>Israel
possibility A</th><th>Israel
possibility B</th></tr>
<tr><td rowspan="3">Shalmaneser III
6</td><td rowspan="3">Jehoshapat
17</td><td rowspan="2">853</td><td>Ahab
21</td><td>Ahaziah
1</td></tr>
<tr><td>22</td><td rowspan="3">2</td></tr>
<tr><td rowspan="4">852</td><td rowspan="3">Ahaziah
1</td></tr>
<tr><td rowspan="4">7</td><td rowspan="4">18</td></tr>
<tr><td>Joram
1</td></tr>
<tr><td>2</td><td rowspan="3">2</td></tr>
<tr><td rowspan="2">851</td><td rowspan="2">1
(2)</td></tr>
<tr><td>8</td><td>19</td></tr>
</table>

Table 10

Assyria	*JUDAH*		*Year BCE*	*ISRAEL* possibility A	possibility B
Shalmaneser III 8	*Jehoshaphat* 19	*Jehoram* Accession year	851	*Joram*	*Joram*
				2 (3)	3
9	20	1	850	3 (4)	4
10	21	2	849	4 (5)	5
11	22	3	848	5 (6)	6
12	23	4	847	6 (7)	7
13	24	5	846	7 (8)	8
14	25	6	845	8 (9)	9
15	- - - - - - -	7	844	9 (10)	10
16		8 *Ahaziah* Accession year	843	10 (11)	11
17		1	842	11 (12)	12
	Accession year	Accession year			
18	*Athaliah* 1	*Jehoash* 1	841	*Jehu* 1	

CHAPTER FOUR

ISRAEL AND JUDAH FROM THE REBELLION OF JEHU TO THE CONQUEST OF SAMARIA

The Biblical and external sources indicate with certainty that the rebellion of Jehu took place between the fourteenth year of Shalmaneser III (845/4), the year in which Ben-hadad II ("Adad-idri") still reigned in Damascus, and the eighteenth year of the Assyrian king (841/40), in which Jehu gave tribute to Assyria.[1] King Hoshea of Israel was probably deposed by the Assyrian monarch Shalmaneser V (II Kings 17:4) in 722 at the latest, for Shalmaneser died in this year, in the month of Tebeth (Babylonian Chronicle, col. I, l. 29).[2] Consequently, no more than 123 years passed from the coronation of Jehu to the removal of Hoshea.[3] In contrast, the count of the years of the kings of Judah from the installation of Athaliah until year 4 of Hezekiah, which in my opinion was the last year of Hoshea, totals 164 years of reign,[4] and the count of the years of the kings of Israel from year 1 of Jehu to year 9 of Hoshea totals 143 years and 7 months.[5] Consequently, there is a discrepancy of more than forty years between the chronological framework, which is based mainly on the extra-Biblical sources, and the years of reign data in the Bible.

---

[1] For a discussion of this topic, see above, Chapter Three.

[2] For the period of Hoshea, see: Borger and Tadmor, 244–249; Na'aman 1986, 71–74; also see below, Chapter Five.

[3] Scholarly opinion is unanimous on this issue. It is commonly accepted that no more than 123 years elapsed between the crowning of Jehu and the deposition of Hoshea. Those positing an earlier date assume that Hoshea ruled until 724/3 (Lewy, Begrich, Albright, Tadmor, Yeivin and others) and those in favor of a later date argue that he reigned until 722/1 (Kleber, Mowinckel, Vogelstein, Schedl, Pavlovsky and Vogt, Andersen and others). Most researchers are of the opinion that Jehu rebelled between 843 and 841, with the exception of Begrich and Jepsen, who date the revolt to 845; however, in their opinion as well, ca. 122 years passed from the revolt of Jehu to the removal of Hoshea, since they claim that Hoshea was deposed in 724 or in 723.

[4] The following are the years of reign of the kings of Judah in the period under discussion: Athaliah – 7; Jehoash – 40; Amaziah – 29; Uzziah – 52; Jotham – 16; Ahaz – 16; Hezekiah – 6 (II Kings 11:3–4; 12:2; 14:2; 15:2, 33; 16:2; 18:10).

[5] The years of reign of the kings of Israel in this period are as follows: Jehu – 28; Jehoahaz – 17; Joash – 16; Jeroboam – 41; Zechariah – 6 months; Shallum – 1 month; Menahem – 10; Pekahiah – 2; Pekah – 20; Hoshea – 9 (II Kings 10:36; 13:1, 10; 14:23; 15:8, 13, 17, 23, 27; 17:1).

Many proposals for resolving the discrepancies between the sources have been advanced. Researchers who argue that there were no coregency periods, or that they were of short duration, such as, e.g., Albright, Andersen, and recently Hughes, are forced to suggest radical changes in the data of the years of reign,[6] while those who are of the opinion that all or most of the years of reign data are accurate, such as, e.g., Thiele, propose protracted coregency periods.[7] In my opinion, the discrepancy results from two main causes: (1) some of the kings of Israel and Judah were crowned during the reigns of their predecessors; (2) the years of the reigns of King Joash of Judah and Pekah apparently were counted retroactively. The rebellion of Jehu apparently took place in 842/1, while Hoshea was deposed by Shalmaneser V in 722; consequently, these two events were separated by ca. 120 years.

It is quite certain that Athaliah would not have succeeded in seizing power in Judah if she had not been supported by the army and at least a portion of the government ministers. It is also clear, however, that other circles within the Judahite leadership, headed by the Jerusalem priesthood, very strongly opposed her rule, and in the end they were responsible for her removal. Her history was written by those who deposed her, and it therefore is not surprising that the description in the Book of Kings of her actions is tendentious and does not reflect the reality.[8] In the seventh year of her rule her opponents gained the upper hand, and Athaliah was murdered on the Temple Mount (II Kings 11:4–16, cf. II Chronicles 23:1–15). It is hardly conceivable that the insurgents counted the years of Joash from the murder of Athaliah, thus acknowledging the legality of her reign. To the contrary, it is to be assumed that Jehoiada and the ministers of Judah, who

---

[6] Albright proposed amending most of the years of reign data, as follows: Jehoash ruled for 38 years, and not 40; Amaziah – 18 and not 29; Uzziah – 42 instead of 52; Ahaz – 21 and not 16, and other changes (Albright 1963, 126–127). Andersen proposed in 1969 (111–112) the following changes for the data of the years of the kings of Israel and Judah in this period: Jeroboam – 32 years, instead of 41; Uzziah – 29, and not 52; Jotham – 8, and not 16; Hezekiah – 19, instead of 29. In 1989 (2–3, 16–25, 45) Andersen changed his view; and altered only the number of Uzziah's years (from 52 to 36). Hughes argues that Jehoash ruled for 38 (and not 40) years; Amaziah, 28 (not 29) years; Uzziah, 26 (and not 52); and Jotham, 11 (and not 16) years (Hughes, 275).

[7] Thiele (1983, 219) proposes the following coregency periods: Jeroboam and Joash reigned jointly for 12 years; Uzziah and Amaziah – 24 years, etc.

[8] For the reign of Athaliah, see: H. Reviv, "About the Period of Athaliah and Joash," *Beit Mikra* 16 (1971), 541–548 (Hebrew) and loc. cit. for additional literature.

were the *de facto* rulers of the land during Joash's minority, did not recognize the legitimacy of Athaliah's rule, and counted the years of the young king from the assassination of his father,[9] like the Egyptian king Tuthmosis III, who did not acknowledge the legality of the rule of his stepmother Hatshepsut, and counted his years from the death of his father, despite the fact that his stepmother was the *de facto* ruler of the country for more than twenty years.[10] The year in which Hatshepsut was deposed, in which Tuthmosis began to rule in fact, is counted as his twenty-second year.[11]

During the reign of Jehu, King Hazael of Aram conquered portions of the Israelite territory east of the Jordan.[12] It may be presumed that Hazael's conquests took place in the second half of the reign of Jehu. In 841 and in 838 the army of Aram suffered defeats at the hands of the Assyrians; especially the Aramean chariot force suffered severe losses.[13] The defeats of Aram on the battlefield did not lead to its surrender, Assyria was not successful in conquering Damascus, and Hazael did not become an Assyrian vassal. The Assyrian threat,

---

[9] For this assumption, see: Mowinckel, 271; Vogelstein, table III; Shea 1985, 11–12.

[10] For this subject, see: Tadmor 1962, 281; Murnane, 32–44; Na'aman 1986, 79 and loc. cit. for additional literature.

[11] Tadmor (ibid.) concedes that there is no known instance in the ancient East in which the period in which a queen ruled during the lifetime of her successors was regarded as the period of her independent rule. Accordingly, it is possible that Joash called his first year: "year 7" of his reign. In his opinion, however, this assumption raises a number of difficulties: (1) it requires shortening the reign of Jehu from 28 to 22 years; (2) if 28 years are allocated to Jehu and 17 to his son, and if it is assumed that Amaziah son of Jehoash was crowned in year 2 of Joash, the grandson of Jehu, then the number of years of Jehoash must be raised to ca. 44–45, instead of the 40 counted for him by the Bible; (3) if Joash was crowned in year 37 of Jehoash and died in year 15 of his son Amaziah, and Jehoash reigned for 44–45 years, the count of Joash's years rises to 23 (instead of the 16 counted by the Bible). The three difficulties raised by Tadmor are in actuality only a single problem, for if the reign of Jehu is reduced to 22 years, the years of Jehoash will no longer exceed 40, and the discrepancy regarding the years of Joash will obviously no longer exist. Furthermore, if we accept the hypothesis (which has been raised by many scholars, including Tadmor) that Jehoahaz was crowned in the lifetime of his father Jehu, all these difficulties may be resolved.

[12] The description in II Kings 10:32–33 of the conquest of the territory east of the Jordan in the time of Hazael raises a number of problems: (1) the Mishor had been conquered by Mesha following the death of Ahab, and there is no evidence of its return to Israel; (2) the Bashan had been under Aramean control in the time of Ahab, and there is no proof that Jehu had restored it to Israel. It therefore is doubtful whether the territorial model describing the conquests of Hazael reflects the reality. This apparently is a literary model reflecting the reality from the time of the united kingdom.

[13] For the campaigns of Shalmaneser III, see above, Chapter Three, n. 1.

however, was not lifted from Damascus, and it took Aram several years to recover from the blows it had endured. Jehu, in contrast, gave tribute to the Assyrians in 841; in return for his dependence upon them, the Assyrians provided Jehu with protection. It therefore is difficult to assume that Hazael would have attacked Jehu before the death of Shalmaneser III (824), and certainly not before the revolt in Assyria, which erupted in 826/25. This uprising, which continued without respite for seven years at the end of Shalmaneser's reign and the beginning of his son's rule, as well as the death of Shalmaneser, the great conqueror, weakened Assyria and made possible the ascent of Aram, which succeeded in gradually gaining dominion over Israel, Judah, and Gath, apparently the Gath of the Philistines. Indirect support for establishing these events during the time of Shamshi-Adad V appears in the inscriptions of Adad-nirari III, the son of Shamshi-Adad. These inscriptions indicate that Assyrian rule in the west had collapsed during the reign of Shamshi-Adad (the Saba'a inscription, ll. 13–15; and possibly also a fragment of a stone slab from the time of Adad-nirari III first published by Scheil, ll. 2'–3').[14]

The proposed reconstruction of these events is likely to correspond with the Biblical testimony. The text in II Kings 12:7 indicates that repairs were made to the Temple in Judah "in the three and twentieth year of King Jehoash" (12:7). After describing the repairs, the chapter continues: "Then Hazael king of Aram went up, and fought against Gath" (v. 18).[15] On the one hand, it cannot be inferred with certainty from this passage that the campaign of Hazael occurred in the same year, for it is possible that the report of the campaign was inserted in its new place from a different context, while in the original chronicle this information did not appear in a single descriptive continuum relating to year 23 of Jehoash. On the other hand, this possibility may not be rejected out of hand, and the source from which the passage in v. 18 was taken may possibly have established Hazael's campaign in year 23 of Jehoash.[16] The inscriptions of the kings of Assyria contain

[14] For this issue, see: Millard and Tadmor, 61.

[15] The description of the campaign in II Kings 12:18 mentions only the conquest of Gath, while it is possible that Hazael may also have conquered additional Philistine cities. Some researchers argue that Hazael captured Gath-Gittaim, which apparently is to be identified with Tell Ras Abu Hammid near Ramleh (see Mazar, Canaan and Israel, 261; Yẹivin, 237, n. 102). This assumption, however, is not to be accepted, and it is more likely that the Arameans seized Gath of the Philistines, apparently Tell eṣ-Ṣafi.

[16] For the assumption that the campaign of Hazael against Gath and Judah oc-

the formula "in those days" (*ina umēšūma*), which may be regarded as a parallel to the word "then" ("אז") in v. 18, mainly in summary inscriptions, which were not necessarily arranged in chronological order, but rather along geographical or associative lines. This formula, however, as well as the parallel formula ("*ina šattima*"), also appears in annalistic inscriptions.[17]

If Hazael in fact conquered territories east of the Jordan River at the beginning of the reign of Shamshi-Adad V, taking advantage of the death of Shalmaneser III and the revolt against Assyria, it is not inconceivable that the next phase in Aramean expansion took place a number of years later, possibly in year 23 of Jehoash = 819/18. Of special importance is the fact that year 23 of King Jehoash of Judah was marked by the coronation in Samaria of Jehoahaz, the son of Jehu (II Kings 13:1). In my opinion, this was year 23 of Jehu; Jehoahaz was crowned during the lifetime of Jehu, and he ruled with his father for five or six years (see table 13 – p. 73). His presumed coronation is likely to be explained by the harsh circumstances that preceded it, including the conquest of territories east of the Jordan and the submission of Israel to Aram. The investiture apparently was intended to strengthen Jehu and ensure the continuity of the new dynasty.[18]

The description in II Chronicles 24:17–25 would seem to indicate that the campaign of Hazael against Judah took place towards the end of Jehoash's reign; some researchers even distinguish between the campaign in year 23 against Jehoash and the campaign at the end of Jehoash's reign.[19] There is no foundation, however, for this conjecture, and the history of the reign of Jehoash and the order of the wars of Hazael cannot be reconstructed on the basis of the tendentious description of the author of Chronicles. The reworking of history in accordance with the principles of personal and immediate recompense led to the combining of two different events (Hazael's campaign against

---

curred in year 23 of Jehoash, see: Mazar, loc. cit.; Tadmor, Jehu, 477. In their opinion, the campaign was conducted in 815/14. Cf. Bright, 255.

[17] For the formula "*ina umēšūma*" in the annalist inscriptions, see, e.g., Cameron, 14, II, l. 60; 15, III, ll. 3, 11, 26; for the formula "*ina šattima*," see, e.g., Michel, 146–148, l. 50. Cf. M. Cogan and H. Tadmor, "Ahaz and Tiglath-Pileser in the Book of Kings-Historiographic Considerations," *Eretz-Israel* 14 (1978), 56 ff. (Hebrew).

[18] For the coronation of Jehoahaz in the lifetime of Jehu, see: Vogelstein, table III; Tadmor 1962, 280; Yeivin 84, 101; Na'aman 1986, 92.

[19] For the Aramean campaign conducted at the end of Jehoash's reign, see: Mazar, Cities and Districts, 236. The Chronicler does not name Hazael in connection with the Aramean campaign, but this undoubtedly is the intent of the Biblical text, since Hazael reigned concurrently with Jehoahaz, the son of Jehu.

Judah, the death of Jehoash) and their presentation as punishment for the sins of Jehoash and Judah (idolatry and the murder of Zechariah son of Jehoiada—II Chronicles 24:18, 21–22). The Aramean campaign against Jerusalem and the murder of Jehoash were most likely unrelated. Many years probably elapsed between the two events.[20]

Jehu apparently died in 815/4, after a reign spanning 28 years.[21] The Aramean pressure against Israel increased during the time of Jehoahaz. The Israelite army was reduced to a symbolic guard (II Kings 13:7), and regions west of the Jordan were occupied by the Arameans (ibid., 13:25).[22]

II Kings 13:22 states that Hazael exerted pressure on Israel "all the days of Jehoahaz," which apparently indicates that Ben-hadad the son of Hazael was crowned only after the death of Jehoahaz. Verse 25, however, reports that this is only a generalization, and that Ben-hadad assumed the throne in the time of Jehoahaz. The meaning of "all the days of Jehoahaz" is therefore: all the days of Jehoahaz that Hazael ruled,[23] or that "Hazael" is a general representation for Aramean rule over Israel; the Biblical text indicates that Israel was dominated by Aram during the entire reign of Jehoahaz, and shook off Aramean rule only in his last year (see below).[24]

The major prophetic source inserted in I Kings 17–II Kings 9 relates two times of an Aramean siege imposed on Samaria (I Kings 20:1–25; II Kings 6:24–7:20). The order of the Book of Kings and the content of these descriptions indicate that the first siege was imposed in the time of Ahab, and the second in the time of his son Joram.

---

[20] For this topic, cf. Myers, 138–139.

[21] There is almost unanimous scholarly acceptance of this datum. Tadmor, e.g., counts 29 years for Jehu (see Tadmor 1962, 280). Mowinckel (271) and Vogelstein (19, 21), on the other hand, allot him only 22 or 23 years. Their hypothesis is based on the following assumptions: (1) Jehoash counted his years from the death of his father, and not from the assassination of Athaliah; (2) Jehoahaz son of Jehu was crowned in year 23 of Jehoash (= year 22 or 23 of Jehu); (3) Jehoahaz was crowned after the death of Jehu. There is no justification, however, for shortening the years of Jehu. Jehoash apparently did count his years from the death of his father, but the datum about the length of Jehu's reign appears to be accurate, thus leading to the conclusion that Jehoahaz was installed in the time of his father, as suggested above.

[22] For the boundaries of the Israelite kingdom in the ninth-eighth centuries BCE, see: B. Oded, "Darb el-Hawarneh—an Ancient Route," *Eretz-Israel* 10 (1971), 191–197 (Hebrew); Mazar, Cities and Districts, 235; and recently: S. A. Irvin, "The Southern Border of Syria Reconstructed," *CBQ*, 56 (1994), 21–41; N. Na'aman, "Rezin of Damascus and the Land of Gilead," *ZDPV*, 111 (1995), 105–117.

[23] Oded 1972, 33.

[24] For the dates of the coronation of Hazael and his son Ben-hadad, see: Pitard 1988, 3 ff. and loc. cit. for additional literature.

But the two descriptions are similar. In each, Aram is led by a king named Ben-hadad; the prophets play a crucial role; and Samaria is saved in a miraculous fashion. It is difficult to assume that the Arameans attacked Samaria in the time of Ahab. The Israelite-Aramean border ran through Gilead in this period, and Israel was at the peak of its military and economic power. Consequently, it is preferable to assume that the siege of Samaria occurred during the time of the kings from the line of Jehu, and that these two traditions are merely two versions of a single historical episode.[25] Many legends about the sudden withdrawal of the Aramean army from Samaria apparently were prevalent in Israel (like the legend related about the sudden retreat of the army of Sennacherib from Jerusalem in 701 BCE).

The historical background of the siege of Samaria and the reason for the retreat from the city are unclear. It may be supposed that Ben-hadad was Ben-hadad son of Hazael; it is possible that the reason for the siege was an Israelite revolt, for it is difficult to assume that without cause the Arameans would have attacked the capital of the Israelite kingdom, which was under their power. Of great importance is the information that the siege of Samaria was unsuccessful, and that its failure led to Israel freeing itself of Aramean dominance. Perhaps there is a connection between the presumed revolt, siege, and deliverance, and the campaigns of Adad-nirari III to the West? (See the discussion below).

Jehoahaz son of Jehu was crowned in the twenty-third year of Jehoash, and ruled for 17 years (II Kings 13:1–2);[26] Joash his son was installed in the thirty-seventh year of Jehoash (ibid., v. 10). These data indicate that Joash son of Jehoahaz was crowned during his father's lifetime. Joash was probably enthroned in 805 (= year 37 of Jehoash), ca. two years before the death of his father Jehoahaz. In this year the Assyrian king, Adad-nirari III, set forth to wage war with the kings of the West. Apparently there was fighting in the West also in

[25] Many researchers are of the opinion that the description in II Kings 6–7 reflects the time of the Jehu dynasty. See, e.g., Mazar, Cities and Districts, 235, n. 19; Lipinski 1979, 85 ff. For the assumption that the siege described in I Kings 20 and the battle of Aphek were conducted in the time of the house of Jehu, see: Whitley, 137–152; Rofe 1982, 54; Pitard 1988, 8–9.

[26] Most scholars are of the opinion that Jehoahaz reigned ca. 17 years. Albright allots him only 14 years (Albright, 21 and n. 20; idem 1970, 34–35). A similar conclusion was also reached by Aharoni (94 ff., 100). Tadmor counts 18 years for Jehoahaz (Tadmor 1962, 280), and Vogelstein surmises that he ruled for 19 years (Vogelstein, 21 and table III).

804–802 and in 796.[27] The summary nature of the inscriptions of Adad-nirari III does not permit a precise determination of (1) when "Je(ho)ash of Samaria" presented tribute to the Assyrian king; (2) how many campaigns to the West were conducted in the time of Adad-nirari III; and (3) when these campaigns took place. Some scholars advance the giving of the tribute to 805,[28] others are of the opinion that Joash offered it in 803 or in 802,[29] while the proponents of a later date postpone the giving of the tribute to 796.[30]

The Eponym Chronicles indicates that Adad-nirari III apparently set out for the West four or five times within the space of a decade (in 805, 804, 803, 802?, 796). The inscriptions from Saba'a, Tell al-Rimah, and from Calah (Nimrud) are summary inscriptions, and the information they provide is partial and tendentious. Even the Assyrian achievements are reported only in an incomplete fashion. They make no mention of, e.g., the victory in the battle of Paqirahubana, and the surrender of Arpad (see the Sheikh Hammad inscription and the Pazarcik inscription).[31] Consequently, any reconstruction of the wars of Adad-nirari III must remain in the realm of conjecture. The following is a tentative reconstruction of the events in the West at this time. The preparations for the campaign of Adad-nirari III to the West apparently began at the end of his fifth year (806/5).[32] The campaign itself was conducted in the sixth year of his reign (805), as is indicated by the Eponym Chronicles. This probably was preceded by an attack by the alliance headed by the kings of Damascus and Arpad against Zakur king of Hamath and La'ash, and by the besieging of Hadrach. The exact timing of the siege and its reasons are unclear, but not its results. Zakur definitely overcame his enemies.[33] There most likely was a connection between the failure of the siege of Hadrach and the Assyrian campaign of 805. In the battle that was waged in Paqirahubana, west of the Euphrates, probably in this year,

---

[27] For the campaigns of Adad-nirari III, see: Dalley 1968; idem 1969; Cody; Oded 1972; Millard, 161 ff.; Millard and Tadmor; Tadmor 1973; Lipinski 1979, 85–93; Shea 1985.

[28] Lipinski 1979, 88 ff.; Cody, 332–337; Shea 1978a, 101 ff.

[29] Albright 1970, 34 ff.; Bright, 256.

[30] Millard and Tadmor, 61–64; Thiele 1983, 111–113.

[31] For an analysis of the inscriptions, see: Millard and Tadmor, 57 ff.; Donbaz, 5 ff.

[32] See the Saba'a stele, ll. 11 ff.; cf. Tadmor 1973, 147 ff.

[33] For the Zakur inscription, see: J. C. L. Gibson, *Textbook of Syrian Semitic Inscriptions*, 2, Oxford 1975, 6–17.

the Assyrians faced a coalition headed by Atarsumki king of Arpad (the Pazarcik inscription). The Assyrian victory led to the submission of Arpad and its allies, and the resolution of the border dispute between Gurgum and Kummuh. Probably dating to the same period is the Antakya inscription, which testifies to the intervention of Adad-nirari III in the conflict between Zakur and Atarsumki, the king of Arpad. It is surprising that the Assyrians favored Atarsumki, who fought against them, over the king of Hamath, who apparently did not participate in the anti-Assyrian coalition headed by the king of Arpad.[34] It cannot be determined if the king of Damascus took part in the battle of Paqirahubana, and when the Assyrians succeeded in taking Damascus. The Assyrians probably were compelled to fight the West an additional number of times after 805 (in 804, and probably also in 803–802). It therefore may be assumed that their victory in 805 was not as decisive as is seemingly indicated by the Assyrian inscriptions.[35]

The renewed appearance of the Assyrians in the West apparently did not escape the notice of the Israelite king. Joash was probably crowned by his father Jehoahaz in the year in which the war against Arpad was waged (805). Jehoahaz presumably sought to take advantage of the great historical opportunity that presented itself to him. He rebelled against Aram, and hoped that Assyria would come to his assistance in his hour of need. During the course of Adad-nirari III's wars in Syria, Joash, the young king, was sent to him bearing the tribute of the Israelite kingdom and a request for Assyrian help against the Aramean attack which soon materialized. The presumed coronation of Joash was part of a far-reaching political plan by Jehoahaz, who had been an Aramean vassal during his entire reign, and now had found the opportune time to rebel against his masters. The Arameans laid siege to Samaria in response to the Israelite insurrection. The siege apparently was not short-lived, as is indicated from the harsh descriptions of the famine that swept the city at the time (II Kings 6:25–29). The Bible relates that the siege of Samaria was a failure, but the reason for the sudden withdrawal of the Arameans from the city is unclear. It may be presumed that this withdrawal was linked to the war of the Assyrians against Aram in 803 or in 802. It is most

[34] Galil 1992b, 59.

[35] The inscriptions from Tell al-Rimah and from Sheikh Hammad indicate that the West was defeated in a single year; however, this too is a literary pattern not reflective of the reality. See Tadmor 1973, 143; Millard and Tadmor, 58.

likely that the kingdoms of Tyre, Sidon, and Philistia also submitted to Assyria at this time.

The Assyrian inscriptions clearly indicate that Adad-nirari III succeeded in overwhelming Damascus, but the date of this event is unclear. Two main proposals may be presented on this point: (1) Damascus surrendered in 803 or 802. At this time Joash restored to Israel territories that had been taken from it by Hazael and Ben-hadad III. The latter did not accept the severe defeats he had suffered at the hands of Assyria and Israel. He rebuilt his army, and ca. six years after the conquest of Damascus, when Adad-nirari was occupied with his protracted wars in the east and the north, Ben-hadad rose up against Assyria in 797/6. In response to the uprising, Adad-nirari returned to the West and succeeded in suppressing the revolt in 796; (2) in 803–802 the Aramean army suffered losses, but Damascus was not conquered and did not surrender to Assyria (as had been the case in 841 and in 838); it fell to the Assyrians only in 796. At that time Israel had already become a vassal kingdom of Assyria, like the situation in 838, in which the Assyrians marched against Damascus about three years after Israel had submitted to them.

The first possibility presented above points to similarities between the campaigns of Tiglath-pileser III to the West and the stages of Adad-nirari III's domination of the West: (1) the two kings were compelled to first do battle with Arpad (Adad-nirari in 805–804; Tiglath-pileser in 743–740); (2) in the wake of the defeat of Arpad, the Assyrians succeeded in bringing about the surrender of most of the kings of the West: Tiglath-pileser, without resorting to force (the Iran stele – 740, see below), while Adad-nirari had been forced to fight for Damascus, and its conquest was followed by the surrender of additional kingdoms (803?); (3) in the next phase, the conquest of the West was completed: Tiglath-pileser waged a campaign against Unqi, Hamath, and the northern Phoenician cities, including Arvad (738), and Adad-nirari had marched along the coast and erected a stele in Arvad (802); (4) a number of years later, Damascus acted against Assyrian interests: in the time of Tiglath-pileser, after ca. six years (734), and also during the time of Adad-nirari, most probably after six years (797/6?). The hostile activities of Damascus were followed by Assyrian campaigns: in the time of Tiglath-pileser in 733/2, and in the time of Adad-nirari in 796 ("against Manṣuate"). Along with these similarities, there obviously are many differences between the two periods, including the nature of the relations between Israel and Aram, and the attitude of Hamath toward Assyria (see the discussion below).

In contrast with the reconstruction proposed above, Millard and Tadmor conjectured that Damascus and Israel submitted only in 796.[36] They argue that the Assyrian king was active in 805–803 (802?) in northern Syria, and only in 796 he fought in southern Syria and defeated Damascus. In their opinion, Joash offered his tribute only in 796. Their theory is based on two main arguments: (1) in 802 Joash had not yet ascended the Israelite throne; and (2) it is unlikely that the king of Aram rebelled against Assyria only a few years after his capitulation. These two arguments, however, are not decisive. First, it has already been demonstrated that Joash could already have been crowned by 806/5; in our opinion, this proposal is more likely (if the Biblical chronological data are in fact correct). Similarly, Aram's rebelling ca. six years after its original surrender is a distinct possibility. The history of the ancient Near East in the eighth-sixth centuries BCE is replete with examples of rebellion coming on the heels of surrender: thus, e.g., Hoshea offered tribute to Assyria in 731, to be followed by his rebellion only about six years later (see below, Chapter Five); Jehoiakim submitted to Nebuchadrezzar of Babylon "and he became his servant three years; then he turned and rebelled against him" (II Kings 24:1); Zedekiah was placed on the throne by the Babylonian king, but nevertheless rebelled against him about nine years later (ibid., 24:17, 20); Baʿal, the king of Tyre, submitted to Esarhaddon in 671, giving the Assyrian monarch a heavy tribute. Notwithstanding this, only a few years later, at the beginning of the reign of Ashurbanipal (668 or shortly thereafter), he rose against Assyria once again, and Ashurbanipal marched against him and defeated Tyre, but nevertheless maintained Baʿal as king.

The proposal by Millard and Tadmor clearly contradicts the Biblical testimony that the Lord saved Israel in the time of Jehoahaz, for they claim that Israel shook off Aramean domination only during the reign of Joash.

It is widely accepted by scholars that the savior of Israel during the time of Jehoahaz was Adad-nirari, the Assyrian king.[37] The proposed coregency of Joash with his father Jehoahaz makes it possible to assume that this deliverer was Joash, who smote Aram (II Kings 13:19, 25) and restored to Israel territories that had been occupied

---

[36] Millard and Tadmor, 61 ff.; Millard, 162.
[37] Yeivin, 105.

by Aram.[38] One of the battles was undoubtedly waged in Aphek (ibid., v. 17), which may be the battle described in I Kings 20:26–34.

If Joash, king of Israel, began to reign in the thirty-seventh year of Jehoash (who ruled for 40 years), and if Amaziah son of Jehoash ascended the throne in year 2 of Joash, then Amaziah was crowned in the last years of his father, at the very latest in the first half of year 39 of Jehoash, and at the earliest in the second half of year 37 of Jehoash.[39] In my opinion, the second possibility should be preferred, and Amaziah was probably crowned in 805/4, a few months after the investiture of Joash (see table 14 – p. 74).

It may be assumed that at the beginning of their reigns Amaziah and Joash renewed the cooperation between Israel and Judah. This is indicated by the fact that Joash agreed to hire out an Israelite contingent to the Judaean army. The exact date of Amaziah's campaign against Edom cannot be determined, nor that of the war between Joash and Amaziah that erupted after Amaziah's partial victory over Edom. At any rate, there is no evidence connecting this war with the investiture of Uzziah in the time of Amaziah (see below).[40]

Joash apparently died in 790, after having ruled for 16 years, and he was succeeded by his son Jeroboam, in the fifteenth year of Amaziah (II Kings 14:23).[41] Amaziah was assassinated 15 years later, ca. 776/5.[42]

---

[38] Cf. Shea 1985, 19.

[39] Kleber, 178.

[40] For the campaign of Amaziah to Edom, see: Yeivin, 106–107; Na'aman 1985, 214–215.

[41] Scholarly opinion is divided regarding the years of Joash's reign. Tadmor presumes that Joash ruled for 17 years, and that Jeroboam was crowned in 783 (Tadmor 1962, 281). Other researchers, including Kleber (188), Thiele (1983, 116), Yeivin (84), Schedl (1962a, 100), Gray (1964, 65, 74), and Pavlovsky and Vogt (347), are of the opinion that Jeroboam ruled as coregent in the time of Joash and was crowned between 794 (Gray) and 787 (Yeivin). Joash's death was established between 790 and 781. Most researchers, with three exceptions, state that Joash ruled for 16 years: Tadmor (as above); Aharoni counted 15 years (Aharoni, 100); and Gray (1964, 74) allots him 20 years.

[42] Most researchers are of the opinion that the datum that Amaziah died 15 years after the death of Joash is erroneous. In Begrich's opinion, Amaziah ruled only 16 years, and he died ca. two years after the death of Joash; the latter died in year 14 of Amaziah, and he was succeeded by Jeroboam (Begrich, 155). Albright presumes that Amaziah reigned for only 18 years and died ca. three years after the death of Joash (Albright, 21). These proposals are based on the assumption that Uzziah was crowned by "the people of the land" after the death of his father Amaziah. These researchers were forced to shorten the reign of Uzziah and to amend many Biblical chronological data. Thus, e.g., Jepsen, who assumed that Uzziah was crowned in year 15 of Amaziah, at the end of Joash's lifetime, was compelled to change 14 of the 34 chronological data relating to the period from the rebellion of Jehu to the conquest of Samaria (Jepsen, 32–39).

The synchronisms in the Book of Kings indicate that Jeroboam was crowned only after the death of his father, for Amaziah began to rule in year 2 of Joash, and Jeroboam was installed in year 15 of Amaziah = the last year of Joash. If Zechariah was in fact crowned in year 38 of Uzziah and Jeroboam ruled for 41 years, then Uzziah was installed in the time of Jeroboam and not that of Joash; and if Jeroboam did not begin to rule in his father's lifetime, then it may not be assumed that Uzziah was crowned when Amaziah was taken captive, but rather a number of years later.[43] The investiture of Uzziah was probably unrelated to the war between Amaziah and Joash, and Uzziah was crowned only after the death of Joash. If it is assumed that Uzziah was crowned in the lifetime of Joash, then it must be assumed that a number of chronological data are erroneous, first and foremost the datum that Jeroboam reigned for 41 years, for if Zechariah began to rule in year 38 of Uzziah, and Jeroboam was installed in year 15 of Amaziah, i.e., about a year after the investiture of Uzziah, then the reign of Jeroboam totaled at most 37 years. If the count of Jeroboam's years is correct, then it must be surmised that the synchronisms relating to the time of Uzziah are incorrect. Furthermore, the assumption that Uzziah was installed in the wake of the war between Joash and Amaziah is at variance with the Biblical testimony, for v. 14 indicates that Joash took hostages from Jerusalem, most probably to ensure that the Southern Kingdom would honor its commitments. It is highly questionable if there was any reason to take hostages if Joash had resolved to keep King Amaziah of Judah captive. Moreover, if he intended to depose Amaziah, it is likely that he would have installed another king in his stead (as Rezin and Pekah had intended to do). It therefore must be assumed that Amaziah was restored to his throne. Opposition to Amaziah increased after the defeat, and a few years later, when Uzziah reached the age of 16, he was installed alongside his father by "the people of Judah" (II Kings 14:21).

The investiture of Uzziah in the lifetime of Amaziah is not stated explicitly in the Bible, but it may be deduced from the Biblical data. If it is assumed that Uzziah was crowned only after the death of his

[43] For the assumption that Uzziah was crowned after his father was taken into captivity, see: Tadmor 1962, 282.

[44] For the coregency of Uzziah and Amaziah, see: Aharoni, 95, who emphasizes that the words "after that the king lay with his fathers" indicate that Uzziah ruled beforehand as well.

father, then it must be further assumed that Jeroboam son of Joash ruled for 52 or 53, and not 41 years (for the Biblical synchronisms indicate that he reigned from year 15 of Amaziah to year 38 of Uzziah, i.e., presumably 14–15 years in the reign of Amaziah and 38 years in the reign of Uzziah); or we will be forced to assume that Uzziah ruled for less than 52 years. Indeed, some researchers shorten the reign of Uzziah to 42, 29, or even 26 years.[45]

Jeroboam apparently was crowned in 790, and ruled for 41 years until 750/49. Very little is known of this protracted period. Jeroboam succeeded in defeating Aram of Damascus and restoring Israelite sovereignty up to Lebo'-Hamath (II Kings 14:25–28). The conquests of Jeroboam most probably took place after the campaign of Shalmaneser IV against Damascus in 773 (Pazarcik inscription, rev., ll. 4–10; the Eponym Chronicles).[46] Israelite dominion of Damascus therefore continued for ca. 20 years.

Concurrent with Jeroboam's conquests in Syria, Uzziah was successful in occupying parts of Philistia and in regaining control of the port of Ezion-geber, and at this time Jotham may have subdued Ammon (see below). These actions, especially the renewed dominance of Ammon, probably would not have been possible without cooperation between the Northern and Southern Kingdoms. Such cooperation is indicated by the difficult passage in II Kings 14:28: ". . . and how he recovered Damascus, and Hamath, for Judah in Israel," and from I Chronicles 5:17, which indicates that a census was taken in the areas east of the Jordan controlled by Israel in the time of Jotham and Jeroboam. There is no reason to assume that this synchronism was an invention of the Chronicler. This information also plays a crucial role in determining the time of Jotham's reign. It is commonly accepted that Jotham was crowned in the lifetime of his father Uzziah. This assumption is based on the explicit passage in II Kings 15:5 which indicates that Uzziah contracted leprosy, left his palace, and

---

[45] Thus, e.g., Albright argued that Uzziah ruled 42 years (Albright, 21; idem 1963, 116); Andersen assumed in 1969 (95) that Uzziah reigned for 29 years; see also: Jagersma, 155 (in 1989 Andersen changed his mind; see above, 47, n. 6); and Hughes counted 26 years for Uzziah (Hughes, 275).

[46] For the determination of the conquests of Jeroboam after 773, see: Olmstead, Assyria, 169; Tadmor 1961, 239 ff. There is no proof for the assumption that Jeroboam began his conquests only towards the end of his lifetime. For this conjecture see: M. Haran, *Biblical Periods and Institutions*, Tel Aviv 1973, 240 ff. (Hebrew). Haran is of the opinion that the period in which Jeroboam enjoyed mastery over Damascus extended for only 7–8 years (ca. 755–748/7).

dwelt in "a house set apart," while his son Jotham ruled the kingdom: "And Jotham the king's son was over the household, judging the people of the land." It is clear from this text that before his investiture as king Jotham held the important administrative post: "אשר על הבית." The words "the king's son" apparently do not denote any official title, like the words "judging the people of the land," which indicates merely that Jotham was a "judge," i.e., governor, the ruler of Judah at the time. Jotham's title after his presumed crowning in his father's lifetime probably was "king," like all the coregents in Israel and in the ancient Near East. He ruled for 16 years (ca. 758 to 743/2), and died a number of years before his father. Jotham was probably installed in year 32/3 of Jeroboam, and ruled ca. 9 years during the reign of the latter. It is most likely that during this period Jotham gained control of Ammon, and conducted a census east of the Jordan in conjunction with Jeroboam the son of Joash (these two events probably occurred in the 750s BCE).

Uzziah probably was crowned in year 3 or 4 of Jeroboam. The synchronism establishing the investiture of Uzziah in year 27 of Jeroboam (II Kings 15:1) is in total contrast with all the other data, and probably is erroneous.[47] Uzziah's extended reign may be divided into four subperiods: (1) his coregency with his father, extending for ca. 12 years (788/7–776/5); (2) his reign as sole monarch (ca. 17 years, 776/5–758/7); the years in which he ruled together with his son Jotham (ca. 15 years, 758/7–743/2); (4) the last years of Uzziah,

---

[47] The datum in II Kings 15:1 attesting that Uzziah was crowned in year 27 of Jeroboam contradicts the following Biblical data: (1) the investiture of Jeroboam in year 15 of Amaziah, who ruled 29 years (II Kings 14:2, 23). This datum presumes that Uzziah the son of Amaziah was crowned, at the latest, in year 15 of Jeroboam; (2) Amaziah lived 15 years after the death of King Joash of Israel (ibid., v. 17); (3) the investiture of Zechariah in year 38 of Uzziah (II Kings 15:8) and all the other synchronisms relating to Uzziah and Israelite kings (II Kings 15:17, 23, 27). These data indicate that Uzziah began to rule ca. year 3 of Jeroboam, if it is assumed that Jeroboam ruled 41 years. Thiele's proposal for reconciling all these data (p. 79 ff.) is improbable. It presumes that the datum in question refers not to the investiture of Uzziah but to the death of Amaziah (or in Thiele's opinion, to the beginning of his reign as an independent monarch), i.e., that Amaziah died in year 27 of Jeroboam. Thiele also claims that Jeroboam began to reign in year 15 of Amaziah as an independent king, while he had already been crowned in the lifetime of his father. Thiele's thesis is problematic, for it entails the assumption that Amaziah and Joash installed their successors in year 5 of their reign. Furthermore, Thiele's hypothesis is not consistent with the important testimony regarding the conducting of a census east of the Jordan in the time of Jotham and Jeroboam. In Thiele's opinion, this datum is not reliable, because Jeroboam died ca. 3 years before the investiture of Jotham. For this question, see also: Kleber, 183 ff.; Aharoni, 95; Andersen, 91.

in which his grandson Ahaz ruled (ca. 8 years, 743/2–736/5). The major undertakings of Uzziah mentioned in the Bible probably took place in period (2), when he was approx. 28–45 years of age. II Kings 14:22 states explicitly that Uzziah built Elath and restored it to Judah, "after that the king lay with his fathers," i.e., after the assassination of Amaziah. The Book of Kings mentions only his illness that forced him to remove himself to "a house set apart," while Chronicles contains important information regarding Uzziah's activities, including his conquests in Philistia, his domination of the Me'unites and the Arabs who roamed south of Philistia, and his construction projects in Jerusalem, Judah, and possibly also in the Mishor. The majority of these activities apparently took place in the 760s.

It has recently been shown that Uzziah had no connection with the affair of Azriyau mentioned in the annals of Tiglath-pileser III.[48] It also is extremely doubtful if Judah took advantage of the weakness of Israel after the death of Jeroboam to increase its borders.[49] Judah did not overpower Israel in this period, and Israel obviously did not form an alliance with Assyria in order "to cast off the overbearing Judean superiority". In 836 King Uzziah was an old (approximate 66 years of age) and infirm man and he had no connection to the revolt against Assyria that erupted in northern Syria.

Zechariah son of Jeroboam was crowned in year 38 of Uzziah (apparently 750/49), and was assassinated in year 39 of Uzziah by Shallum, who reigned for a single month before being murdered in turn by Menahem in year 39 of Uzziah. Menahem ruled for ten years, and was succeeded by his son Pekahiah in year 50 of Uzziah (II Kings 15:8, 10, 13, 14, 17, 23). Pekahiah ruled for two years before he was assassinated by Pekah in year 52 of Uzziah (ibid., 21:27).[50] We shall first attempt to establish the time frame for this period, in the light of the Biblical data. This information would seem to be contradictory, for if Menahem seized power in year 39 of Uzziah, and then ruled for 10 years, we would expect that his son would have been crowned as his successor in year 49 of Uzziah, and not in year 50; similarly, if Pekahiah assumed the throne in year 50 of Uzziah, and was in

---

[48] Na'aman 1974, 36 ff.

[49] Tadmor 1961, p. 251.

[50] For the improbable assumption that Pekah is actually Pekahiah, see: Wellhausen, 630–631. Reade recently rediscovered this possibility (see: Reade, 5). The text, however, emphasizes that Pekah was the son of Remaliah, and he cannot be identified with Pekahiah son of Menahem, who was assassinated by his official, Pekah.

power for two years of reign, then Pekah should have been crowned in year 51, and not year 52, of Uzziah. Tadmor attempted to resolve these difficulties by assuming that the redactor of the Book of Kings rounded off the numbers of years of reign in his sources, arguing that in actuality Menahem ruled for 11 years, and Pekahiah for 3 years.[51]

The solution apparently lies in a change in the system of counting years of reign in Israel from antedating to postdating, which probably had already taken place in the time of Joash, following his submission to Assyria. The years of Jeroboam son of Joash apparently were postdated. Menahem ruled from 749 (= year 39 of Uzziah) until 738, and his son Pekahiah reigned from 738 to 736. This reconstruction coincides with the Assyrian sources (see below).

An additional difficulty is generated by the data pertaining to the coronation of Zechariah and Shallum. If there was a discrepancy of six months between the beginning of the new year in Israel and that in Judah, then it should be assumed that there was an interregnum before and/or after the short reign of Shallum. We prefer the possibility that Shallum ruled in the month of Elul and the beginning of Tishri (see table 20 – p. 80).

Following the publication of the stele of Tiglath-pileser III from Iran, we now possess two lists of kings who offered tribute to the Assyrian monarch which include the name of Menahem "of Samaria."[52] In one he is mentioned before Ethbaal (Tubaʾil) of Tyre (The Stele from Iran, IIIA, l. 6 [henceforth: List A]), and in the second he appears before Hiram of Tyre (Tadmor, *ITP*, Ann. 13*, l. 11 = Ann. 27, l. 2 [henceforth: List B]).[53] The different names of the kings of Tyre indicate that List A preceded List B, because Hiram king of Tyre is explicitly mentioned in inscription ND 4301 + in connection with Rezin and the campaigns of Tiglath-pileser III to the West in 734–732: "Hiram of Tyre, who with Rahianu (= Rezin) of [Damascus . . .]" (Tadmor, *ITP*, summ. 9, rev. ll. 5–8).[54]

We shall now attempt to determine the exact time of these two lists. The first step is to clarify the scope, composition, and order of the segments of the annals of Tiglath-pileser III. The section including List B is present, in Tadmor's opinion, in two series of annals (A

[51] Tadmor 1962, 283–284; and before him, Lewy, 16. For the assumption that Menahem reigned 11 years, see also: Aharoni, 96.

[52] For the Iran stele, see: Levine, 11–24; Tadmor, *ITP*, 91–110.

[53] Tadmor, *ITP*, 68–69, 89, 106–107.

[54] Cogan 1973, 96–99; Tadmor, *ITP*, 186–187.

and B). Thanks to the research conducted by Tadmor, it is now clear that sections 3, 9, IIIR (Rost, ll. 123–159) are merely the eclectic text of G. Smith, and further discussion must be based on the copies of Layard and not on Smith's work.[55] Tadmor demonstrated that list B comprises a list of the kings of the West who gave tribute to Assyria in 738/7.[56] In 739 the Assyrian king was in the area of the Upper Tigris (Ulluba), thereby leading to the conclusion that List A is only a list of those giving tribute to Assyria in 740/39, the year in which the Assyrians conquered Arpad.[57]

The following is a concise reconstruction of the events in 745–738, which will clarify the manner in which the submission of Menahem to Assyria fits into these occurrences:

1. In the time of Ashur-nirari V, who preceded Tiglath-pileser III, the Assyrians still ruled northern Syria, including Arpad, and apparently also Unqi. The kings of Arpad and Unqi were accused by Tiglath-pileser III of violating the oath they had made during the reign of his predecessor. The kingdom of Urarṭu extended its rule in the area and controlled Kummuh, Carchemish, and the Aleppo region; the kingdom of Hamath may possibly still have been under Israelite influence at the time.

2. In 743/2 the Assyrians defeated a coalition headed by Sarduri II of Urarṭu and Mati'il of Arpad and which included additional kings, among them the kings of Melid, Gurgum, and Kummuh. The victory on the battlefield in the land of Kummuh was followed by an Assyrian siege of the city of Arpad. The city fell after three years, and the kingdom of Arpad became an Assyrian province.

3. After the fall of Arpad in 740, most of the kingdoms of the West submitted to Assyria (the Iran stele). The list of tribute-givers to Assyria includes, *inter alia*, Israel, Damascus, Tyre, and the Arabs. On the other hand, two major groups are missing from the list: (a) the kingdoms located south of Damascus and Israel, including Judah, the kingdoms east of the Jordan, and the Philistine city-states; (b) the kingdoms of northwestern Syria, headed by Hamath and Unqi, as well as the Phoenician cities to the south of Unqi and to the west of Hamath,

[55] Tadmor 1967, 124; idem, *ITP*, 31, 216 ff.
[56] Tadmor 1961, 257, 271; idem, *ITP*, 234–235, 263 ff., 273–276; see also: Loretz and Mayer, 226.
[57] For a different view, see: Thiele 1983, 143 ff.

including Usnu, Zimarra, Arvad, Ṣimirra (Ṣumur), Arqa, Siannu, and Kashpuna. At least one of these kingdoms was regarded as rebelling against Assyria (Unqi). The nonsubmission of the others, however, was undoubtedly perceived by the Assyrians as a hostile act which could not go unanswered.

4. II Kings 15, 19–20 relates of the arrival of the Assyrian king in the land of Israel and his acceptance of the tribute from Menahem, apparently referring to the submission of the latter in 740/39. Menahem faced challenges at the time, and his joining with Assyria was intended to strengthen the new dynasty. The money for the Assyrians was not paid from the royal treasury, but was collected from the landed classes who apparently opposed Menahem. The Assyrian sources contain no evidence of Tiglath-pileser's arrival in the land of Israel in the time of Menahem, but the inscriptions of Tiglath-pileser are silent regarding events during the years 742–740, and therefore the Biblical testimony is not to be rejected out of hand.

5. After the conquest of Arpad and the acceptance of tribute from the kings of the West, the Assyrian army marched to the Upper Tigris region and fought against Ulluba (739/8).

6. In 738/7 the Assyrian army returned to the West and defeated the coalition apparently headed by Azriyau (the king of Hamath?) and Tutamu the king of Unqi. The Assyrians conquered these kingdoms and transformed them into Assyrian provinces. Of the kingdoms against which the Assyrians marched in 736, only Hamath did not become a province, as is indicated by the mention by name of Eni-il king of Hamath in the list of kings offering tribute in 738. The omission of Hamath from the stele from Iran is not coincidental, it rather seems to indicate that Hamath did not submit to Assyria in 740.[58] Furthermore, if Hamath remained loyal to Assyria in 738 and did not join the coalition of Azriyau, and was itself harmed by the latter's actions (since its cities were occupied), why was it punished by the Assyrians, who stripped it of nineteen of its districts? The king of Hamath could have expected to be rewarded for his loyalty after the suppression of the revolt, and certainly not to have parts of his kingdom annexed by Assyria. In light of the above-mentioned facts, it is more likely that Azriyau was the king of Hamath. His

[58] Cf. Na'aman 1977, 178–180.

name probably indicates Israelite influence upon Hamath in the 750s.[59] Azriyau either died in battle or was deposed in a coup d'etat, to be succeeded by Eni-il. The presumed coup in Hamath and the ascension of a pro-Assyrian clique may have been the reason for Assyrian approval of the continued semi-independent existence of the kingdom, within a reduced territory (cf. the circumstances surrounding the seizure of power by Hoshea, the last Israelite king).

7. The king of Arvad is not listed among the kings offering tribute to Assyria in 738, thereby indicating that Arvad did not surrender, not even after the defeat of the kings of Unqi and the Phoenician kingdoms to the north of Byblos in 738. The Assyrians succeeded in overwhelming Arvad only during their campaign of 734, as is indicated from the mention of the king of Arvad among those giving tribute in this year (K 3751 = Tadmor, *ITP*, Summ. 7, rev., l. 10'). The submission of Arvad apparently also is mentioned in the summary inscription ND 400 (= Tadmor, *ITP*, Summ. 8, ll. 1'–7'), which speaks of the surrender of a city located "in the midst of the sea."[60]

Pekah undoubtedly did not reign for 20 years as a sole monarch, since ca. 7 years elapsed between the giving of tribute by Menahem (year 8 of Tiglath-pileser III – 738) and by Hoshea in year 15 of Tiglath-pileser III (731), and therefore it is perfectly clear that Pekah could not have reigned as sole monarch for two decades. Even if it is assumed that Menahem died in 738, and that Hoshea was crowned in 731, it cannot be accepted that Pekah ruled as sole monarch for more than 5 years, for in the first two of these seven years Pekahiah son of Menahem ruled. It therefore may be concluded that the datum that Pekah reigned for 20 years is erroneous (this is probably the only instance of an erroneous Biblical datum regarding years of reign). Scholars have surmised that Pekah was crowned towards the end of Jeroboam's lifetime, and ruled in Gilead also during the reigns of Zechariah, Shallum, Menahem, and Pekahiah.[61] This hypothesis must be rejected, however, because II Kings 15:25 defines Pekah as a captain ("שליש") of Pekahiah, and therefore it is inconceivable that he ruled in conjunction with Pekahiah. At the most, it may be surmised

[59] For the Israelite influence in Hamath, see: Dalley 1990, 27 ff.

[60] Alt, KS, II, 152–153; Oded 1974, 46; but cf. Tadmor, *ITP*, 176.

[61] For the thesis that Pekah reigned in Gilead during the time of his predecessors, see: Lewy, 18–19; Cook, 128–135 and loc. cit. for additional literature.

that he was the official appointed over Gilead by the Israelite king. It is possible, however, that after his investiture, Pekah counted the years of his reign retroactively, from his appointment in the time of Jeroboam II.

The Israelite synchronisms stating that Jotham was crowned in year 2 of Pekah, and Ahaz in year 17 of Pekah (II Kings 15:32; 16:1), are most likely erroneous, and were probably calculated by a redactor in the following way: the first datum is based on the report that Pekah began to rule in year 52 of Uzziah (his last year). If year 1 of Pekah = year 52 of Uzziah, then year 1 of Jotham, who succeeded his father, would be year 2 of Pekah. The datum that Hoshea was installed in year 20 of Jotham was reached by a similar calculation. It is based on the assumption that Pekah reigned for 20 years. In year 20 of Pekah, Hoshea was crowned, and therefore year 1 of Hoshea = year 20 of Jotham (see the table below). The datum that the investiture of Ahaz was in year 16 of Pekah is derived from three data: Jotham reigned for 16 years; he was crowned in year 2 of Pekah; the latter ruled for 20 years. If year 1 of Jotham = year 2 of Pekah, then year 16 of Jotham = year 17 of Pekah, and in this year Ahaz was crowned (the last calculation may possibly have been made by a redactor, after the composition of the Book of Kings).

Uzziah 52	*Jotham 1*	2	3	4	5	6	7	8	9	10	11	12	13	14	15	16	17	18	19	*20*
Pekah 1	*2*	3	4	5	6	7	8	9	10	11	12	13	14	15	16	*17*	18	19	20	*1 Hoshea*
																1 Ahaz				

Since Pekah was not the *de facto* sovereign during his first 15 years, and, at most, it may be assumed that he counted the years of his reign retroactively, after his coronation, it is clear that the datum that Jotham was crowned in year 2 of Pekah cannot be original. It may be assumed that the sources of the author of the Book of Kings contained the correct data pertaining to this period, but he could not reconcile them with the datum that Pekah reigned for 20 years. The author of the Book of Kings therefore proposed an alternative system of data, without expunging the previous system. The Assyrian synchronisms indicate that the reverse was not the case.

In the time of King Ahaz of Judah, Israel and Aram marched against Jerusalem and sought to install a puppet as king. In the wake of the Aramean-Israelite attack, Ahaz sent messengers and tribute to the Assyrian king, stating: "I am your servant and your son; come up, and save me out of the hand of the king of Aram, and out of the hand of the king of Israel, who rise up against me" (II Kings 16:7). Verse 9 relates that Tiglath-pileser III responded favorably to the petition by Ahaz: he attacked Aram, conquered Damascus, and killed Rezin. It is not clear from these texts when Judah became an Assyrian satellite, before or after Ahaz's appeal.[62]

In the inscriptions of Tiglath-pileser, Ahaz is mentioned by name only in a clay inscription from Calah (K 3751 = Tadmor, *ITP*, Summ. 7, rev., l. 11'), in which "Jehoahaz of Judah" is listed among those presenting tribute to Assyria, along with other kings, including those of Ammon, Moab, and Edom, and the Philistine kings: [Mi]tinti of Ashkelon and [Ha]nun of Gaza. This summary inscription was composed after the seventeenth year of Tiglath-pileser III (= 729/8). The events it describes appear in geographic, and not chronological order: rev., ll. 1'–6' tell of the surrender of the Arabs and the nomads and the appointment of Idibiʾilu, apparently reflecting events occurring in 733–732; rev., ll. 7'–9' contain an up-to-date list of those giving tribute to Assyria in 738.[63] Missing from this list are the names of a number of kings, including those of Aram and Israel. Lines 10'–13' (rev.) list kings of Phoenicia, Philistia, the lands east of the Jordan, and Judah, who were not mentioned in the list of tribute-givers in 738, and l. 14' ff. (rev.) mention two additional events apparently dating to the end of this period: the payment of the offering by Metenna of Tyre, and the deposition of Uassurme king of Tabal. Since the latter was also included in rev., l. 9' of this inscription among the givers of tribute, it is clear that rev., l. 14' ff. were added to the nucleus of the inscription, which was formulated from the joining together of a number of passages. The inclusion of Panammu king of Samʾal and of [Mi]tinti of Ashkelon in inscription K 3751 indicates that the tribute was given in 734, because Panammu of Samʾal was killed during the siege of Damascus in 733/2 (*KAI*, 215,

[62] For the Syrian-Ephraimite war see: Oded 1972b, 153 ff.; Lipinski 1979, 97–101; H. Tadmor and M. Cogan, "Ahaz and Tiglath-Pileser in the Book of Kings: Historiographic considerations," *Biblica* 60 (1979), 491–508; R. Bickert, "König Ahaz und der Prophet Jesaja. Ein Beitrag zum Problem des syrisch-ephraimitischen Krieges," *ZAW* 99 (1987), 361–384; S. A. Irvin, *Isaiah, Ahaz, and the Syro-Ephraimitic Crisis*, Atlanta 1990; E. Ben-Zvi, "Tracing Prophetic Literature in the Book of Kings: The Case of II Kings 15, 37," *ZAW* 102 (1990), 100–105; Becking, 5–20; Galil 1992b, 60–61; Tadmor, *ITP*, 279–282.

[63] Tadmor 1990, 186–187; idem, *ITP*, 170–171, 265–268.

ll. 16–18), and [Mi]tinti of Ashkelon was deposed in 733 or in 732 (Tadmor, *ITP*, Ann. 18, ll. 8'–9'; Ann. 24, 12'–16').

The order of Tiglath-pileser III's campaigns in 734–732 is problematic, because of three main reasons: (1) the majority of the Assyrian inscriptions are of a summary nature, and the few surviving annalist fragments provide only minor help in determining the order of the campaigns; (2) the Assyrian inscriptions are contradictory; (3) the Biblical testimony is insufficiently clear, and cannot be employed in deciding among the various reconstruction possibilities.

From among the various proposals raised by researchers, the following reconstruction is to be preferred:

1. *The campaign in 734/3.* The goal of the Assyrian campaign to the Mediterranean coast is insufficiently clear. It most probably was economic: the Assyrians sought to take control of the wealthy coastal cities.[64] The following is the most likely course of events of this campaign:

a. the conquest of Arvad (?) and the annexation of Kashpuna to the province of Ṣumur (ND 400 = Tadmor, *ITP*, Summ. 8, ll. 1'–9').
b. the conquest of the Tyrean cities, including Mahalab (ND 4301 + = Tadmor, *ITP*, Summ. 9, rev., ll. 5–8).
c. the Assyrian army then continued south along the coastal highway towards Philistia.
d. the conquest of Gaza (IIIR 10, 2 = Tadmor, *ITP*, Summ. 4, ll. 8'–15'; ND 4301 + = Tadmor, *ITP*, Summ. 9, rev., ll. 13–16; ND 400 = Tadmor, *ITP*, Summ. 8, ll. 14'–18').
e. the erection of a monument in "the city of the brook of Egypt" (ND 400 = Tadmor, *ITP*, Summ. 8, ll. 18'–19').
f. the submission of Siruatti the Meʿunite (ND 400 = Tadmor, *ITP*, Summ. 8, ll. 22'–23').

During the course of the campaign, Assyria accepted the surrender of most of the kingdoms of the West, including Judah and Ashkelon (K 3751 = Tadmor, *ITP*, Summ. 7, rev., 1'–13'). At the conclusion of the campaign, the Assyrians returned to their own land.

2. After the departure of the Assyrians from the region, Aram and Israel attacked Judah, on the background of the conflicts between the

[64] Cf. H. Tadmor, "Philistia Under Assyrian Rule," *BA*, 29 (1966), 88; Oded 1974, 42–49; B. Otzen, "Israel under the Assyrians," *Annual of the Swedish Theological Institute*, 11 (1977/78), 101 ff.

kingdoms, with the Arameans intending to overrun the kingdom of Judah. At this time Elath was conquered (II Kings 16:6), and the Philistines occupied areas in the Judean Shephelah (II Chronicles 28:18). The Aram-Israel alliance apparently was joined by additional kings, including, *inter alia*, Hanun of Gaza, Hiram of Tyre, and Samsi the queen of the Arabs.

3. Following the attack on Judah, Ahaz sent emissaries to the Assyrian king, seeking his protection and his intervention in the conflict. This request, which coincided with Assyrian interests, apparently only marginally influenced the decision of the Assyrian monarch to shorten his stay in Urarṭu (before the siege of Ṭushpa had been concluded) and divert the major thrust of his war effort to the West, in order to stop the erosion of Assyrian status and to prevent the expansion of the Aramean-Israelite coalition.

4. *The campaigns in 733/2* were directed mainly against Aram and Israel. It is difficult to reconstruct the elements of these campaigns, and the following order must remain mere conjecture:

a. at the start of the campaign, parts of the Aramean kingdom were conquered, and Damascus was besieged (Tadmor, *ITP*, Ann. 23, 1'–17').
b. the territory east of the Jordan was then occupied, and Israelites from the tribes of Reuben, Gad, and Manasseh were exiled to Assyria (II Kings 15:29; I Chronicles 5:6, 22, 25–26).
c. the annals of Tiglath-pileser (Rost, l. 210 = Tadmor, *ITP*, Ann. 23, 18') indicate that the warfare against the Arabs followed the conquest of parts of the kingdom of Damascus. The surrender of Samsi queen of the Arabs apparently occurred in late 733 or early 732.[65] The surrender of the queen of the Arabs was closely followed by that of the other nomadic tribes listed in the Assyrian inscriptions, including Massa', Tema', ʿEphah, and others. At that time the Assyrians appointed Idibi'ilu over the Egyptian border region.
d. the conquest of Israel was completed during the campaign. The Assyrian army occupied Galilee (II Kings 15:29; Tadmor, *ITP*, Ann. 18, 2'–7'; Ann. 24, 1'–11'?) and the cities of Ephraim and Manasseh, and laid siege to Samaria (732?).

---

[65] Cf. I. Ephʿal, *The Ancient Arabs*, Jerusalem and Leiden 1982, 82 ff.; Tadmor, *ITP*, 80–81, 222 ff.

e. Damascus was conquered in 732. Rezin was put to death, and the kingdom of Aram was divided into four Assyrian provinces (II Kings 16:9; ND 4301 + = Tadmor, *ITP*, Summ. 9, rev. ll. 3–4; IIIR 10, 2 = Tadmor, *ITP*, Summ. 41 ll. 6'–8').

f. The fall of Damascus led to the submission of Samaria and Ashkelon as well, accompanied by coups d'etat in the latter two cities (the name of the deposed king of Ashkelon was probably Mitinti, who was replaced by Rukibtu). Hoshea seized the throne in Israel and executed Pekah (II Kings 15:30; ND 400 = Tadmor, *ITP*, Summ. 8, ll. 10'–13'; ND 4301 + = Tadmor, *ITP*, Summ. 9, rev., ll. 9–11; IIIR 10, 2 = Tadmor, *ITP*, Summ. 4, ll. 15'–19'; and apparently Tadmor, *ITP*, Summ. 13, ll. 17'–18').[66] Hoshea was crowned in 732/1; evidence for this date comes from an Assyrian inscription (ND 4301 + = Tadmor, *ITP*, Summ. 9, rev., ll. 9–11) indicating that Hoshea gave tribute to the Assyrian king in the city of Sarabanu in 731.[67]

---

[66] Na'aman 1986, 72–73; Tadmor, *ITP*, 202–203.
[67] Borger and Tadmor, 244 ff.; Tadmor, *ITP*, 188–189, 277.

Table 11

Assyria	*JUDAH*		*Year BCE*	*Israel*
Shalmaneser III	*Athaliah*	*Jehoash*	841	*Jehu*
18	1	1		2
			840	
19	2	2		3
			839	
20	3	3		4
			838	
21	4	4		5
			837	
22	5	5		6
			836	
23	6	6		7
			835	
24	7	7		8
			834	
25		8		9
			833	
26		9		10
			832	
27		10		11
			831	
28		11		

Table 12

Assyria	*Judah*	*Year BCE*	*Israel*
Shalmaneser III 28	*Jehoash* 11	831	*Jehu* 12
29	12	830	13
30	13	829	14
31	14	828	15
32	15	827	16
33	16	826	17
34	17	825	18
35 *Shamshi-Adad V* Accession year	18	824	19
1	19	823	20
2	20	822	21
3	21	821	

Table 13

Assyria	*Judah*	*Year BCE*	*I S R A E L*	
Shamshi-Adad V 3	*Jehoash* 21	821	*Jehu* 22	
4	22	820	23	*Jehoahaz* 1
5	23	819	24	2
6	24	818	25	3
7	25	817	26	4
8	26	816	27	5
9	27	815	28	6
10	28	814		7
11	29	813		8
12	30	812		9
13	31	811		

Table 14

Assyria	*JUDAH*		*Year BCE*	*ISRAEL*	
Adad-nirari III Accession year	*Jehoash* 31		811	*Jehoahaz* 10	
1	32		810	11	
2	33		809	12	
3	34		808	13	
4	35		807	14	
5	36		806	15	*Joash* 1
6	37	*Amaziah* Accession year	805	16	2
7	38	1	804	17	3
8	39	2	803		4
9	40	3	802		5
10		4	801		

Table 15

Assyria	*Judah*	*Year BCE*	*Israel*
Adad-nirari III 10	*Amaziah* 4	801	*Joash* 6
11	5	800	7
12	6	799	8
13	7	798	9
14	8	797	10
15	9	796	11
16	10	795	12
17	11	794	13
18	12	793	14
19	13	792	15
20	14	791	

Table 16

Assyria	*JUDAH*		*Year BCE*	*Israel*
Adad-nirari III 20	*Amaziah* 14		791	*Joash* 16
21	15		790	*Jeroboam II* Accession year
22	16		789	1
23	17	*Uzziah* Accession year	788	2
24	18	1	787	3
25	19	2	786	4
26	20	3	785	5
27	21	4	784	6
28 *Shalmaneser IV* Accession year	22	5	783	7
1	23	6	782	8
2	24	7	781	9

Table 17

Assyria	*JUDAH*		*Year BCE*	*Israel*
Shalmaneser IV	*Amaziah*	*Uzziah*		*Jeroboam II*
2	24	7	781	10
3	25	8	780	11
4	26	9	779	12
5	27	10	778	13
6	28	11	777	14
7	29	12	776	15
8		13	775	16
9		14	774	17
10 *Ashur-dan III* Accession year		15	773	18
1		16	772	19
2		17	771	

Table 18

Assyria	*Judah*	*Year BCE*	*Israel*
Ashur-dan III 2	*Uzziah* 17	771	*Jeroboam II* 20
3	18	770	21
4	19	769	22
5	20	768	23
6	21	767	24
7	22	766	25
8	23	765	26
9	24	764	27
10	25	763	28
11	26	762	29
12	27	761	

Table 19

Assyria	*JUDAH*		*Year BCE*	*Israel*
Ashur-dan III 12	*Uzziah* 27		761	*Jeroboam II* 30
13	28		760	31
14	29		759	32
15	30	*Jotham* Accession year	758	33
16	31	1	757	34
17	32	2	756	35
18 *Ashur-nirari V* Accession year	33	3	755	36
1	34	4	754	37
2	35	5	753	38
3	36	6	752	39
4	37	7	751	40
5	38	8	750	

Table 20

Assyria	*J U D A H*		*Year BCE*	*Israel*	*Retroactive count of the years of Pekah*
Ashur-nirari V	*Uzziah*	*Jotham*	750	*Jeroboam II* 40	1
5	38	8		41	2
6	39	9	749	*Zechariah*	
				Shallum	3
7	40	10	748	*Menahem* Accession year	

Table 21

Assyria	*JUDAH*		*Year BCE*	*Israel*	*Retroactive count of the years of Pekah*
Ashur-nirari V 7	*Uzziah* 40	*Jotham* 10	748	Accession year	4
8	41	11	747	*Menahem* 1	
9	42	12	746	2	5
10 *Tiglath-pileser III* 1 Accession year	43	13	745	3	6
2 (1)	44	14	744	4	7
3 (2)	45	15	743	5	8
4 (3)	46	16 *Ahaz* Accession year	742	6	9
5 (4)	47	1	741	7	10
6 (5)	48	2	740	8	11
7 (6)	49	3	739	9	12
8 (7)	50	4	738	10 *Pekahiah* Accession year	13

Table 22

Assyria	*JUDAH*		*Year BCE*	*Israel*	*Retroactive count of the years of Pekah*
Tiglath-pileser III 8 (7)	*Uzziah* 50	*Ahaz* 4	738	*Pekahiah* 1	14
9 (8)	51	5	737	2 *Pekah* Accession year	15
10 (9)	52	6	736	1	16
11 (10)		7	735	2	17
12 (11)		8	734	3	18
13 (12)		9	733	4	19
14 (13)		10	732	5 *Hoshea* Accession year	20
15 (14)		11	731	1	
16 (15)		12	730	2	
17 (16)		13	729	3	
18 (17)		14	728		

CHAPTER FIVE

THE LAST YEARS OF THE KINGDOM OF ISRAEL AND THE FALL OF SAMARIA

The Assyrian conquest of Samaria in the last quarter of the eighth century BCE brought about the end of the kingdom of Israel and the exile of tens from the land of Israel of thousands of Israelites. This historical event has received a great deal of attention in the scholarly literature, while the causes leading to the fall of the Israelite kingdom have not been properly clarified: the historical sources describing the event are contradictory, and Biblical scholarship has not provided satisfactory answers to the many questions raised by these sources. The following is a critical survey of the leading approaches presented in the scholarly literature, accompanied by a proposed reconstruction of the stages of the last campaign against Samaria and the process of the fall of the Northern Kingdom.

The Bible provides two descriptions of the last campaign against Samaria: (1) II Kings 17:3–6; (2) II Kings 18:9–12. The first description begins with the march against Israel by Shalmaneser king of Assyria, and the bringing of tribute by Hoshea (v. 3); v. 4 mentions the Israelite rebellion leading to the Assyrian campaign, in the course of which Hoshea was captured and imprisoned. It is not clear whether these two verses refer to one or two campaigns; if this is a description of only a single campaign (the prevailing scholarly opinion), why is the Assyrian king's march against Israel mentioned twice? And why does the description of the campaign precede the description of the roots of the crisis? How can the delivering of the tribute be reconciled with the arrest of Hoshea? Furthermore, v. 5 apparently relates to two events preceding the imprisonment of Hoshea: the king of Assyria marches against the Israelite cities ("Then the king of Assyria came up throughout all the land"), and only afterwards does he advance against Samaria and lay siege to it. The circumstances of Hoshea's arrest are not related, and it is not stated explicitly whether he was imprisoned before, during, or at the end of the siege of the city. The conqueror of Samaria is not identified. The context of the narrative would imply that Shalmaneser captured it, but his name is not explicitly stated in

v. 6. It is similarly unclear who exiled the Israelites. The author mentioned only the duration of the siege (three years) and the date of the city's capture—the ninth year of Hoshea. It may be concluded from this, in accordance with the perspective of the author, that Hoshea was imprisoned at the conclusion of the siege of the city, for according to II Kings 17:1, Hoshea ruled for nine years. The relationship between the scope of the historical description and that of the didactic speech in 17:7–23 indicates what, in the eyes of the author, was of primary importance in the Book of Kings and what was secondary: the historical facts are cited in a concise manner, which is not the case for the educational-religious lesson to be learned from this specific event.

No mention is made in chap. 18 of the rebellion and imprisonment of Hoshea, but two synchronisms absent from chap. 17 are added: the last siege of Samaria began in the fourth year of Hezekiah and was completed with the conquest of the city and the exile of its inhabitants in the sixth year of Hezekiah. This passage as well does not identify the conqueror of Samaria, nor who sent the Israelites into exile. The synchronisms in chapter 18 indicate that the city fell in the last year of Hoshea.

The extra-Biblical sources apparently attribute the conquest of Samaria to two different kings. The Babylonian Chronicle, written in the twenty-second year of Darius I, king of Persia (500 BCE) indicates that Samaria was conquered by Shalmaneser V, king of Assyria (727–722 BCE) while the Assyrian royal inscriptions attribute the conquest of the city to Sargon II, king of Assyria (722–705 BCE).

The capture of Samaria is the only event in the reign of Shalmaneser V recorded by the Babylonian Chronicle (I, ll. 27–30).[1]

> On the twenty-fifth day of the month Tebeth, Shalmaneser ascended the throne in Assyria [and Akkad]. He ravaged (*iḫ-te-pi*) Samaria.
>
> ---
>
> The fifth year: Shalmaneser died in the month Tebeth. For five years Shalmaneser ruled Akkad and Assyria.

The description of the reign of Shalmaneser is divided by a line into two clauses, and as will be discussed below, some scholars regarded this division as testifying to the time of the conquest of Samaria (in the beginning of the reign of Shalmaneser; or, in the opinion of

---

[1] K. Grayson, *Assyrian and Babylonian Chronicles*, Locust Valley, NY 1975, 73.

other scholars, at the end of his reign). The term "Samaria" in this passage is unclear. On the one hand, it may be assumed that it refers to the city of Samaria; on the other hand, however, there is a possibility that it represents the entire Northern Kingdom. It is well known that the term "Israel" is rare in the extra-Biblical sources; the kingdom, kings, or inhabitants of Israel are referred to, in most instances, by the toponym "Samaria," or by the phrase "the house of Omri," from which the appellation "the son of Omri" is derived.[2]

In the inscriptions of Sargon, the conquest of Samaria is mentioned many times. In the annals, the conquest of Samaria is placed in the accession year of Sargon.[3] The continuation of the annals speaks of the repression of a revolt in the second year of Sargon (720 BCE), in which Samaria also participated.[4] These sources apparently do not contradict one another, and they could be accepted at face value. Some scholars, however, thought otherwise (see below). In the Nimrud prism the description of the conquest of Samaria begins with a reference to the revolt of the Samarians:[5]

> [LÚ^{URU} *Sa*]*-me-ri-na-a-a ša it-ti* LUGAL [LÚ.KÚR]*-ia a-na la e-peš ar-du-ti* [*ù la na*]*-še-e bil-ti* [ḪUL-*t*]*ú ig-me-lu-ma e-pu-šú ta-ḫa-zu*
>
> [The Sa]marians—who requited (me with) [evil] with a king [hostile] to me, not to be (my) servants, [and not to de]liver tribute stood (against me) in battle.

This passage raises a number of questions: why is there a general reference to the Samarians, without (as was usual) mentioning the name of their king? Who is the hostile king with whom the Samarians were allied? Does the term "Samarians" refer only to the inhabitants of the city, or does it generally encompass all the inhabitants of the kingdom?[6]

---

[2] I. Eph'al, "'The Samarian(s)' in the Assyrian Sources," in: M. Cogan and I. Eph'al (eds.), *Ah Assyria . . . : Studies in Assyrian History and Ancient Near Eastern Historiography Presented to Haim Tadmor* (*Scripta Hierosolymitana* 33), Jerusalem 1991, 36–45. Menahem, king of Israel, is called in Tiglath-pileser III's stele from Iran: "^{m}*Mi-ni-hi-im-*⌜*me*⌝ ^{KUR}*Sa-*⌜*me*⌝*-ri-i-na-a-*⌜*a*⌝," yet in the Annals he is called "^{m}*Me-ni-hi-im-me* ^{URU}*Sa-me-ri-na-a-a.*" Cf. Tadmor, *ITP*, 68, 106.

[3] Lie, 4–7, II.2–3, ll. 10–17. Cf. recently Becking, 37–45. In his opinion the city, whose conquest is described in the Annals (II.2–3, ll. 10–17), cannot be identified. Cf. A. Fuchs, *Die Inschriften Sargons II. aus Khorsabad*, Göttingen, 1993, 87–88.

[4] Lie, 6–7, II.3, ll. 23–25; Fuchs, ibid., 89.

[5] C. J. Gadd, "Inscribed Prisms of Sargon II from Nimrud," *Iraq* 16 (1954), 179–180, frag. D, IV, ll. 25–28; Becking, 28–31.

[6] For the proposal to read: "against the king my [predecessor]," see: Dalley 1985, 36; Na'aman 1990, 209–210.

The conquest of Samaria during the reign of Sargon is also mentioned in his "summary inscriptions" from Khorsabad, including the inscription of Salon XIV, the Bull inscriptions[7] and the pavement inscriptions[8] ("the conqueror of Samaria and all the land of the house of Omri"); and similarly, in the Cylinder inscription ("the conqueror of the large land of the house of Omri."[9] The "Display inscription" makes mention both of the siege of Samaria and its becoming a province, and of the repression of the revolt of Hamath, in which Samaria also participated;[10] while "the Assur Charter" mentions only Samarian participation in the revolt of the king of Hamath.[11]

There are a number of clearly-delineated approaches in the research of the last years of the Israelite kingdom. Some researchers are of the opinion that Shalmaneser conquered Samaria and exiled the Israelites to Assyria.[12] In their view, the last siege of Samaria began in the second year of Shalmaneser (725 BCE) and concluded in the fourth or fifth year of his reign (723 or 722). In 720 a revolt was put down which had erupted in Samaria as well, but at that time it was already an Assyrian province. In the continuation of this hypothesis, the scholars restored "aga[inst Samaria]," in the corresponding lines for the years 725–723 in the Eponym Chronicles. They assert that the last king of Israel was imprisoned only in the ninth year of his reign, close to the fall of the city. Support for this view is provided by the fact that the Bible mentions only Shalmaneser, making no mention of Sargon. Thiele supposed that the conquest of the city is not to be dated to the sixth year of Hezekiah, because Hezekiah's invitation to the Israelites to celebrate the Passover was extended during the first year of his reign (II Chronicles 29:3; 30:1).[13]

This approach raises many difficulties and appears incorrect, for the following reasons: (1) the conquest of Samaria and the exile of its inhabitants during the time of Shalmaneser is indicated only in the

---

[7] Fuchs (above, n. 3), 63, l. 21; 76, l. 15.

[8] Idem, ibid., 261, ll. 31–32.

[9] Idem, ibid., 34, l. 19.

[10] Idem, ibid., 197, ll. 23–25.

[11] H. W. F. Saggs, "Historical Texts and Fragments of Sargon II of Assyria, 1. The 'Assur Charter'," *Iraq* 37 (1975), 11–20.

[12] A. T. Olmstead, "The Fall of Samaria," *AJSL* 21 (1904/5), 179–182; idem, *Western Asia in the Days of Sargon of Assyria, 722–705 B.C.*, New York 1908, 45–47; Olmstead, Assyria, 205; Hallo, 51; Jepsen 1968, 43; Reade, 4; Thiele 1983, 163–172; Hughes, 205–209.

[13] Thiele 1983, 168–171.

context of the surrounding events, and is not explicitly mentioned in the Bible (and the textual connection does not necessary indicate a chronological connection between the events); (2) there is no basis for the completion of the text in the Eponym Chronicles;[14] (3) we cannot ignore the numerous testimonies to the conquest of Samaria in the time of Sargon, and assume that they are all false; (4) if Hoshea was indeed imprisoned only at the end of the siege of the city, why was this fact noted before the description of the campaign and the beginning of the siege? (5) this proposal is not consistent with the data establishing the conquest of Samaria in the sixth year of Hezekiah; (6) no historical or chronological reconstruction can be based on the tendentious chronological data of the Chronicler, who sought to emphasize the righteousness of Hezekiah who, already in the first year of his reign, had instituted ritual reforms, purified the Temple, and gathered in the remnant of Israel.[15]

Other scholars state that the last siege of Samaria began during the time of Shalmaneser (in 724, which, in their opinion, is the ninth year of Hoshea), but it was completed only during the reign of Sargon, in the beginning of his reign, between Tebeth and Adar 722/1.[16] Hoshea was imprisoned at the beginning of the siege of the city, and until its fall no king ruled in Samaria. The siege began during the reign of Ahaz, and not during that of Hezekiah, who ascended the throne only in 715. In 720 Samaria joined the rebellion that had began in the West, but the city and the region already constituted an Assyrian province at this time. In their opinion, the Bible attributes only the beginning of the siege to Shalmaneser, while the description of the conquest of the city mentions an anonymous Assyrian king, who is to be identified with Sargon.

This theory raises two main difficulties: (1) this approach is in contradiction to the synchronisms establishing the conquest of Samaria during the reign of Hezekiah; (2) the accession year of Sargon lasted only ca. two and a half months (from 12 Tebeth to 29 Adar, 722/1), and it is difficult to assume that in such a short period Sargon succeeded in freeing himself for the conquest of Samaria, the exile of its inhabitants, and its reorganization as a province.[17] Furthermore, at

---

14 Tadmor 1958, 33, n. 100; Millard, Eponyms, 45–46.

15 Cogan 1980, 165–172; idem 1985, 179–209; Halpern, Chronology, 130 ff.

16 Lewy, 15–16; Mowinckel, 196; Albright, 22; Andersen, 97; idem 1989, 3, 8–14.

17 Thiele 1983, 166.

this time revolts broke out in various regions of the empire, and even Assyria itself was not free of opponents to Sargon, who had usurped the throne.[18]

Many researchers have accepted the approach of H. Tadmor.[19] In his opinion Samaria was conquered twice: during the last year of Shalmaneser (722) and again in the second year of Sargon (720). The first siege began in 724: Hoshea was imprisoned in its beginning, and during the course of four years, Samaria was not ruled by a king. In 722 Shalmaneser conquered the city, but died shortly after the conquest; following his death, the Assyrian army withdrew from Israel. In 720 the Assyrians once again seized Samaria, after it had joined the rebellion of the king of Hamath. Sargon exiled the inhabitants of the city, which he made the capital of the province of Samaria. In Tadmor's opinion, the first siege began in the fourth year of Hezekiah, although Samaria fell and became a province only in the eighth year of Hezekiah. Sargon's scribes, who sought to mark a military victory in each of the years of his reign, established the conquest of Samaria in his accession year and not in his second year.

Although Tadmor's approach resolves many problems, it too entails a number of difficulties: (1) it is difficult to assume that after the first conquest (following a protracted and difficult siege lasting more than two years), the Assyrian army would abandon the city without harming its fortifications, without exiling its inhabitants, and without turning it into a province, or at the very least leaving behind limited military units to complete the mission. It cannot be assumed that during a crisis all the Assyrian units would retreat from the provinces and leave them to their own devices. Despite the widespread rebellion at the beginning of Sargon's reign, there is no proof for the conjecture that the Assyrian military presence in the West totally collapsed (see below); (2) the partial destruction of Samaria (as is shown by the archaeological excavations) is inconsistent with the hypothesis of the double conquest;[20] (3) the establishment of the fall of Samaria in the eighth year of Hezekiah (720) creates, in effect, a

[18] Dalley 1985, 33.

[19] Tadmor 1958, 33–40; Cogan and Tadmor, II Kings, 195–201; Tadmor's hypothesis was accepted by many scholars. Recently it was defended, with minor variations, by Becking (53–56).

[20] For the excavations in Samaria, see: J. W. Crowfoot et al., *The Buildings at Samaria*, London 1942, 110; and recently N. Avigad, "Samaria," in: E. Stern (ed.), *The New Encyclopedia of Archaeological Excavations in the Holy Land*, Jerusalem 1993, vol. 4, 1300–1310, with additional bibliography.

two-year interregnum between Hezekiah and Manasseh (or between Manasseh and Amon, or between Amon and Josiah).

N. Na'aman has recently raised a new proposal,[21] the main points of which are: (1) the Assyrians waged three campaigns against Israel in the years 727/6–720: campaign I was conducted in the accession year of Shalmaneser's reign. This campaign is mentioned in II Kings 17:3 and in the Babylonian Chronicle (since the campaign is mentioned before the line separating the two clauses describing the reign of Shalmaneser, it must be dated close to his coronation, and not at the end of his reign). This campaign was in response to the (first) rebellion of Hoshea. Campaign II was conducted at the end of Shalmaneser's reign, in the wake of the (second) rebellion of Hoshea (II Kings 17:4–5).[22] Campaign III—in the second year of Sargon, Samaria was conquered (after it had rebelled a third time). The conquest of the city is attributed to Sargon, for literary reasons (thus following Tadmor); (2) Hoshea surrendered to the Assyrians during the course of the second campaign, and Samaria remained without a king during the years 722–720. It is not at all clear if Shalmaneser besieged the city; (3) the siege of Samaria did not last three years, rather three years elapsed between campaign II and campaign III (the duration of the siege is only an interpretation of the Deuteronomistic editor who found in his sources a report that Samaria had been conquered three years after it rebelled); (4) all the chronological data in II Kings 17:3–6; 18:9–12 are not accurate. In his opinion, Hezekiah was crowned in 728 and ruled for 43 years;[23] the description in II Kings 18:9–12 is totally lacking in historical value, and is based on 17:3–6.

Na'aman's proposal raises many difficulties: (1) there is no real basis for the claim that the Babylonian Chronicle indicates that the campaign against Samaria began at the start of Shalmaneser's reign. This is the only event in his reign which is mentioned, and it cannot be determined if it occurred in the beginning of, during the course of, or at the end of his reign;[24] (2) there is no evidence that Hoshea

---

[21] Na'aman 1990, 212–225.

[22] For the proposal that Shalmaneser conducted two campaigns against Israel, see: H. Goedicke, "The End of 'So, King of Egypt'," *BASOR* 171 (1963), 64; Katzenstein, 226–228.

[23] For a similar opinion, see: Gray 1970, 75.

[24] Dalley (1985, 33), supposed that it occurred at the end of the reign of Shalmaneser. In 1986 Na'aman held the same opinion as Dalley (Na'aman 1986, 74).

rebelled against Assyria in the beginning of the reign of Shalmaneser. This hypothesis is based on a faulty reading of II Kings 17:3; (3) it is difficult to imagine that Samaria escaped total destruction, despite the fact that three campaigns had been directed against it in a period of less than eight years; (4) the attribution of II Kings 17:5 to Sargon is problematic; (5) the passage in II Kings 18 is of great importance, containing as it does original material which could not be understood from what is stated in chapter 17; (6) it cannot be assumed that Shalmaneser was able to conduct a campaign against the Israelite kingdom in his accession year, which lasted ca. two months (25 Tebeth-29 Adar). Similarly, in the first year of his reign the king remained "i[n the land]" (the Eponym Chronicles, B 3:8').[25]

The following is a reconstruction of the main stages of the last siege of Samaria, in my opinion: Hoshea was crowned during the reign of Tiglath-pileser III (732/1), and remained loyal to Assyria until ca. 723. At that time he rebelled against Assyria, with the aid of the king of Egypt (II Kings 17:4. The name of the Egyptian king has not been preserved, and apparently we may reconstruct the text: "to So [to the] king of Egypt").[26] The reason of his rebellion is unclear. It may possibly have had its roots in the failure of the Assyrians and their allies in the naval battle against Tyre, which apparently was waged during the course of the second campaign against the city (Josephus, *Antiquities* 9:285–286). The first campaign against Tyre apparently had taken place in 725, and the second in 724 or 723. In the wake of Hoshea's rebellion, Shalmaneser invaded the Northern Kingdom, conquered its cities, and besieged Samaria (II Kings 17:5, and also the Babylonian Chronicle referring to the conquest of the Kingdom of Israel. The term "Samaria" is a general term representing the kingdom as a whole, as explained above). At that time Hoshea probably went forth from Samaria to meet the king of Assyria in a last-minute attempt to attain a compromise and prevent the conquest of the Israelite cities and the fall of Samaria. But the Assyrian king imprisoned Hoshea and continued his belligerent acts against

---

[25] Millard, Eponyms, 45, 59; for a new discussion of the subject, contrast J. H. Hayes and J. K. Kuan, "The Final Years of Samaria (730–720 B.C.)," *Biblica* 72 (1991), 153–181.

[26] For the identity of "So", see: D. L. Christensen, "The Identity of 'King So' in Egypt (2 Kings XVII 4)," *VT* 39 (1989), 140–153; J. Day, "The Problem of 'So, King of Egypt' in 2 Kings XVII 4," *VT* 42 (1992), 289–301; A. W. Green, "The Identity of King So of Egypt—An Alternative Interpretation," *JNES* 52 (1993), 99–108.

Samaria and its cities. Shalmaneser apparently arrived in Israel in the fourth year of Hezekiah (which was the fifth and last year of the Assyrian king), which began in the spring of 722 (Hoshea apparently was imprisoned before 1 Tishri 722).[27] Samaria did not fall, nor was another king installed in place of Hoshea; his ministers and officers remained loyal to him, and successfully withstood the Assyrian pressure for ca. two and a half years following the imprisonment of their king.

The Assyrians laid siege to Samaria probably in the summer of 722. A few months later, Shalmaneser died and was succeeded by Sargon. It is unclear how the Assyrian army deployed to deal with the revolts that erupted throughout the empire following Sargon's seizure of power. In any event, it may not be assumed that the troops garrisoned in the provinces withdrew from them, leaving the local Assyrian administration at the mercy of the rebels. To the contrary, the garrisons were probably reinforced with Assyrian troops or with auxiliaries recruited from among the vassal states. Furthermore, it is known that some of the provinces (mainly in frontier regions) possessed large military forces, which could be used independently against both domestic rebels and external threats (such as, e.g., the action of the prefect of Que against the king of Phrygia during the reign of Sargon II).[28] The Assyrian army encamped in Samaria was probably of limited scope, and the siege may possibly have turned into a blockade. It is inconceivable, however, that the Assyrians withdrew from Samaria, thereby permitting the Israelites to reorganize and become an unsettling and hostile element in the region. The Assyrians adopted a similar strategy at that time in their war against Tyre. The military activity against the city-state apparently began in 724 and continued for five years, until 720. The Assyrians initially engaged in offensive actions. Since their naval operations did not lead to the defeat of their enemy, the Assyrians contented themselves with the imposition of a blockade, cutting off the city's water supply (from its source near Usu).[29] It may be assumed that the enforcement of the blockade of Tyre (and, similarly, that of Samaria) required relatively small forces, and the blockade apparently continued during the ac-

[27] The pattern: "And it came to pass in the fourth year of king Hezekiah," was probably copied from a Judaite Chronicle, as the patterns in II Kings 12:7, 25:1 and in I Kings 14:25.

[28] Lie, 66–67, II.34, ll. 445–446.

[29] For the blockade on Tyre in the days of Shalmaneser and Sargon, see: Oded 1975, 206–208.

cession year of Sargon and also during the first and second years of his reign. It is possible, as was mentioned, that during the course of the military actions against Samaria the Assyrians also mobilized auxiliary forces from the neighboring vassal kingdoms (like the mobilization of the fleet of the Phoenician city-states against Tyre). It should be emphasized that most of the administrative and political units in the west remained loyal to Assyria in 722–720, including all the kingdoms in Trans-jordan; most of the kingdoms of Philistia (excluding Gaza); and most of the Phoenician city-states, among them Sidon and Byblos;[30] nor may it be assumed that Judah rebelled against Assyria at that time.[31]

In the second year of Sargon, the conquest of Samaria was completed: the city fell to the Assyrians, its inhabitants—and apparently also the inhabitants of additional cities—were exiled, and the Israelites were replaced by exiles from other regions.[32] It is unclear (a) whether the number of exiles from Samaria (27,280 or 27,290) also included Israelites who did not dwell in the city; (b) whether there were additional exiles; (c) how many Israelites were not exiled.[33] After its conquest, the city became the capital of the province of Samaria founded on the ruins of the Kingdom of Israel. The fighting over Samaria therefore lasted ca. three years (722–720 = the fourth-sixth years of Hezekiah king of Judah), and the city did indeed fall "at the end of" ca. three years. Sargon's scribes set the fall of Samaria in his accession year for literary-ideological reasons, as has been shown by Tadmor.[34]

The identity of the "Samarians" who fought Assyria in 722–720 cannot be decisively determined. This term may possibly apply, not

---

[30] Thirty-eight administrative and political units were included in the western parts of the Assyrian empire at the beginning of the reign of Sargon (Cf. E. Forrer, *Die Provinzeinteilung des assyrischen Reiches*, Leipzig 1920, 68–84). Only four vassal kingdoms rebelled or did not surrender to Assyria: Hamath, Gaza, Tyre, and Israel, and at least four provinces rebelled against Sargon: Arpad, Ṣumur, Damascus, and probably also Hadrach (Tadmor 1958, 37). It is not clear whether the Assyrian troops which were situated in the provinces succeeded in suppressing the rebellion; and how many troops from those provinces actually came to aid the king of Hamath.

[31] For the relations between Assyria and Judah in the days of Sargon II, see: Galil 1992a, 111–133.

[32] For the question whether all the Israelites were exiled from the land see: B. Oded, "II Kings 17: Between History and Polemic," *Jewish History* 2 (1987), 37–50.

[33] For the deportations to Samaria see: Oded 1979, 66; N. Na'aman, "Population Changes in Palestine following Assyrian Deportations," *Cathedra* 54 (1989), 56 (Hebrew).

[34] Tadmor 1958, 30–32.

only to the inhabitants of the city of Samaria who attempted to extricate themselves from the blockade, but also to the inhabitants of the outlying Israelite cities, who apparently attempted to bring supplies to their besieged compatriots and even to attack the Assyrian army encamped on Israelite soil. The "remnant of Israel" at that time undoubtedly drew extra strength from the rebellions that plagued the Assyrian empire, and it is possible that the Israelites, along with soldiers from the provinces of Damascus, Ṣumur, Arpad, and probably also Hadrach, volunteered to aid the king of Hamath in his revolt against Assyria.

In the opinion of the author of the Book of Kings, who lived ca. 150 years after the conquest of Samaria, and who wrote both the description in 17:3–6 and that in 18:9–12, Shalmaneser was the Assyrian king who imprisoned Hoshea, conquered Samaria after the three-year siege, and exiled the Israelites to Assyria. It appears that the author had knowledge only of Shalmaneser. It is noteworthy that the information he possessed regarding relations between Israel/Judah and Assyria was highly fragmentary, as is demonstrated by the fact that the description in the Book of Kings indicates that Judah was to no degree under Assyrian rule in the time of Manasseh, Amon, and Josiah (in the opinion of the author of Kings, Assyrian rule in Judah came to an end with the failure of Sennacherib's campaign).[35] His knowledge of the last years of the Northern Kingdom apparently also was fragmentary and hazy; it is in this context that the purpose of 17:3 is to be explained. It seems that he wrote this verse to explain the revolt of Hoshea, for in his opinion, Hoshea had not been an Assyrian vassal before the reign of Shalmaneser, but only after the campaign that the later apparently conducted against Hoshea (as is stated in v. 3); the existence of such a campaign is not supported by any extra-Biblical source. In the author's opinion, Menahem offered tribute to Tiglath-pileser. It is clear, however, that he supposed that this was a one-time tribute of submission in order to maintain his rule over Israel, after which the Assyrian king left Israel. Furthermore, there is no evidence in the Book of Kings that Pekah was an Assyrian vassal, and there is no connection between the campaigns of Tiglath-pileser III and the coup d'etat of Hoshea. Consequently, in the author's opinion, Hoshea, at the beginning of his reign, was not an Assyrian vassal, while in his sources he found that Hoshea

[35] Galil 1988, 1–12.

rebelled against Assyria. This inconsistency was resolved by him in v. 3, which is merely an interpretation by the author, who sought to clarify his sources and explain how Hoshea rebelled against Assyria if previously he had not been its vassal. In his opinion, Israel became an Assyrian vassal state only during the time of Shalmaneser (and not immediately upon the coronation of Hoshea). Together with this, however, it is clear that the author possessed reliable testimonies which apparently originated in the Book of the Chronicles of the Kings of Judah;[36] it is unlikely that he also possessed an Israelite source (in the description of the reign of Hoshea and the conquest of Samaria there is no mention of the Book of the Chronicles of the Kings of Israel. For an estimated reconstruction of the chronicles of Judah, see table 24).[37] In his descriptions, the author intermittently inserted interpretive additions which he had composed and reworked passages from the original chronicle. It is likely that the purpose of the repetition in the Book of Kings of the description of the fall of Samaria was to emphasize that this occurred during the reign of Hezekiah.

---

[36] Snaith, 291; Gray 1964, 583 ff.

[37] Many exegetes claimed that II Kings 17:3–6 and II Kings 18:9–12 are almost identical parallels. Cf. Montgomery and Gehman, 465, 482; T. R. Hobbs, *2 Kings* (*WBC*), Waco 1985, 224–226, 228–231, 253–254; Cogan and Tadmor, II Kings, 195–201, 217–222. For recent discussions of this subject, see: C. Hardmeier, *Prophetie im Streit vor dem Untergang Judas*, Berlin and New York 1990, 110, 117; S. L. McKenzie, *The Trouble with Kings*, Leiden 1991, 101–102.

Table 23

Assyria	*Judah*	*Year BCE*	*Israel*
Tiglath-pileser III 18 (17)	*Ahaz* 14	728	*Hoshea* 4
19 (18) *Shalmaneser V* Accession year	15	727	5
1	16 *Hezekiah* Accession year	726	6
2	1	725	7
3	2	724	8
4	3	723	9
5 *Sargon II* Accession year	4	722	*The last siege of Samaria* 1st year
1	5	721	2nd year
2	6	720	3rd year
3	7	719	
4	8	718	

Table 24

2 Kings 17	*Reconstruction of the Judaean Chronicle*	*2 Kings 18*
Addition (1) /1/ In the twelfth year of Ahaz king of Judah began Hoshea the son of Elah to reign in Samaria over Israel nine years. /2/ And he did that which was evil in the sight of the Lord, but not as the kings of Israel that were before him /3/ Against him came up Shalmaneser king of Assyria; and Hoshea became his servant, and gave him presents.		*Source* (1)
Source (1) /4/ and . . . the king of Assyria found conspiracy in Hoshea . . . for he had sent messengers to So . . . king of Egypt and brought no present to the king of Assyria as he had done year by year. Therefore the king of Assyria shut him up, and bound him in prison /5/ Then the king of Assyria came up throughout all the land, and went up to Samaria, and besieged it three years.	and it came to pass in the fourth year of King Hezekiah. And [Shalmaneser] the king of Assyria found conspiracy in Hoshea [king of Israel] for he had sent messengers to So [to the] king of Egypt and brought no present to the king of Assyria as he had done year by year. Therefore the king of Assyria shut him up, and bound him in prison. Then the king of Assyria came up throughout all the land, and went up to Samaria, and besieged it and at the end of three years they took it.	/9/ and it came to pass in the fourth year of King Hezekiah *Addition* (1) which was the seventh year of Hoshea son of Elah king of Israel. *Source* (2) that Shalmaneser king of Assyria came up against Samaria and besieged it. /10/ And at the end of three years they took it, even in the sixth year of Hezekiah. *Addition* (2) that is the ninth year of Hoshea king of Israel
Addition (2) /6/ In the ninth year of Hoshea	in the sixth year of [the king] Hezekaiah the king	*Source* (3) Samaria was taken /11/ And the king of Assyria did carry away

Table 24 (*continuation*)

2 Kings 17	*Reconstruction of the Judaean Chronicle*	*2 Kings 18*
Source (2) the king of Assyria took Samaria, and carried Israel away into Assyria, and placed them in Halah and in Habor by the river of Gozan, and in the cities of the Medes.	of Assyria took Samaria, and carried Israel away into Assyria, and placed them in Halah and in Habor by the river of Gozan, and in the cities of the Medes. And the king of Assyria brought men from Babylon, etc.	Israel unto Assyria, and put them in Halah and in Habor by the river of Gozan and in the cities of Medes.
Addition (3) vv. 7–23.		*Addition* (3) /12/ Because they obeyed not the voice of the Lord their God but transgressed His covenant, and all that Moses the servant of the Lord commanded, and would not hear them, nor do them.
Source (3) /24/ and the king of Assyria brought men from Babylon, etc.		

CHAPTER SIX

THE CHRONOLOGY OF THE KINGS OF JUDAH FROM HEZEKIAH TO JOSIAH

There are differences of opinion regarding the time of King Hezekiah of Judah. Extra-Biblical sources indicate that Hezekiah ruled in 701, the year in which Sennacherib of Assyria conducted his campaign to the West.[1] It also is clear, from both the Bible and the inscriptions of Sennacherib, that Hezekiah was not deposed in this year, and he continued to reign in Jerusalem after the departure of the Assyrians from the land. Two other extra-Biblical testimonies indicate (1) that Hezekiah was crowned after 734, the year in which his father Ahaz offered tribute to Tiglath-pileser III of Assyria (K 3751, rev., 11'); and (2) ca. 677/6 his son Manasseh already occupied the throne (Esarhaddon, Nineveh Prisms A and F, 55). Hezekiah is mentioned by name in the "Azekah inscription" (apparently in the form "*Ha-zaq-ia-a-u*");[2] I assumed that this inscription describes the conquests of Hezekiah in Philistia ca. 713 and the campaign of Sargon II against Judah and Ashdod in 712. If we were to possess only the extra-Biblical sources, we would assume that Hezekiah reigned for at least 13 years (713–701), that he was crowned after 734, and that he died before 677/6. This conclusion is not at variance with the Biblical testimony that counts 29 years for Hezekiah (II Kings 18:2). On the other hand, there are contradictory Biblical testimonies regarding the year of Hezekiah's investiture. The text in II Kings 18:13 (= Isaiah 36:1), which testifies that Sennacherib conducted his campaign in the fourteenth year of Hezekiah, indicates that he was crowned in 715; while the synchronisms connecting Hezekiah and Hoshea, the last Israelite

[1] For recent discussions of the campaign of Sennacherib to the West, see: H. Tadmor, "Sennacherib's Campaign to Judah: Historical and Historiographical Considerations," *Zion* 50 (1985), 65–80 (Hebrew); E. Vogt, *Der Aufstand Hiskias und die Belagerung Jerusalems 701 v. Chr.*, Rome 1986; Galil 1988, 1–12 and loc. cit. for additional literature; B. Halpern, "Jerusalem and the Lineages in the Seventh Century BCE: Kingship and the Rise of Individual Moral Liability," in: B. Halpern and D. W. Hobson (eds.), *Law and Ideology in Monarchic Israel* (*JSOT* supp. 124), Sheffield 1991, 11–107, esp. 20–49.

[2] Galil 1992a, 111 ff.

king (II Kings 18:1, 9–10), indicate that Hezekiah was installed in the 720s. Some researchers prefer to accept the data in vv. 1, 9–10, and they surmise that Hezekiah was crowned between 728 and 725, and that he ruled until ca. 699/7.[3] Other scholars, based on the information in v. 13, surmise that Hezekiah was crowned only in 715 and died in 697/6[4] or in 687/6.[5] A third group argues that there is no contradiction between all these data.[6] They theorize that Hezekiah was in fact crowned in the 720s, in the lifetime of his father King Ahaz. In 715, after the death of Ahaz, a new count of his years began. The campaign of Sennacherib was conducted in year 14 of his reign as sole king (after the death of his father), and these researchers also count the 29 years of his reign from 715. In their opinion Hezekiah's reign extended in practice for 42 or 43 years. All the above-mentioned scholars assumed the reliability of at least a portion of the chronological data in II Kings 18:1–13. In contrast, Hughes has recently revived the assumption that these data are not accurate, and cannot be used in calculating the years of Hezekiah.[7] This approach assumes that Hezekiah was crowned in 722, the year in which Shalmaneser V of Assyria and Ahaz of Judah died. This hypothesis relies upon the prophecy in Isaiah 14:28–32: "In the year that king Ahaz died was this burden. Rejoice not, O Philistia, all of you, because the rod that smote you is broken. . . ." This last assumption, however, is improbable. The prophecy in Isaiah 14:28–32 is likely to support the assumption that Ahaz died and Hezekiah was crowned in 727 or in 726, close to the death of Tiglath-pileser III, for it was he who had attacked Philistia. This was not the case regarding Shalmaneser V; there is no proof of his presumed action against the Philistines.[8]

The supposition that Hezekiah ruled 42 or 43 years is improbable.

---

[3] This opinion is held by many scholars, including Lewy (15, 32), Begrich (155), Jepsen (36–38), Schedl 1962a (112–119), Pavlovsky and Vogt (342–343), Vogelstein (2–3), Tadmor 1962 (277–279), Aharoni (96–97, 100), and Jenkins (286). It also reflects the view of the researchers agreeing with Begrich and Jepsen, and that of the scholars who accept Tadmor's reconstruction (see above, Chapter One).

[4] Mowinckel (214–220, 271); Andersen (98, 112), and those accepting Andersen's 1969 reconstruction, including Herrmann, Lemche (9), Jagersma, and Jones; yet in 1989 (14 ff., 45) Andersen changed his mind (see below).

[5] This is the opinion of Kleber (181–188), Thiele 1983 (174), Albright (22), and all the researchers accepting the theses of Thiele or of Albright.

[6] For this assumption, see: Horn 1964, 47–50; Gray 1970, 74; Kitchen, 494; Na'aman 1986, 84–85, 90 and loc. cit. for additional literature.

[7] Hughes, 212–218, 222 and loc. cit. for additional literature.

[8] For this assumption see, e.g.: Tadmor 1962, 278; Pavlovsky and Vogt, 342–343.

It cannot be assumed that a new count was initiated for the coregent after the death of his father. In fact, the Egyptian testimonies indicate (1) that the years of a king were counted from his coronation, whether he was crowned in the lifetime of his father, or whether his investiture followed his father's death; and (2) that a new count did not begin after the death of the father.[9]

The supposition that Hezekiah was crowned in 715 raises many difficulties and contradicts seven chronological data:

1. The text in II Kings 16:2 indicates that Ahaz ruled 16 years. If Hezekiah was installed in 715, it consequently must be assumed that Ahaz reigned ca. 20 years, for the summary inscription K 3751 indicates that Ahaz offered tribute to Tiglath-pileser III in 734 (see the detailed discussion of this inscription in Chapter Four, above).[10] Those scholars who claim that Hezekiah was crowned in 715 allot 20 years to Ahaz.[11] Outstanding in this respect is Kleber, who argues that there was an interregnum between Ahaz and Hezekiah.[12]

2. If it nevertheless is assumed that Ahaz reigned for 16 years, as stated in II Kings 16:2, and that Hezekiah succeeded him in 715, it follows that the investiture of Ahaz took place in 731 or in 730, thereby contradicting the testimony of inscription K 3751.

3. If Hezekiah was crowned only in 715, and each of his forefathers, Ahaz and Jotham, ruled for 16 years, then Jotham was installed ca. 747. Jeroboam of Israel apparently died before 747, which contradicts the chronological data in I Chronicles 5:17 that a census was conducted east of the Jordan in the time of Jotham and Jeroboam. Therefore, in Thiele's opinion, on the one hand, and that of Andersen, on the other, Jeroboam died ca. three years before the investiture of Jotham.[13]

4. If Hezekiah was crowned in 715 and Josiah died in 609, then the count of Mannaseh's years (or that of Hezekiah, or of Josiah) must be reduced by ca. 11 years, for the count of their years totals 117 years

[9] For this issue, see the extensive discussion in Murnane; and recently Na'aman 1986, 85–88 and loc. cit. for additional literature. For an exception, see: Murnane, 57–87.

[10] For this difficulty, see: Hughes, 212.

[11] See, e.g.; Thiele 1983, 133; Andersen, 111–112.

[12] Kleber, 181.

[13] Thiele 1983, 116, 131; Andersen, 111–112. In 1989 (14 ff.) Andersen changed his mind, and claimed that Hezekiah was crowned in 726/25, and died in 697/96.

(Hezekiah – 29; Mannaseh – 55; Amon – 2; Josiah – 39), while only 106 calendar years elapsed between 715 and 609. Some researchers do indeed surmise that Manasseh reigned for only 45 years,[14] while Mowinckel assumed that Hezekiah ruled 19, and not 29, years.[15] There are scholars who resolve this difficulty by assuming that Manasseh ruled as coregent ca. 11[16] or 10[17] years. This assumption as well has no basis (see the discussion below).

5. If Hezekiah was crowned in 715, the synchronism linking Hezekiah with Hoshea cannot be maintained.[18]

6. If the year of Hoshea's investiture (732, or 731 at the latest) is year 12 of Ahaz (II Kings 17:1), and if Hezekiah began to reign only in 715, then it must be assumed that Ahaz ruled at least 28 years.

7. The hypothesis that Hezekiah was crowned only in 715 contradicts the tradition that Samaria was conquered during the reign of Hezekiah. The conquest of Samaria was one of the most important events in Israelite history in the Biblical period, and it may safely be assumed that the inhabitants of Judah and their descendants would clearly remember who reigned in Judah at the time of the fall of the Northern Kingdom.[19]

Advancing the investiture of Hezekiah to the 720s contradicts the text of II Kings 18:13 that Sennacherib conducted his campaign in year 14 of Hezekiah, as well as the datum that Hezekiah began to rule at the age of 25, for if this report is correct, then it must be assumed that Ahaz was only 11 or 12 years old when he fathered Hezekiah, which is highly unlikely. Alternatively, it has been proposed that Hezekiah was 15 and not 25 at his investiture, or that Ahaz was 25 years old and not 20 when he began to rule (as is asserted by the Septuagint for II Chronicles 25:1).[20] Thiele argued that advancing

---

[14] Albright, 22.
[15] Mowinckel, 271.
[16] For this opinion, see, e.g.: Thiele 1983, 176; Na'aman 1986, 90.
[17] Horn 1964, 51.
[18] This opinion is held by all the scholars who advance Hezekiah's investiture to 715 (see, e.g., Thiele 1983, 176) and of additional researchers, including Tadmor 1962 (287–288); see also the discussion below.
[19] Cf. Vogelstein, 2; Aharoni, 96; Jenkins, 286. For a different opinion, see: Wellhausen, 635 ff.
[20] H. Tadmor, "Hezekiah," *EB* 3 (1958), 95 (Hebrew); Tadmor 1962, 303–304; cf. Hughes, 224, n. 128.

the coronation of Hezekiah also contradicts II Chronicles 29:3; 30:1, which reports that in his first year Hezekiah celebrated the Passover for all the tribes of Israel, from which he concluded that the Northern Kingdom had ceased to exist by this time.[21] Cogan, however, has already shown that this date is tendentious, with the sole purpose of stressing "that Hezekiah cared for the Temple and its affairs from his first day as king."[22]

A number of proposals have been raised for the explanation of the datum establishing the campaign of Sennacherib in year 14 of Hezekiah: (1) "the number 14 of Hezekiah is a corruption of 24, and establishes the beginning of the revolt against Sennacherib in 703;"[23] (2) the date refers to the campaign of Sargon against Judah and Philistia which was conducted in 713–712;[24] (3) Hezekiah undertook his reform in 715, and a new count of his years began in this year;[25] (4) the date is derivative and is based, on the one hand, on the count of Hezekiah's years (29) and, on the other hand, on the report that "in those days" Hezekiah was mortally ill and that in this year Isaiah delivered a prophecy to him that he would live an additional 15 years, thus leading to the conclusion that these events occurred in year 14 of Hezekiah.[26] In a similar vein, Tadmor surmised that in his fourteenth year (714/13) a delegation came to Hezekiah from Merodach-baladan: "the date 'year 14 of Hezekiah' which is written at the beginning of the narrative of the war of Sennacherib against Hezekiah is the creation of a redactor, who combined the story of the Assyrian campaign against Judah with another narrative, that of the miracle performed for Hezekiah during his illness, in that God granted him an additional 15 years of life."[27]

The third campaign of Sennacherib most likely was not conducted in year 14 of Hezekiah. This date apparently is not original, rather it was based, as proposed above, on the calculation of the redactor of the Book of Kings who possessed data, from which he concluded that the Assyrian campaign took place in the fourteenth year of Hezekiah.

---

[21] Thiele, 150 ff.; idem 1983, 169 ff., 175–176, 201 ff.

[22] Cogan 1980, 169; contrast Halpern, chronology, 130 ff.

[23] Aharoni, 97; cf. H. H. Rowley, "Hezekiah's Reform and Rebellion," *BJRL* 44 (1961–2), 410–413.

[24] J. Lewy, "Sanherib und Hizkia," *OLZ* 31 (1928), 158–159; Jenkins, 284–298.

[25] Vogelstein, 2–4.

[26] Schedl 1962a, 114; Jepsen, 29–32; Pavlovsky and Vogt, 343.

[27] Tadmor 1962, 279; see also: Tadmor and Cogan, 198–199. For a critique of this assumption, see: Hughes, 212.

His calculation was based on the following data: (1) Hezekiah reigned 29 years; (2) Sennacherib conducted his campaign during the time of Hezekiah; (3) "In those days" (II Kings 20:1)—i.e., in the redactor's view, at the time of the campaign of Sennacherib, Hezekiah was sick unto death, and the prophet Isaiah informed him that he would live an additional 15 years. The redactor presumed that the prophecy was fulfilled, and concluded that the campaign was conducted in year 14 of Hezekiah.

The conjecture that Hezekiah was crowned in 728 raises an additional difficulty, for this assumes that 119 years elapsed from the investiture of Hezekiah to the death of Josiah (609), while the count of years of reign from the coronation of Hezekiah to the death of Josiah totals only approximately 117 years (Hezekiah – 29; Mannaseh – 55; Amon – 2; Josiah 31).[28] Lewy sought to resolve this discrepancy by suggesting that Hezekiah reigned in effect for 31 years proposing that the first two years of his reign he served as coregent.[29] In Lewy's opinion, the scribes who calculated the synchronisms connecting Hezekiah and Hoshea counted the years of the former from his investiture in the time of his father. This hypothesis is difficult and convoluted and cannot be accepted.[30]

Another proposed resolution of this difficulty was raised by Tadmor, who assumed that the count of the years of Hezekiah, Amon, and Mannaseh consists of the whole years counted for these kings, "but in addition to their whole years, each of them ruled a few months (but less than a year) at the end of his reign, rather [the latter] were omitted from the calculation by the orderer of the chronological system, even though they had been included in the official count during the time of the kings themselves as a normative year."[31] In his opinion, Hezekiah ruled 30 years, Mannaseh 56 years, and Amon 3 years. Tadmor was also forced to surmise that the years of Mannaseh were calculated by the antedating system, while those of Amon were counted in accordance with the postdating system, for the latter system came into use at this time. He argues that "the author of the chronological system was unaware of the fact that the postdating system was adopted when Amon ascended the throne, and consequently he deleted the

[28] Cf. Hughes, loc. cit.
[29] Lewy, 19–20, 32.
[30] For criticism of this assumption, see also: Tadmor 1962, 277.
[31] Ibid.

last year from the reigns of Mannaseh and Amon, even though, for the purposes of the count, their fragmentary years are of equal weight with the whole years."[32] Tadmor's hypothesis is problematic, and it cannot be assumed that the author of the Book of Kings (or "the author of the chronological system") rounded off the years of the kings of Judah. His hypothesis is arbitrary and inconsistent (see Chapter One). Moreover, the claim that the postdating system was adopted specifically for the investiture of Amon is not supported by any written testimony. Judah became an Assyrian vassal state ca. 90 years before Amon ascended the throne.

The key to resolving this chronological problem apparently lies in the data regarding the last siege of Samaria (see the comprehensive discussion in the preceding chapter). The siege probably began in year 4 of Hezekiah and was completed in his sixth year (= 720 BCE). Hezekiah was crowned in 726 and reigned 29 years, until 697/6. After his death, he was succeeded by his son Mannaseh, who ruled 55 years from 697/6 to 642/1. The latter's son Amon ruled for two years (642/1–640/39), and Josiah reigned for 31 years (640/39–609). The final siege of Samaria began in year 4 of Hezekiah (722), and Samaria fell in his sixth year, in 720. In 713 (= year 13 of Hezekiah), Judah fought Philistia and conquered Ekron.[33] It is most likely that in year 14 of Hezekiah (= 712), the Babylonian expedition came to Judah (II Kings 20:12–19 = Isaiah 39).[34] In that same year the Assyrians conducted a punitive campaign against Ashdod and Judah, in the course of which Azekah was conquered. Sargon died in year 21 of Hezekiah (705), and Judah rebelled against Assyria. The campaign of Sennacherib to the West began in year 25 of Hezekiah, ca. 4 years before he died.

[32] Ibid.

[33] Galil 1992a, 130–131.

[34] Idem, ibid., 125–127, 131 and loc. cit. for additional literature.

Table 25

Assyria	*Year BCE*	*Judah*
Sargon II	718	*Hezekiah*
4		8
	717	
5		9
	716	
6		10
	715	
7		11
	714	
8		12
	713	
9		13
	712	
10		14
	711	
11		15
	710	
12		16
	709	
13		17
	708	
14		18

Assyria	*Year BCE*	*Judah*
Sargon II	708	*Hezekiah*
14		18
	707	
15		19
	706	
16		20
	705	
17 *Sennacherib* Accession Year		21
	704	
1		22
	703	
2		23
	702	
3		24
	701	
4		25
	700	
5		26
	699	
6		27
	698	
7		28

Table 26

Assyria	*Year BCE*	*Judah*
Sennacherib	698	*Hezekiah*
7		28
8	697	29 *Manasseh* Accession Year
9	696	1
10	695	2
11	694	3
12	693	4
13	692	5
14	691	6
15	690	7
16	689	8
17	688	9

Asyria	*Year BCE*	*Judah*
Sennacherib	688	*Manasseh*
17		9
18	687	10
19	686	11
20	685	12
21	684	13
22	683	14
23	682	15
24 *Esarhaddon* Accession Year	681	16
1	680	17
2	679	18
3	678	19

Table 27

Assyria	*Year BCE*	*Judah*
Esarhaddon	678	*Manasseh*
3		19
	677	
4		20
	676	
5		21
	675	
6		22
	674	
7		23
	673	
8		24
	672	
9		25
	671	
10		26
	670	
11		27
	669	
12 *Ashurbanipal* Accession Year		28
	668	
1		29

Assyria	*Year BCE*	*Judah*
Ashurbanipal	668	*Manasseh*
1		29
	667	
2		30
	666	
3		31
	665	
4		32
	664	
5		33
	663	
6		34
	662	
7		35
	661	
8		36
	660	
9		37
	659	
10		38
	658	
11		39

CHAPTER SEVEN

THE CHRONOLOGY OF THE LAST KINGS OF JUDAH

The chronology of the last kings of Judah is discussed extensively in the scholarly literature. Researchers have raised many hypotheses for the resolution of the complicated chronological problems of this period. No hypothesis which has been proposed, however, is consistent with all the information we possess. All the scholars, without exception, establish the date of the surrender of Jehoiachin, king of Judah, as the second day of Adar, the seventh year of Nebuchadrezzar II, king of Babylon (March 16, 597 BCE), following the Babylonian chronicle published by D. J. Wiseman in 1956 (BM 21946, rev., ll. 11–13).[1] This unique which date is undoubtedly the most precise in Israelite history during the Biblical period, constitutes one of the cornerstones of the Biblical chronology. Is it possible that this date has been interpreted incorrectly, and that this is the reason why the scholars have not been able to propose a hypothesis providing a reasonable explanation of all the Biblical and external data relating to the period under discussion?

We will precede the discussion itself with a critical survey of the various reconstruction proposed by scholars. Among scholars there is wide agreement regarding the two following issues: (1) most researchers are of the opinion that the reckoning system in practice in Judah at the time was postdating;[2] (2) in the opinion of many scholars, Josiah died in Megiddo in the month of Sivan, or at the latest, at the beginning of Tammuz 609 (BM 21901, ll. 66–75).[3] On the other hand,

---

[1] D. J. Wiseman, *Chronicles of Chaldaean Kings (626–556 B.C.)*, London 1956, 72–73.

[2] For a different opinion, see: Cazelles 1983, 427–435. Cazelles supposed that the Egyptian system, in which the king's official first year begins with his accession day, was also in use in Judah. For this system in Egypt, see: A. H. Gardiner, "Regnal Years and Civil Calendar in Pharaonic Egypt," *JEA* 31 (1945), 11–28; Finegan, 77 ff.; W. Barta, "Das Jahr in Datumsangaben und seine Bezeichnungen," in: M. Görg and E. Pusch (eds.), (*Festschrift Elmar Edel: Aegypten und Altes Testament*, I), Bamberg 1979, 35–41.

[3] C. J. Gadd, *The Fall of Nineveh*, London 1923, 36, 41–42. The Egyptian army crossed the Euphrates in Tammuz, and their march from Megiddo to the Euphrates took about 30 days. Cf. Clines 1972, 30–31, 34; I. Eph'al, "On Warfare and Mili-

scholars are divided on two questions: (1) did the new year fall in Judah, at the end of the First Temple period, on 1 Nisan, 1 Tishri, or 1 Heshvan? (2) In which year was Jerusalem destroyed: 587 or 586? Many are of the opinion that the new year fell on 1 Nisan: some propose a later date for the fall of the city, in 586,[4] while others support an earlier date, in 587.[5] In contrast, all the scholars who establish Tishri 1[6] or Heshvan 1[7] as the date of the new year hold that Jerusalem was destroyed in 586. We will first examine the positions of the scholars who maintain that the new year fell on 1 Nisan. The proponents of the earlier date are of the opinion that Zedekiah was crowned in Adar 597 and the first year of his reign began less than a month later, in Nisan 597. The proponents of the later date, on the other hand, are of the opinion that the count of the years of Zedekiah's reign began only after 1 Nisan 597, and that the first year of his reign began in 1 Nisan 596. The approach of the proponents of the earlier date is not reasonable. Such an assumption clearly contradicts the synchronisms between Zedekiah and Nebuchadrezzar (II Kings 25:8; Jeremiah

---

tary Control in the Ancient Near Eastern Empires," in: H. Tadmor and M. Weinfeld (eds.), *History Historiography and Interpretation*, Jerusalem 1983, 99.

[4] H. Tadmor, "Chronology of the Last Kings of Judah," *JNES* 15 (1956), 226–230; idem 1962, 274–276; Schedl 1962b, 209–213; Barnes, 195, 200; Cogan and Tadmor, II Kings, 303–324, 341.

[5] Begrich, 141–146, 197 ff.; Mowinckel, 199–203; W. F. Albright, "The Seal of Eliakim and the Latest Preexilic History of Judah, with Some Observations on Ezekiel," *JBL* 51 (1932), 77–106, esp. 85; idem, "The Nebuchadnezzar and Neriglissar Chronicles," *BASOR* 143 (1956), 28–33; Freedman 1956, 50–60; Noth 1958, 133–157; E. Kutsch, "Zur Chronologie der letzten jüdäischen Könige (Josia bis Zedekia)," *ZAW* 71 (1959), 270–274; idem 1974, 520–545; Jepsen, 21–28; E. W. Heaton, *The Hebrew Kingdoms*, Oxford 1968, 126–132; Zimmerli, 564; Andersen 108–112; idem 1989, 42; K. E. Pohlmann, *Studien zu Jeremiabuch: Ein Beitrag zur Frage der Entstehung des Jeremiasbuches* (*FRLANT* 118), Göttingen 1978, 205; Ackroyd, 3 ff.; Bright, 324–330; Jones, 27; H. Donner, *Geschichte des Volkes Israel und seiner Nachbarn in Grundzügen*, II, Göttingen 1986, 375 ff.; Reade, 1–9; Hughes, 230 ff.

[6] E. R. Thiele, "New Evidence on the Chronology of the Last Kings of Judah," *BASOR* 143 (1956), 22–27; idem 1983, 179–192; A. Malamat, "A New Record of Nebuchadrezzar's Palestinian Campaigns," *IEJ* 6 (1956), 246–256; idem, "The Twilight of Judah: In the Egyptian-Babylonian Maelstrom," *VT* supp. 28 (1975), 124 ff.; Kitchen and Mitchell (above 3, n. 8), 212–223; de Vries, 580–599, esp. 594 ff.; Horn, 12–27; H. S. Gehman, "Chronology," *The New Westminster Dictionary of the Bible*, Philadelphia 1970, 162 ff., esp. 167–172; Freedy and Redford, 462–485; Weippert, Edom, 351 ff., 649 ff.; Green 1982, 57–73.

[7] E. Auerbach, "Die Babylonische Datierung im Pentateuch und das Alter des Priester-Kodex," *VT* 2 (1952), 334–342, esp., 336; idem, "Der Wechsel des Jahres-Anfangs in Juda im Lichte der Neugefundenen Babylonischen Chronik," *VT* 9 (1959), 113–121, esp., 118; idem, "Wann eroberte Nebukadnezar Jerusalem?" *VT* 11 (1961), 128–136.

52:12; 32:1): the tenth year of Zedekiah would be congruent with the seventeenth (and not the eighteenth) year of Nebuchadrezzar, and similarly, the last year of Zedekiah's reign would not begin in the nineteenth, but rather in the eighteenth year of Nebuchadrezzar. Some of the scholars maintaining this assumption argue that the above-mentioned synchronisms are faulty, and that the testimony of Josephus is to be preferred to them.[8] Other conjecture that to the west of the Euphrates a different reckoning of the years of Nebuchadrezzar was in effect. This count began at the end of the twentieth year of Nabopolassar, from the time that Nebuchadrezzar was put in command of the army.[9] The chronology of this period, however, cannot be based on the calculations of Josephus.[10] Similarly, it is extremely difficult to assume that in the west the count of the reign of Nebuchadrezzar began about a year before he was crowned.[11] Nor does the determination of the destruction of the Temple in 587 correspond with the chronological datum in Ezekiel 33:21 which indicates that the fall of Jerusalem was known to the exiles in Babylonia in the twelfth year of the exile of Jehoiachin: "And it came to pass in the twelfth year of our captivity, in the tenth month, in the fifth day of the month, that one that had escaped out of Jerusalem came unto me saying the city is smitten."[12] Most scholars, including the proponents of the advanced Nisan hypothesis, suppose that the count of the exile of Jehoiachin began on 1 Nisan 597. Consequently, the refugee informed Ezekiel of the conquest of Jerusalem about seventeen months after the fall of the city, which is a completely unreasonable assumption.[13]

Like the approach of the proponents of the early date, the approach maintaining a later date seemingly at least contradicts a number of chronological data: (1) II Kings 25:1 (= Jeremiah 52:4) indicates that the final siege of Jerusalem began in the ninth year of the reign

---

[8] Begrich, 145 ff.; Josephus established the destruction of Jerusalem in the eighteenth year of Nebuchadrezzar (*Antiquities* 10:146).

[9] Albright 1956, 32; Freedman 1956, 57; Noth 1958, 155.

[10] For the chronology of Josephus, see: Thiele 1951, 204–227.

[11] Cf. Horn, 23; Green 1982, 61–62.

[12] Cf. Freedy and Redford, 468. Other scholars prefer the version of the Lucianic recension of the LXX, the Syriac and a few Hebrew MSS "בעשתי" instead of "בשתי" (See: G. Fohrer, *Ezechiel* (*HAT*), Tübingen 1955, 187; Zimmerli, 810. Cf. also Kutsch 1985, 41–45. In his opinion the version of the MT should be preferred.

[13] Cf. Vogt 1975, 228.

of Zedekiah, in the tenth month, in the tenth day of the month. A similar date is given in Ezekiel 24:1–2: "Again in the ninth year, in the tenth month, in the tenth day of the month, the word of the Lord came unto me, saying, son of man, write thee the name of the day even of this same day: the king of Babylon set himself against Jerusalem this same day." If the dates in the Book of Ezekiel are counted from the exile of Jehoiachin, then the chronological datum in Ezekiel 24:1–2 contradicts the proponents of a later date, who supposed that the ninth year of Zedekiah would begin in the tenth, and not the ninth, year of the exile of Jehoiachin. This difficulty can be resolved if we assume that this date, in contrast with other dates in the Book of Ezekiel, is not counted from the exile of Jehoiachin but rather by the reign of Zedekiah.[14] The language of the verse, which is identical with the language of the date cited in II Kings 25:1 (=Jeremiah 52:4), and the uniqueness and importance of the date do provide some basis for the assumption that in this instance the official reckoning of the kingdom of Judah was employed, and not the reckoning of the exile of Jehoiachin; (2) the proponents of the later date are of the opinion that the reckoning of the reign of Zedekiah began only after 1 Nisan 597, about a month after the deposition of Jehoiachin. It is difficult, however, to assume that Zedekiah was crowned before 1 Nisan but counted his years only after Jehoiachin's departure from the land of Israel;[15] similarly, there is no support for the conjecture that Zedekiah's coronation was postponed by a month.[16] To the contrary, it may be assumed that Nebuchadrezzar installed Zedekiah close to the deposition of Jehoiachin, returning afterwards to his land for the new year celebrations.[17] The first contradiction therefore can be resolved, but no reasonable hypothesis has yet been proposed for resolving the second contradiction; accordingly, the view proposing a late Nisan would seem to be impossible.[18]

---

[14] See the commentary of Rashi on Ezekiel. His proposal was adopted by the following scholars: Freedy and Redford, 468; Zimmerli, 559 ff. Kutsch 1985, 61–63, 70; J. W. Wevers, *Ezekiel* (*NCB*), London 1969, 189.

[15] Tadmor 1962, 276.

[16] Vogt 1975, 227.

[17] Cf. E. Vogt, "Die neubabylonische Chronik uber die Schlacht bie Karkemisch und die Einnahme von Jerusalem," *VT* supp. 4 (1956), 67–96, esp. 94; Noth 1958, 152; Malamat, 23; Green 1982, 60.

[18] Another chronological datum which is not in accordance with the Nisan reckoning is Dan. 1:1. Yet no historical or chronological reconstruction should be based on the date mentioned in the first verse of the Book of Daniel. For a similar attitude towards this date, see: Tadmor 1962, 266; Malamat, 256–257; J. E. Goldingay,

The scholars who are of the opinion that the new year fell on 1 Tishri suppose that Jehoiakim was crowned after 1 Tishri 609.[19] Malamat raised the alternative possibility that Jehoiakim was crowned before 1 Tishri 609.[20] Both proposals are difficult. Establishing the coronation of Jehoiakim after 1 Tishri contradicts the chronological datum in Jeremiah 46:2, which indicates that the battle of Carchemish took place in Jehoiakim's fourth year. If we establish the coronation of Jehoiakim after 1 Tishri 609, then the battle of Carchemish took place in the third year of Jehoiakim. If, on the other hand, we assume that Jehoiakim was crowned before 1 Tishri, this difficulty would be resolved, but as a consequence we would count twelve years, and not eleven, for the reign of Jehoiakim. A number of proposals have been offered to resolve these difficulties. Researchers conjectured that the chronological data in the Book of Jeremiah (which have no parallel in the Book of Kings) count the years of the reign of the kings of Judah from 1 Nisan.[21] Another scholar is of the opinion that contradictory traditions regarding the coronation of Jehoiakim were prevalent. Some of them established his coronation before 1 Tishri, and other traditions established his coronation only after 1 Tishri, while in practice Jehoiakim was crowned close to the new year which fell on 1 Tishri (in his opinion, it is not clear whether the coronation took place before or after 1 Tishri).[22] These forced arguments do not resolve the above-mentioned difficulty, for if we assume that Jehoiakim was crowned before 1 Tishri, this would contradict the count of the years of his reign; if we assume that he was crowned after 1 Tishri, the datum in Jeremiah 46:2 cannot be maintained.

Other scholars have adopted a position integrating the above-mentioned proposals. They are of the opinion that during the entire period of the Divided Kingdom, the new year fell in Judah on 1 Tishri (or on 1 Heshvan), while during the reign of Jehoiakim the date of the new year was changed to 1 Nisan. The fifth "year" of Jehoiakim lasted seventeen months[23] (alternatively, the sixth "year" of Jehoiakim lasted eighteen months).[24] From the seventh year of Jehoiakim on,

---

Daniel (*WBC*), Dallas 1989, 14–15; But cf. M. K. Mercer, "Daniel 1:1 and Jehoiakim's Three Years of Servitude," *AUSS* 27 (1989), 179–192.

[19] Thiele 1983, 182 ff.; Horn, 19.

[20] Malamat, 246–247.

[21] Thiele 1983, 183 ff.

[22] Green 1982, 71–73.

[23] Auerbach (see above, n. 7); Finegan, 203.

[24] Pavlovsky and Vogt, 346.

this reconstruction is identical to that maintaining Nisan as the new year by the proponents of the later date. Yet these conjectures also are difficult. There is no supporting evidence for the assumption that the new year in Judah was changed from 1 Tishri or 1 Heshvan to 1 Nisan, and certainly not that this change took place in the time of Jehoiakim.[25]

All the scholars assumed that the Babylonian calendar corresponded to the Judahite, and that 2 Adar in the seventh year of Nebuchadrezzar—a date undoubtedly given in the Babylonian chronicle according to the Babylonian calendar—fell on 2 Adar according to the calendar of Judah. But it can be positively established that there is no proof for the presumed correspondence between the calendars. To the contrary, since there was no fixed intercalation of years in Babylonia (see below), it is certainly possible that at times the calendars diverged. We shall attempt to show that in the seventh year of Nebuchadrezzar the possibility of divergence was more probable than the possibility that the calendars corresponded, followed by a discussion of the implications of this conclusion for a reconstruction of the chronological frame of the events in the last years of the kingdom of Judah.

We shall first discuss our knowledge of the calendars in Babylonia and Judah at the time. It is well known that the Babylonian calendar was lunar-solar, and that in the seventh-sixth centuries BCE a fixed system for intercalation had not yet been introduced. Only in a later period, apparently in the fourth century BCE, was an intercalation cycle of nineteen years introduced in Babylonia, in which seven fixed years (years 3, 6, 8, 11, 14, 17, 19) were intercalated.[26] Parker and Dubberstein's research revealed that in the seventh-sixth centuries BCE a flexible cycle evolved. In the course of this cycle, nineteen years on average, between six and eight years were intercalated.[27] Now, after the publication of a catalogue of more than 35,000 economic documents from the city of Sippar in the collections of the British Museum,[28] it is clear that most of Parker and Dubberstein's

---

[25] Clines 1972, 33.

[26] Parker and Dubberstein, 1–9; See also: H. Hunger and E. Reiner, "A Scheme for Intercalary Months From Babylonia," *WZKM* 67 (1975), 21–28.

[27] Parker and Dubberstein, esp. 6, Pl. I.

[28] E. Leichty, *Catalogue of the Babylonian Tablets in the British Museum, VI: Tablets from Sippar 1*, London 1986; E. Leichty and A. K. Grayson, *Catalogue of the Babylonian Tablets in the British Museum, VII: Tablets from Sippar 2*, London 1987; E. Leichty, J. J. Finkelstein and C. B. F. Walker, *Catalogue of the Babylonian Tablets in the British Museum, VIII:*

findings are still valid; two points, however, require emendation: (1) following Goetze, Parker and Dubberstein supposed that the nineteenth year of Nabopolassar was intercalated.[29] But in the sole document on which their supposition is based (NCBT 1156), the king's name is not specified. It is more likely that this document is from the time of Kandalanu, the nineteenth year of whose reign was definitely intercalated. (2) It can be established that the first year of Nabopolassar was intercalated (BM 54209), consequently the number of intercalated years in the cycle beginning in 633 was at least six. We therefore can establish with a great deal of certainly the years intercalated in Babylonia during that period, as well as the Julian dates of the years in Babylonia from the last third of the seventh century BCE on (see the complete listing in table 31 – p. 122).

In contrast with our detailed knowledge regarding the Babylonian calendar, our knowledge of the calendar of Judah is sparse. It may reasonably be assumed, as is accepted in the scholarly literature, that the calendar in Judah was lunar-solar, and that in Judah as well there was some sort of mechanism for adjusting the 12-month lunar year to the solar one with intercalation cycles averaging nineteen years, as was the practice in Babylonia, or eight year cycles in which three years were intercalated, as was the practice in Greece before the institution of the Metonic cycle in the fifth century B.C.E., or in another manner—for otherwise it would not have been possible to observe the festivals in their proper times.[30]

We will now turn our attention to the seventh year of Nebuchadrezzar. It can be definitely established that this year was intercalated and that the intercalated month was Elul.[31] Similarly, 2 Adar (in the Babylonian calendar) fell in this year on March 16, 597, and 1 Nisan (in the Babylonian calendar) in the eighth year of Nebuchadrezzar

---

Tablets from Sippar 3, London 1988; for a list of the Neo-Babylonian and Late-Babylonian tablets published after the publication of Parker and Dubberstein's last edition of their book (1956), see: M. A. Dandamaev, *Slavery in Babylonia*, DeKalb, IL 1984, 6–18; see also: G. J. P. McEwan, *Late Babylonian Texts in the Ashmolean Museum*, Oxford 1984; F. Joannès, *Les Tablettes Néo-Babyloniennes de la Boldeian Library*, Oxford 1990; R. H. Sack, *Cuneiform Documents from the Chaldean and Persian Periods*, London and Toronto 1994; idem, *Neriglissar—King of Babylon*, Neukirchen-Vluyn 1994.

[29] Parker and Dubberstein, 4, and n. 9 there.

[30] For intercalation in Israel and in Judah in Biblical times, see: J. B. Segal, "Intercalation and the Hebrew Calendar," *VT* 7 (1957), 250–307; idem, *EB* 8 (1982), 197–209, esp. 204–205, with earlier literature (Hebrew).

[31] An intercalary Elul in the 7th year of Nebuchadrezzar is mentioned in three tables: (1) J. N. Strassmaier S.J., *Inschriften von Nebuchodonosor*, Leipzig 1889, no. 61; (2) H. F.

fell on April 13, 597.[32] Is it possible to determine the Julian date on which 1 Nisan in Judah fell in that year? Based on our knowledge of the Babylonian calendar and the calendar of Judah, two main possibilities may be proposed. The first is that 1 Nisan fell also by the calendar of Judah on April 13; the other possibility is that 1 Nisan by the calendar of Judah fell about a month before 1 Nisan by the Babylonian calendar, i.e., close to March 15.[33] It seemingly is not possible to decide in favor of one of these two possibilities. If, however, we prefer the first (i.e., that the two calendars corresponded to each other), we must then assume that Zedekiah was crowned by Nebuchadrezzar close to the surrender of Jehoiachin, but numbered his years only after Jehoiachin's departure from the land of Israel. This is unreasonable. Similarly, the other hypotheses raised to resolve the above difficulty also are extremely difficult. More reasonable is the assumption that Zedekiah counted his years from his coronation, which occurred—according to the Babylonian calendar—at the beginning of the month of Adar, and according to the calendar of Judah, at the beginning of Nisan. This proposal resolves the Biblical and external chronological data for the period under discussion and provides an opportunity for the possible reconstruction of the events in the last years of the kingdom of Judah. An outline of the chronological frame of this period follows:

1. In the month of Sivan, or, at the latest, the beginning of Tammuz 609 (according to the Babylonian calendar), in the thirty-first year of his reign, Josiah fell in battle at Megiddo.[34] His sudden death and

---

Lutz, *Neo-Babylonian Administrative Documents from Erech*, Berkeley 1927, 84, no. 10 (= idem, *Selected Cuneiform Texts, University of California Publications in Semitic Philology*, vol. 9, Berkeley 1931); (3) BM 49685 (see note 28, above: Leichty, *Catalogue*, vol. VI, 14).

[32] Parker and Dubberstein, 27. The Julian dates in Parker and Duberstein's book were established at times on the basis of only one tablet indicating the intercalation of a month in a specific year (and in few cases even the single tablet was not found and they were obliged to propose tentative suggestions). The publication of a catalogue of more than 35,000 tablets enables us to base each intercalary year on at least two tablets and often on more than three tablets (see Table 31 – p. 122). Forty-four from the forty-seven intercalary years mentioned in this table are established on the basis of more than two tablets.

[33] It is less reasonable to suppose that the Passover in this year was celebrated on May 28th (and that 1 Nisan = May 13). In Babylon (after 609 BCE), 1 Nisan never occurred after April 26.

[34] Bright, 324; Malamat, 237–238; see also: Halpern and Vanderhooft, 221 ff. Other scholars assume that no battle took place at Meggido and that Josiah was executed. See: A. C. Welch, "The Death of Josiah," *ZAW* 43 (1925), 255–260; and recently

the hasty departure of Necho from the land left a vacuum, which was well used by the supporters of Jehoahaz, who crowned him in place of his father.

2. About three months later, Jehoahaz was imprisoned in Necho's headquarters in Riblah, and his brother Jehoiakim was crowned in his stead.

3. In the spring/summer of 605, in the fourth year of Jehoiakim, the Babylonians defeated the Egyptians near Carchemish and conquered the land of Hamath.[35] On 8 Av 605 Nabopolassar died, in the twenty-first year of his reign. His son Nebuchadrezzar returned to Babylonia and was crowned on 1 Elul 605.

4. In the first year of Nebuchadrezzar, the Babylonian army invaded Judah. At that time, in the fifth year of Jehoiakim, in the ninth month (Kislev), during which Nebuchadrezzar conquered Ashkelon, a fast was proclaimed in Jerusalem and Jehoiakim summoned an emergency session of his council of ministers in which they possibly discussed surrender to Babylonia (Jeremiah 36:9 ff.).[36] It is not clear whether Judah surrendered to Babylonia in that year, or only a year later (603).[37]

5. In the winter of 601/600 a battle was waged between the Egyptians and the Babylonians which apparently ended indecisively. It may be assumed that the results of the battle reinforced the assessment in Judah that Babylonian rule in Judah was drawing to an end, and the decision was taken in Jerusalem to revolt. The Babylonian response was not long in coming. Nebuchadrezzar, who remained in his land in this year (609), sent his troops together with the auxiliary forces mobilized in the neighboring countries, and Jerusalem was besieged (II Kings 24:2, 10).

N. Na'aman, "The Town-Lists of Judah and Benjamin and the Kingdom of Judah in the Days of Josiah," *Zion* 54 (1989), 63 ff. (Hebrew), with earlier literature.

[35] For the reconstruction "Ha[ma]th" instead of "Hatti," see: Oded 1966, 104.

[36] For a possible connection between the general fast day and the Babylonian campaign against Ashkelon, see: Malamat, 257; D. J. Wiseman, *Nebuchadrezzar and Babylon*, Oxford 1985, 23. For a different view, see: A. Baumann, "Urrolle und Fasttag," *ZAW* 80 (1968), 350–373; N. Luhfink, "Die Gattung der 'Historischen Kurzgeschichte' in den letzten Jahren von Juda in der Zeit des Babylonischen Exils," *ZAW* 90 (1978), 319–347.

[37] For the exact date of the Babylonian subjugation of Judah, see: Pavlovsky and Vogt, 345 ff.; Oded 1966, 103 ff.

6. Jehoiakim died during the siege and his son Jehoiachin was crowned in his stead, on 22 Kislev (according to the presumed calendar of Judah, which corresponded to about 22 Heshvan in the Babylonian calendar).[38] Shortly after the coronation of Jehoiachin, in the month of Kislev according to the Babylonian calendar, Nebuchadrezzar set forth from his land at the head of his army and came to Jerusalem (BM 21946, l. 11).

7. Only a few weeks after the arrival of the Babylonian king and his forces in Jerusalem, on 2 Adar, the seventh year of Nebuchadrezzar, according to the Babylonian calendar (which probably corresponded to 2 Nisan in the calendar of Judah, i.e., the day after the new year), Jerusalem surrendered and opened its gates to Nebuchadrezzar. Jehoiachin was deposed, after reigning for 100 days, and his uncle Zedekiah was crowned in his stead. The time which elapsed from the crowning of Zedekiah in the month of Nisan (according to the presumed calendar of Judah) until the end of the month of Adar 596 is reckoned as the accession year of Zedekiah, while the first year of his reign began on 1 Nisan 596.

8. Jehoiachin, and along with him about 10,000 people, were exiled to Babylonia at the beginning of the eighth year of Nebuchadrezzar, which was the first year of the exile of Jehoiachin (II Kings 24:12).[39]

---

[38] For the death of Jehoiakim, see: Horn, 27; Malamat, 262; A. R. Green, "The Fate of Jehoiakim," *AUSS* 20 (1982), 103–109.

[39] This assumption, which is accepted by most scholars, contradicts the chronological datum adduced in the end of Book of Kings regarding the release of Jehoiachin from the Babylonian prison in the thirty-seventh year of his exile, on the 25th/27th day of the twelfth month, in the accession year of Evil-Merodach. It can be established that the accession year of Evil-Merodach began before 5 Tammuz 562 (= July 19, 562 – BM 65270), and lasted about nine months, until the end of Adar 561. Jehoiachin was released from his imprisonment on 25/27 Adar 561 (= April 1–3, 561). If the count of the exile of Jehoiachin began on 1 Nisan 597, then his release is to reckoned in the thirty-sixth year of the exile of Jehoiachin, only a few days before the beginning of the thirty-seventh year of his exile. Perhaps this proximity of dates was intended by the author. Scholars interpreted "בשנת מלכו" as referring to the first year (see: Finegen, 209–210; Jepsen, 21–23). This proposal is not reasonable, and it cannot be assumed that Jehoiachin was released at the end of the first year of Evil-Merodach, i.e., more than twenty months after his coronation. To the contrary, it may reasonably be supposed that Evil-Merodach, like many kings in the ancient Near East, released Jehoiachin within the context of a *duraru* he probably proclaimed close to his coronation. For the *duraru*, see: the recent work of M. Weinfeld: *Justice and Righteousness in Israel and the Nations*, Jerusalem 1985 (Hebrew), 45ff., 84ff. Furthermore, we now possess many economic documents likely to testify to the coregency of Evil-Merodach and Nebuchadrezzar, showing that the

This exile is to be distinguished from that of the 3,023 Judahites in the seventh year of Nebuchadrezzar (Jeremiah 52:28).[40]

9. On 10 Tebeth 587, in the ninth year of Zedekiah, which was the seventeenth year of Nebuchadrezzar, the final siege of Jerusalem began (II Kings 25:1; Jeremiah 52:4; Ezekiel 24:1–2). During the course of the siege, the Egyptian army moved north to the aid of Judah, the Babylonians were forced to lift the siege and concentrate their army for the decisive battle against the Egyptians (Jeremiah 37:5). The Egyptian army was defeated, however, and the Babylonians renewed the siege of Jerusalem.

10. On 9 Tammuz 586, after eighteen months of siege, the walls of the city were breached (Jeremiah 39:2), and about a month later, on 7 or 10 Av 586, Nebuzaradan destroyed the Temple and burnt Jerusalem (II Kings 25:8 ff.).

---

release of Jehoiachin took place a relatively short time after Evil-Merodach was installed as sole ruler (see: R. H. Sack, *Amēl-Marduk: 562–560 B.C.*, Neukirchen-Vluyn 1972, nos. 56, 70, 79; as well as documents BM 65270, 66846, 75322 mentioned in the catalogues published by Leichty—n. 28, above). A new document (BM 5386 = CT 55 138), from the month of Tebeth, the forty-third year of Nebuchadrezzar king of Babylonia, could indicate that Nebuchadrezzar died only in January or February 561. Kutsch (1985, 55–59), is of the opinion that Jehoiachin was released from imprisonment in the thirty-seventh year of his exile, which fell in the accession year of the reign of Evil-Merodach. He advances the exile of Jehoiachin and the beginning of the count of his exile to the seventh year of Nebuchadrezzar. But Kutsch's reconstruction is not reasonable. It clearly contradicts no less than four Biblical chronological data. In his opinion, the first year of Nebuchadrezzar is not the fourth year of Jehoiakim (contrary to Jeremiah 25:1); the exile of Jehoiachin did not occur in the eighth year of Nebuchadrezzar (contrary to II Kings 24:12); the tenth year of Zedekiah is not the eighteenth year of Nebuchadrezzar; and the eleventh year of Zedekiah is not the nineteenth year of Nebuchadrezzar (in opposition to Jeremiah 32:1; 52:12; II Kings 25:8). See: Kutsch 1974, 542, 545; idem 1985, 30 ff.; 74.

[40] Tadmor 1962, 275–276; Malamat, 263 ff.; Vogt 1975, 225. For different views on this problem, see: Thiele, 161 ff.; Weippert, Edom, 356; Horn, 23; Green 1982, 62; Talmon 1958, 64–65.

Table 28

Assyria	*Year BCE*	*Judah*
Ashurbanipal	658	*Manasseh*
11		39
12	657	40
13	656	41
14	655	42
15	654	43
16	653	44
17	652	45
18	651	46
19	650	47
20	649	48
21	648	49

Assyria	*Year BCE*	*Judah*
Ashurbanipal	648	*Manasseh*
21		49
22	647	50
23	646	51
24	645	52
25	644	53
26	643	54
27	642	55 *Amon* Accession Year
28	641	1
29	640	2 *Josiah* Accession Year
30	639	1
31	638	2

Table 29

Babylonia	*Year BCE*	*Judah*
Kandalanu	638	*Josiah*
10		2
	637	
11		3
	636	
12		4
	635	
13		5
	634	
14		6
	633	
15		7
	632	
16		8
	631	
17		9
	630	
18		10
	629	
19		11
	628	
20		12

Babylonia	*Year BCE*	*Judah*
Kandalanu	628	*Josiah*
20		12
21	627	
Interregnum		13
	626	
Nabopolassar Accession Year		14
	625	
1		15
	624	
2		16
	623	
3		17
	622	
4		18
	621	
5		19
	620	
6		20
	619	
7		21
	618	
8		22

Table 30

Babylonia	*Judah*	*Year BCE*	*Egypt*
Nabopolassar 8	*Josiah* 22	618	*Psammetichus I*
9	23	617	47
10	24	616	48
11	25	615	49
12	26	614	50
13	27	613	51
14	28	612	52
15	29	611	53
16	30	610	54 *Necho II* 1
17	31 *Jehoahaz* *Jehoiakim* Accession year	609	2
18	1	608	3

Table 31: Intercalary Months in Babylonia 633–501 BCE*

	1	2	3	4	5	6	7
1	Kn/15 633	*Np/12 A* *22.4.614*	Nk/10 22.4.595	Nk/29 22.4.576	*Nr/3 A* *23.3.557*	Cy/1 24.3.538	*Da/3 E* *23.3.519*
2	Kn/16 632	Np/13 10.5.613	*Nk/11 A* *12.4.594*	Nk/30 12.4.575	Nn/0 11.4.556	*Cy/2 E* *12.3.537*	Da/4 11.4.518
3	Kn/17 631	Np/14 30.4.612	Nk/12 30.4.593	*Nk/31 E* *1.4.574*	*Nn/1 A* *31.3.555*	*Cy/3 E* *31.3.536*	*Da/5 A* *30.3.517*
4	Kn/18 630	*Np/15 E* *19.4.611*	Nk/13 19.4.592	Nk/32 19.4.573	Nn/2 19.4.554	Cy/4 18.4.535	Da/6 18.4.516
5	*Kn/19 E* *8.4.629*	Np/16 8.5.610	*Nk/14 A* *8.4.591*	*Nk/33 A* *8.4.572*	*Nn/3 A* *7.4.553*	Cy/5 8.4.534	Da/7 8.4.515
6	Kn/20 27.4.628	Np/17 27.4.609	Nk/15 27.4.590	Nk/34 26.4.571	Nn/4 26.4.552	*Cy/6 A* *28.3.533*	*Da/8 A* *29.3.514*
7	Kn/21 16.4.627	Np/18 16.4.608	Nk/16 15.4.589	Nk/35 16.4.570	Nn/5 16.4.551	Cy/7 16.4.532	Da/9 16.4.513
8	Np/0 5.4.626	Np/19 5.4.607	*Nk/17 A* *4.4.588*	*Nk/36 A* *4.4.569*	*Nn/6 A* *5.4.550*	Cy/8 5.4.531	Da/10 5.4.512
9	*Np/1 A* *24.3.625*	*Np/20 A* *25.3.606*	Nk/18 23.4.587	Nk/37 23.4.568	Nn/7 23.4.549	*Ca/0 E* *26.3.530*	*Da/11 E* *25.3.511*
10	*Np/2 A* *12.4.624*	Nk/0 12.4.605	Nk/19 13.4.586	Nk/38 13.4.567	Nn/8 13.4.548	Ca/1 12.4.529	Da/12 13.4.510
11	Np/3 1.5.623	Nk/1 2.4.604	Nk/20 2.4.585	Nk/39 2.4.566	Nn/9 2.4.547	Ca/2 1.4.528	*Da/13 A* *1.4.509*
12	Np/4 21.4.622	*Nk/2 E* *22.3.603*	*Nk/21 E* *22.3.584*	Nk/40 22.3.565	*Nn/10 E* *22.3.546*	*Ca/3 E* *21.3.527*	Da/14 20.4.508
13	*Np/5 E* *9.4.621*	Nk/3 10.4.602	Nk/22 10.4.583	*Nk/41 E* *11.3.564*	Nn/11 9.4.545	Ca/4 9.4.526	Da/15 9.4.507
14	Np/6 28.4.620	Nk/4 30.3.601	*Nk/23 A* *30.3.582*	*Nk/42 A* *29.3.563*	*Nn/12 A* *29.3.544*	*Ca/5 A* *29.3.525*	*Da/16 A* *30.3.506*
15	*Np/7 A* *18.4.619*	*Nk/5 E* *19.3.600*	Nk/24 17.4.581	Am/0 17.4.562	Nn/13 17.4.543	Ca/6 17.4.524	Da/17 17.4.505
16	Np/8 7.5.618	Nk/6 6.4.599	Nk/25 6.4.580	Am/1 6.4.561	Nn/14 6.4.542	Ca/7 7.4.523	Da/18 6.4.504
17	Np/9 25.4.617	*Nk/7 E* *27.3.598*	*Nk/26 A* *26.3.579*	*Nr/0 A* *26.3.560*	*Nn/15 A* *26.3.541*	*Da/0 A* *27.3.522*	*Da/19 E* *27.3.503*
18	*Np/10 E* *14.4.616*	Nk/8 13.4.597	Nk/27 14.4.578	Nr/1 14.4.559	Nn/16 14.4.540	Da/1 14.4.521	Da/20 14.4.502
19	Np/11 3.5.615	*Nk/9 E* *3.4.596*	*Nk/28 A* *3.4.577*	Nr/2 4.4.558	Cy/0 4.4.539	Da/2 3.4.520	Da21 2.4.501

* In each square in the table appear in the upper line (from left to right): the king's name; the year of his reign; and the intercalary month. The date given in the bottom line in each square is that of the first day of Nisan of this year. The following abbreviations are used: A = Adar; Am =

Amel-Marduk (= Evil-Merodach); Ca = Cambyses; Cy = Cyrus; Da = Darius; E = Elul; Kn = Kandalanu; Nk = Nebuchadrezzar; Nn = Nabonaid; Np = Nabopolassar; Nr = Neriglissar. The abbreviation Ca/0 marks not only Cambyses' accession year but also Cyrus' last year (the 9th), and so Cy/0 marks also Nn/17, and Np/0 = 22 "*arki Kandalanu*"; Nk/0 = Np/21; Am/0 = Nk/43; Nr/0 = Am/2; Nn/0 = Nr/4 = the accession year of Labashi-Marduk; Da/0 = Ca/8 = the accession year of Bardiya. The following intercalary months are based only on one source: Np/1, Nk/9, Nk/11. The others are based on two or more sources. In the left column we pointed out the fixed intercalary months in Babylon from the 4th century BCE on.

Table 32

Babylonia	*Judah*	*Year BCE*	*Egypt*
Nabopolassar	*Jehoiakim*	608	*Necho II*
18	1		3
19	2	607	4
20	3	606	5
21 *Nebuchadrezzar II* Accession Year	4	605	6
1	5	604	7
2	6	603	8
3	7	602	9
4	8	601	10
5	9	600	11
6	10	599	12
7	11	598	13

Table 33

Babylonia	*Judah*	*Year BCE*	*Egypt*
Nebuchadrezzar II 7	*Jehoiakim* 11 *Jehoiachin*	598	*Necho II* 13
8	*Zedekiah* Accession year	597	14
9	1	596	15
10	2	595	*Psammetichus II* 1
11	3	594	2
12	4	593	3
13	5	592	4
14	6	591	5
15	7	590	6
16	8	589	7 *Apries* 1
17	9	588	2

Table 34

<table>
<tr><th>Egypt</th><th>Babylonia</th><th>Judah</th><th>Year BCE</th><th rowspan="2"></th></tr>
<tr><td rowspan="2">Apries
2</td><td rowspan="3">Nebu-chadrezzar II
17</td><td rowspan="3">Zedakiah
9</td><td>588</td></tr>
<tr><td rowspan="3">587</td><td rowspan="3">The last siege of Jerusalem
1st year</td></tr>
<tr><td rowspan="3">3</td></tr>
<tr><td rowspan="3">18</td><td rowspan="3">10</td></tr>
<tr><td rowspan="3">586</td><td rowspan="3">2nd year
The fall of Jerusalem</td></tr>
<tr><td rowspan="2">4</td></tr>
<tr><td>19</td><td>11</td></tr>
</table>

CHAPTER EIGHT

THE CHRONOLOGICAL DATA IN THE GREEK TEXT OF THE BOOK OF KINGS

The chronological data in the Greek text of the Book of Kings are different from those in MT. The discrepancies are the most striking for the period from the schism to the rebellion of Jehu, and generate alternative chronological structures which cannot be reconciled (see appendix E).[1] Some researchers prefer MT to the Septuagint. E. R. Thiele is one of the outstanding proponents of this view. He assumed that the data in the Septuagint comprise the attempts by early commentators to reconcile the contradictions in MT, and are not based on an original tradition.[2] Thiele's research is founded on a thorough and precise examination of the data in MT. In contrast, his study of the Septuagint, as he himself attests, relies on the data in the book of C. F. Burney.[3] Burney, however, mentions only a portion of the parallels of the Septuagint to MT. Furthermore, he was not precise in determining the differences between the various Greek manuscripts, satisfying himself with a general and erroneous division between the data of the Septuagint (= LXX) and those of the Lucianic manuscripts (= "LUC."). Moreover, he made no mention of the additions in the Septuagint which have no parallel in MT. These shortcomings prevented Thiele from gaining an understanding of the systems of the authors of the various Septuagint manuscripts, and from obtaining any precision in the comparisons he conducted between the Septuagint and MT.[4]

Other researchers have attempted to demonstrate the derivative nature of MT in relation to the Greek text of the Book of Kings. The leading representative of this approach is J. D. Shenkel.[5] Following

---

[1] The chronological data in the Septuagint for the period from the rebellion of Jehu to the destruction of the First Temple are identical to those in MT, with certain exceptions. See: Thiele 1951, 179; Shenkel, 26–27; and below, nn. 10, 15.

[2] Thiele 1951, 167–203; idem 1974, 175–190; idem 1983, 89–94, 209–210.

[3] C. F. Burney, *Notes on the Hebrew Text of the Book of Kings*, Oxford 1903, xlii–xliv.

[4] For a critique of Thiele's approach on this topic, see: Shenkel, 34 ff.; Wifall, 320 ff.; Hayes and Hooker (15) also claimed that MT has preserved the original chronology (see also: Gooding, 118 ff.).

[5] Shenkel, esp. 7–21, 125–129.

in the footsteps of researchers who preceded him, including H. St. J. Thackeray, D. Barthélemy, and F. M. Cross,[6] Shenkel identified four major stages in the history of the Greek text of the books of Samuel and Kings: the original Old Greek translation (OGT), and three recensions of it: the proto-Lucian; the KR recension, and the hexaplaric recension. He divided the chronological data into three historical periods. In his opinion, in the first period (from Jeroboam to Omri), wherever the OGT is extent and free from obvious scribal corruption, it agrees with the proto-Lucian recension against the MT in its chronological data. The second period (from Omri to Jehu), which is in his opinion the most important one, spans the division between I and II Kings. In I Kings the OGT, where extant, agrees with the proto-Lucian text in exhibiting a chronology at sharp variance with the chronology found in the MT. In chapter 22 of I Kings and throughout II Kings, the Old Greek translation has been replaced by the KR, which displays the Hebrew chronology, in the majority of Greek manuscripts, including Codex Vaticanus. The proto-Lucian text continues to follow the Old Greek chronology until the end of the period with but a single exception. In the third period (from Jehu to the fall of Samaria), he found no systematic difference between the chronological data of the Greek texts and the MT. From the study of these three periods he concluded that there is no distinct Lucianic chronology, rather that the Lucianic text has best preserved the Old Greek chronology. In his view the Old Greek chronology, was the earliest chronology in the Greek textual tradition and was already present in the Hebrew *Vorlage* of the earliest translation of the Books of Kings. Shenkel investigated the prophetic narratives in Kings into which the regnal formulae had been inserted, and his conclusion was that the Hebrew chronology was a secondary development. In his opinion "a pious redactor (of II Kings 3) wished to justify Elisha's intervention on behalf of the king of Judah by identifying the latter with the religiously acceptable Jehoshaphat, whose name was inserted into the text. Because this identification conflicted with the existing chronology, however, the Hebrew chronology was

[6] H. St. J. Thackeray, "The Greek Translators of the Four Books of Kings," *JTS* 8 (1907), 262–278; idem, *The Septuagint and Jewish Worship: A Study in Origins*², London 1923, 16–28; D. Barthélemy, *Les Devanciers d'Aquila* (*VT* Supp. 10), Leiden 1963, esp. 126 ff.; F. M. Cross, "The History of the Biblical Text in the Light of the Discoveries in the Judean Desert," *HTR* 57 (1964), 281–299; idem, "The Contribution of the Qumran Discoveries to the Study of the Biblical Text," *IEJ* 16 (1966), 81–95.

devised to make the identification of Jehoshaphat plausible from a chronological viewpoint. Ultimately it was necessary to revise the synchronisms and numbers for the regnal years back to the reign of Omri in I Kings."[7]

Shenkel's conclusions regarding the connection between the various Septuagint manuscripts are to be separated from his comparison of the OGT and MT. His judgments on the former are of great value. Especially noteworthy is his emphasis of the unique nature of MS. c_2 in comparison with the other Lucianic manuscripts, and his determination of the counting system used by the author of c_2. On the other hand, his conjectures (which are based mainly on historical arguments) in which he prefers the chronological data in the OGT to those in MT, cannot be accepted.[8]

In addition to these two approaches, Bible scholars have also raised the possibility of reconstructing the original time frame on the basis of the nonerroneous data in MT and in the Septuagint.[9] This view, however, is to be rejected. It raises methodological problems, and the attempts to apply it are arbitrary and artificial. It is unclear why the proponents of this approach at time select data from MT, and in other instances data preserved in the Septuagint.

The following is a reexamination of the subject. The discussion will focus on the period from the schism to the rebellion of Jehu, since most of the textual variations between MT and the Septuagint pertain to chronological data from this period. The textual variations for other periods are few, and do not together comprise an integrated system. When necessary, these versions will be mentioned below.[10]

---

[7] Schenkel, 111.

[8] For criticism of Shenkel, see: Gooding, 118 ff.; Thiele 1974, 184 ff.; A. R. Green, "Regnal Formulas in the Hebrew and Greek Texts of the Books of Kings," *JNES* 42 (1983), 167–180; cf. Albright 1970, 33–36; Jones, 2–9, 19–21. Jones accepts Shenkel's view, and prefers the chronological data in the Septuagint to those in MT (ibid., 6, 21).

[9] Begrich, 172–173; Miller, 280–288; Wifall, 320 ff., 331, 335–336; Hughes, 123 ff.; for a critique of this approach see: Shenkel, 124, n. 1; see also: below, n. 32.

[10] The most striking difference between the data of MT and those in the Septuagint for the period from the rebellion of Jehu to the conquest of Samaria is the count of the years of Pekahiah. MT and MS. B count 2 years for him; the Lucianic manuscripts boe_2 and MS. Agr, 10 years; and c_2 and many other manuscripts, 12 years. It is inconceivable, however, that Pekahiah ruled 10 or 12 years. These data contradict not only other data stated by these same manuscripts, but also the Assyrian chronological data which indicate that Menahem, the father of Pekahiah, offered tribute to Assyria also in 738, and that Hoshea gave tribute in the city of Sarabanu in 731. Consequently, Pekahiah and Pekah could not have ruled more than 7 years.

We shall first examine the chronological data in the Septuagint. Each manuscript will be examined on its own merits, along with its relationship to the other manuscripts. In the second stage, we will attempt to clarify whether the differences between the various manuscripts are coincidental, or whether they are intentional and reflective of counting systems based on unequivocal principles. If the principles of any system can be discovered, it will then be possible to reconstruct the relative chronology following this system, while comparing it to the MT chronology.[11] We will also attempt to determine if one chronology is to be preferred over the other.

A study of the chronological data in the Greek text of the book of Kings indicates clear differences between MT and the five main Greek manuscripts: Bboc$_2$e$_2$. An examination of connections between the data in these manuscripts revealed a great deal of similarity between the data in B (I Kings 1–21) and those of boe$_2$; beginning with I Kings 22 ff., there is a marked identity between MS. B and MT (with certain exceptions). This conclusion resembles the prevalent assumption that MS. B, until I Kings 21, reflects one translation ("OGT"), while from I Kings 22 on it is replaced by the KR.[12] The second conclusion is that the data of c$_2$ (one of the Lucianic manuscripts) are to be separated from those of the other Lucianic manuscripts (boe$_2$, henceforth L. B, until I Kings 21; and boe$_2$, henceforth BL. see appendix E).

The data in manuscript c$_2$ comprise a clear and consistent system,[13] which seemingly resembles the system of postdating. Similar to postdating, the first year of a king's reign begins only with the first new year following the death of his predecessor. In contrast with postdating, however, the synchronisms do not relate to the day of coronation, rather to the first day of the new year following the coronation.[14]

For the synchronisms between Tiglath-pileser III, Menahem and Hoshea, see above, Chapter Four.

[11] For my exposition of the Biblical chronological principles, see above, Chapter One.

[12] See Shenkel, 110; cf. the critique of Gooding, 124 ff.

[13] Shenkel, 27 ff.; cf. Wifall, 325 and loc. cit., n. 19.

[14] Shenkel (28 ff.), following Thiele (1951, 172 ff.), incorrectly labels this "the inconsequent accession-year system." The term was taken from the works of Löv and of Chapman: G. Löv, "Das sinchronistische System der Königsbücher," *ZWT* 43 (1900), 170 ff.; W. J. Chapman, "The Problem of Inconsequent Post-Dating in II Kings XV 13, 17, and 23," *HUCA* 2 (1925), 57 ff. In their opinion, postdating was used together with inconsistent postdating; the period from the death of the previous king to the first new year following his death was not included in the count of his years, like the system of c$_2$. In contrast to the latter, however, Löv and Chapman

The author of c_2 bases his system on the data pertaining to the years of reign in MT, and on four synchronisms in MT which conclude the proposed chronological system within a time span beginning with the schism and the simultaneous coronation of Rehoboam and Jeroboam, and ending with the siege of Samaria, which began in year 4 of Hezekiah of Judah = year 7 of Hoshea of Israel; and in between, the coronation of Omri of Israel in year 31 of Asa of Judah; and the simultaneous coronation of Jehu and Athaliah in the wake of the rebellion of Jehu and the assassinations of Joram and of Ahaziah.[15] The author of c_2 attempts to confirm, as much as possible, all the data in MT relating to years of reign, while modifying them to conform to the above-mentioned synchronistic system. Thus, e.g., in order to resolve the discrepancy of three years between the count of the years of Israelite kings from the coronation of Omri to the rebellion of Jehu (48) and the count of the Judahite kings in this period (45), he shortened Joram's reign from 12 to 9 years, while extending the reign of Jehoram of Judah by two years, from 8 to 10. In the period between the rebellion of Jehu and the conquest of Samaria, there is a large discrepancy between the years of the kings of Israel and those of Judah, reaching a total of ca. 22 years (Judah – 165 years of reign; Israel – 143 years and seven months). In order to bridge this gap, c_2 extends the reigns of three Israelite kings: Menahem, Pekahiah, and Pekah. He allots 12 years to Menahem, instead of the 10 in MT; 12 years to Pekahiah (MT: 2); and 30 years to Pekah (MT: 20; the seven months in which Zechariah and Shallum reigned are included in the first year of Menahem, just as the seven days of Zimri's rule are included in the first year of Omri). The author of c_2

maintain that the whole year inaugurated by the first new year following the death of the preceding king was called his "accession year," and year 1 of the new king began only with the second new year after the death of his predecessor. Moreover, in contrast to the system of these two researchers, the system of c_2 is consistent.

[15] The data in c_2 indicate that Samaria was conquered in year 10 of Ahaz (II Kings 18:10). This datum is clearly irregular in the system of this manuscript. This difficulty has already been discussed by Shenkel (31) and Wifall (328, n. 23); the latter's proposals to resolve the problem are unconvincing. This inconsistency in the system of c_2 is the exception that proves the rule. Only 2 of the 32 chronological data in c_2 for the period from the schism to the rebellion of Jehu are inconsistent with its system: (1) the coronation of Baasha in year 4 of Asa (I Kings 15:28, and also in MS. bi, but in I Kings 15:33 c_2 provides the version suitable to its system: year 5 of Asa); (2) the investiture of Jehoram in year 5 of Joram (II Kings 8:16; the system of c_2. would call for the investiture of Jehoram in year 1 of Joram. This version appears in MS. i, none of whose data are identical to those of c_2).

based the synchronisms on the years of reign of the respective kings. If there is any degree of correspondence between the synchronisms appearing in MT or in BL and those in c_2, this is purely coincidental. Thus, e.g., for the period from the schism to the rebellion of Jehu, c_2 contains 15 data pertaining to years of reign, 13 of which are identical to the MT data. In contrast, of the 16 synchronisms in this manuscript, 10 differ from both the data of MT and those in BL; of the other data in c_2, some are identical to BL (two), and the rest to both MT and BL (four).

Rehoboam and Jeroboam began to rule simultaneously. The count of the years of Rehoboam (17), Jeroboam (22), and Abijam (3) is identical to the count in MT, as is the synchronism establishing the investiture of Abijam in year 18 of Jeroboam. This apparently was the starting point of the author of c_2, upon which he based his entire system, and in accordance with which he chose all subsequent data. Thus, e.g., in I Kings 15:8 he establishes the death of Abijam in year 20 of Jeroboam in contrast with BL, which maintains: year 24 (MT lacks this datum). The year of Asa's coronation is established in year 21 of Jeroboam (in contrast with BL – year 24; and MT – year 20). At variance with MT and BL, the author of c_2 establishes the reign of Nadab in years 3 and 4 of Asa; accordingly, year 1 of Baasha = year 5 of Asa (in MT and in BL, the reign of Nadab is parallel to years 2 and 3 of Asa). This change can be explained only by the desire of the author of c_2 to adapt the synchronisms to fit his system. Similarly, c_2 matches year 1 of Elah son of Baasha with year 29 of Asa, in contrast with MT (year 26) and BL and others (years 20 or 28), since, in his view, year 1 of Baasha = year 5 of Asa.

Of interest is the fact that in c_2 there is no discrepancy between the date of the death of Zimri and the coronation of Omri; the two events occurred in year 31 of Asa, thus resolving one of the most acute internal contradictions in MT and in BL. In both the latter two versions, Omri was crowned in year 31 of Asa (I Kings 16:23); in the same chapter, however, it is stated (vv. 15–16) that Omri was crowned in year 27 of Asa (so in MT; be_2 establishes the investiture of Omri in year 22 of Asa; cf. BL on I Kings 16:6, 8).[16]

[16] The success of the author of c_2 in avoiding discrepancies in this period is partially coincidental and partially intentional. It ensues primarily from the fact that the count in MT of the years of the Israelite kings from the schism to year 31 of Asa is exactly identical to that of the Judahite kings in this period, assuming that Omri was crowned only in year 31 of Asa, for in Israel Jeroboam ruled 22 years;

From the coronation of Omri on, there is a marked correspondence between c_2 and BL. Both versions count the 12 years of Omri's reign from year 31 of Asa, in contrast to MT. Although both BL and c_2 share a common starting point, the difference between their systems quickly generates discrepancies between them. In the reconstruction of c_2, Jehoshaphat was crowned in year 12 of Omri, while in the chronology of BL, his investiture was in year 11 of Omri. Like L, c_2 states that Ahaziah ascended the throne in year 24 of Jehoshaphat; in this case as well, the correspondence seems to be coincidental. Like BL (but in contrast to MT), the author of c_2 writes "Ahaziah" instead of Jehoshaphat in II Kings 3:9. This change corresponds to his system, which establishes the coronation of Joram after the death of Jehoshaphat (year 2 of Ahaziah = year 25 of Jehoshaphat; year 1 of Joram = year 1 of Jehoram), but he could also have written the name of Jehoram. Consequently, the similarity of c_2 and BL on this point may possibly be more than accidental.

The chronology of c_2 is therefore an artificial adaptation of the MT chronology, indicating that attempts had already been made at a relatively early time to resolve the many discrepancies between the chronological data in MT. The author of c_2 preferred the data of the years of reign, while attempting to reconcile them with the synchronisms whenever possible. The chronology of c_2 is undoubtedly lacking any historical value: in the reconstruction of c_2, the 120 years that elapsed between the rebellion of Jehu (842/1 BCE) and the ouster of Hoshea (722 BCE) grow to 165 years—a discrepancy of 45 years.

We shall now analyze the data of BL. Both Thiele and Shenkel are of the opinion that the data in BL comprise some sort of counting system and are not a random collection of data. Thiele assumed that the counting system employed in the "Greek translations" (following his definition) is alternatively postdating and antedating. He terms this system the "inconsistent postdating system."[17] Shenkel refrains from determining a comprehensive counting system. He main-

---

Nadab – 2 years; Baasha – 24; and Elah – 2 years, for a total of 50 years from the schism to the death of Elah. Consequently (according to the system of c_2), Omri began to rule in the fifty-first year after the schism. Thus too in Judah: Rehoboam reigned 17 years; Abijam – 3 years; and Asa – 30 years, totaling 50 years from the schism through year 30 of Asa. Year 31 of Asa is therefore the fifty-first year after the schism.

[17] Thiele 1951, 172 ff.

tains, however, that the OGT was undoubtedly based on such a system. He notes only that in the period directly following the schism, postdating was in practice in the kingdom of Judah.[18] His proposal, however, entails the assumption that Jeroboam began to rule before Rehoboam, which is in clear contradiction to both MT and the Septuagint.

A study of the data of BL indicates that various data groups seemingly reflect different counting systems. A number of data included in the BL versions presumably indicate that BL's system was antedating;[19] other data apparently indicate that it was postdating.[20] A different data group apparently indicates that the system in Judah was antedating, but in Israel—postdating,[21] while other data cannot be reconciled unless it is assumed that BL's system was like that of c_2.[22] Consequently, it is possible that the data of BL are not based on a consistent system, which by itself is likely to indicate their derivative nature.

We shall now attempt to clarify if the BL system nevertheless was consistent. Theoretically, we cannot rule out the possibility that the system of BL was the original one (if it will be demonstrated below that the data of BL are the original ones). Accordingly, in order to

---

[18] Shenkel, 34–35.

[19] The following two instances support this argument: (a) Nadab, who was crowned in year 2 of Asa, reigned for 2 years before being assassinated by Baasha in year 3 of Asa (MS. Boe_2; MS. b, however, maintains that Baasha began to rule in year 4 of Asa, and this datum was calculated in accordance with the postdating system—see appendix E); (b) Omri began to rule in year 31 of Asa, Jehoshaphat in year 11 of Omri, and Ahab in year 2 of Jehoshaphat.

[20] E.g.: (1) Elah was crowned in year 20 of Asa. He reigned two years and was assassinated in year 22 of Asa (MS. be_2 see appendix E; i.e., year 20 of Asa = the accession year of Elah; year 21 [Asa] = year 1 [Elah]; year 22 [Asa] = year 2 [Elah] = the investiture of Zimri); (2) Abijam was crowned in year 18 of Jeroboam and ruled 6 years, and Asa began to rule in year 24 of Jeroboam (i.e., year 18 of Jeroboam = the accession year of Abijam; year 19 [Jeroboam] = year 1 [Abijam]; year 24 [Jeroboam] = year 6 [Abijam] = the accession year of Asa).

[21] This is the only way to reconcile the following data: the investiture of Ahaziah in year 24 of Jehoshaphat; Jehoshaphat reigned 25 years; Ahaziah ruled 2 years; Joram was crowned in year 2 of Jehoram. This data cannot be reconciled unless it is assumed that year 24 of Jehoshaphat = the accession year of Ahaziah; year 25 of Jehoshaphat = year 1 of Jehoram (and year 1 of Ahaziah), while Joram began to rule in year 2 of Jehoram (= year 2 of Ahaziah).

[22] Thus, e.g., the datum establishing the investiture of Abijam in year 18 of Jeroboam (although Rehoboam ruled only 17 years, and had begun to rule at the same time as Jeroboam, and certainly not later than Jeroboam). It would seem that this datum cannot be reconciled unless it is assumed that year 1 of Jeroboam = year 1 of Rehoboam; year 17 (Jeroboam) = year 17 (Rehoboam); and year 18 of Jeroboam = year 1 of Abijam.

expose the principles of the BL's system all possibilities must be examined, and various elements of the proposed system should not be summarily rejected, such as, e.g., that the new year did not start at the same time in Israel and in Judah, or that the system of counting in both kingdoms was not uniform.

An examination of all the data included in the Lucianic manuscripts (with the exception of c_2) and in MS. B for I Kings 1–21 (with exceptions) indicates that the data in BL are likely to form an integral system (or an attempt to form such a system) based on two principles: (1) the postdating system was employed in both Israel and Judah; (2) the new year in Israel preceded the Judahite new year by half a year. Obviously, this is merely a working hypothesis, and only if the following investigation clearly demonstrates that the data of BL are original will it be possible to assume that there was a BL system. First it is necessary to reconstruct BL's chronology. The double synchronism in I Kings 15:8–9 fixing the death of Abijam and the coronation of Asa in year 24 of Jeroboam (in the BL manuscript) indicates that Jeroboam ruled 25 years (the number of years of Jeroboam is not mentioned in Bboe$_2$). The passage I Kings 14:1–20 is not included in BL in the place in which it is located in MT. A version like vv. 1–18 appears as an addition integrated in BL after I Kings 12:24 (g-n), while vv. 19–20 are absent in these manuscripts.[23] We therefore are presented with two whole, parallel systems. On the one hand, MT maintains that Jeroboam ruled 22 years, and Abijam 3 years, from year 18 to year 20 of Jeroboam; BL, on the other hand, states that Abijam reigned for 6 years, from year 18 to year 24 of Jeroboam. Neither system is to be preferred at this point in time. BL's failure to count the years of Jeroboam cannot be decisive. The source of the change may possibly lie in the early Hebrew version which was possessed by the translator, in which 3 was corrupted to 6. The reverse process, however, also is a possibility. On the other hand, we cannot accept Thiele's assumption that 3 years were added to Abijam's reign in order to bridge the gap between the overall count of years of reign in Judah from the schism to the rebellion of Jehu (95) and those in Israel (98),[24] for 3 years were also added to Jeroboam

[23] For the complex addition inserted in MS. B and in the Lucianic manuscripts after 12:24, and for the midrashic narrative about the rebellion of Jeroboam (which is included in this addition), which differs in many details from the description in MT, see: Z. Telshir, *The Alternative Story: 3 Kingdoms 12:24 A–Z*, Jerusalem 1993.

[24] Thiele 1951, 186–187; Miller, 281.

(as is clearly seen from the synchronistic data of BL).[25]

The reconstruction of BL's chronology from the end of the lifetime of Baasha to the death of Tibni is extremely difficult. The data of BL differ from those of MT, nor are L and B identical. Despite the extreme corruption of the data of BL, it may be assumed that they are based on a whole chronological system clearly different from that of MT. The year of the death of Baasha and the investiture of Elah was established by B as year 20 of Asa. Since Baasha was crowned in year 3 of Asa, he ruled for only 17 years, which clearly contradicts the data appearing in all the Septuagint manuscripts which state, like MT, that Baasha reigned 24 years. Moreover, Elah ruled 2 years, and the investiture of Zimri was established in year 22 of Asa. Although this date is mentioned in only a portion of the Lucianic manuscripts (be_2) it patently corresponds to the datum also appearing in MS. B, i.e., the investiture of Elah in year 20 of Asa.[26] L attests that Zimri reigned 7 days.[27] However, B, a_2 and Ethiopian MSS state that his rule extended for 7 years. It may be assumed that this is a simple corruption that crept into the text, especially since BL on I Kings 16:16 (like MT) states that Omri was crowned in the camp at Gibbethon, close to the assassination of Elah and the investiture of Zimri.[28] Consequently, L (and apparently also BL), states that Omri ascended the throne in year 22 of Asa. However, in both MT and BL, I Kings 16:23 indicates that Omri was crowned only after the death of Tibni,

---

[25] Cf. Begrich, 140, 151.

[26] Thiele 1951 (186–187) is of the opinion that the chronological datum establishing the investiture of Elah in year 20 of Asa is rounded off and was determined in an arbitrary manner, because the author of BL did not know the exact date. This hypothesis, however, is unfounded, as is shown by the synchronism establishing the death of Elah and the investiture of Zimri in year 22 of Asa (be_2). It therefore appears that this datum is an integral part of the BL system of precise dates which are included in the system of L, and it cannot be dismissed as having been rounded off.

[27] Thiele's assumption that L did not establish the length of the reign of Zimri due to uncertainty (Thiele 1951, 175) is factually incorrect, for L explicitly maintains that Zimri ruled 7days (this datum as well is absent from the table of Burney).

[28] Gooding (123–125) is of the opinion that the count by MS. B of 7 years for Zimri is not a chance corruption but an intentional change. He goes so far as to claim that the establishment of 7 years for Zimri is the main reason for the institution of changes in the chronological data in MS. B, and to assert the derivative nature of the changes in the Lucianic manuscripts in relation to the changes of B. But if his assumption is correct, how can he explain the fact that the count of 7 years for Zimri does not correspond to the data of BL, and clearly contradicts the report in I Kings 16:15–16 (also appearing in MS. B) regarding the close proximity between the rebellion of Zimri and his suicide in his castle following Omri's siege of Tirzah?

in year 31 of Asa, thereby raising the question: who, following the BL system, ruled in Israel between year 22 and year 31 of Asa? Two hypotheses have been raised to resolve this issue. The first, that no king ruled in this period; the second, that Omri and Tibni ruled, but the period was accounted solely to Tibni (and, in any event, was not counted to Omri). Consequently, BL establishes that Tibni reigned ca. 8 or 9 years. Support for the second hypothesis may possibly be found in the addition of BL to I Kings 16:22. MT states: "so Tibni died, and Omri reigned," while BL maintains: "so Tibni died . . . and Omri reigned after Tibni," thus indicating that the reign of Omri began only after the rule of Tibni.[29] The chronological system of BL will change if we prefer the datum that Baasha reigned 24 years, rejecting in its favor the synchronism referring to the reign of Nadab. Accordingly, Baasha reigned until year 26 or 28 of Asa. Elah ruled from this year to year 29 (or 30) of Asa, and it would seem that Tibni held power between the murder of Elah/investiture of Zimri and the crowning of Omri in year 31 of Asa.[30] Despite the fact that all the textual versions attest that Omri began to rule in year 31 of Asa, this is only a seeming identity of versions; in actuality, MT maintains that the 12 years of Omri are to be counted from the death of Zimri (year 27 of Asa), while BL maintains that he began to reign in year 31 of Asa (following the death of Tibni).[31]

For this period as well, the superiority of MT or of BL cannot be determined. At the outset, it would seem that MT reflects an attempt to resolve the difficulties in BL, for the data in BL establishing the coronation of Baasha in year 3 of Asa and the investiture of the former's son Elah in year 20 of Asa do not correspond to the count of 24 years to Baasha in BL (there is no discrepancy between these data in MT, which states that Elah was crowned in year 26 of Baasha). Nor can it be claimed, on the other hand, that a later redactor attempted to resolve the contradictions he found in an ancient Hebrew text which is apparently reflected now in the BL manuscripts,

[29] Shenkel, 40. It is not clear from MT if Tibni was crowned or not. It is stated that "half of the people followed Tibni the son of Ginath, to make him king," but the text does not mention whether this intent was realized, or whether Tibni was not crowned at the time of his struggle against Omri (see above, Chapter Two).

[30] It is doubtful whether the testimony of Josephus (30, instead of 31, of Asa – *Antiquities* 8:312) is connected with this discrepancy, because the data of Josephus for this period are identical to those of MT, and it is preferable to assume that the change is merely a copyist's mistake.

[31] This opinion is held by Thiele (1951, 174) and Shenkel (40).

and that the emendations of the redactor are preserved in MT, for the data in MT also seem to be contradictory: Omri was crowned in year 31 of Asa and his son succeeded him in year 38 of Asa (16:29), data which presumably contradict the report that Omri ruled 12 years (ibid., v. 23); it may be assumed that BL resolves this discrepancy by establishing the investiture of Ahab in year 2 of Jehoshaphat. Consequently, the data pertaining to this period as well do not provide a basis for determining which system is preferable.[32] Shenkel argues that the BL version is superior, and that the years of Omri are to be counted from year 31 of Asa, because kings did not count the period of their reign that preceded their official investiture.[33] This claim, however, cannot be accepted. To the contrary: I Kings 16:16 states explicitly that the people crowned Omri as soon as the assassination of Elah became known. The version: "In the X year of Asa, did Zimri reign. Now the people were encamped against . . . and the people that were . . . encamped heard say 'Zimri has conspired, and has also smitten the king'; wherefore they made Omri . . . king . . . that day in the camp" (ibid., vv. 15–16) appears in both MT and in all the Septuagint manuscripts.[34] Consequently, Omri had already been crowned in year 27 of Asa, and be_2 states that the investiture of Omri in the camp occurred in year 22 of Asa. This datum indicates that 20 years elapsed between the investiture of Omri and that of his successor Ahab in year 2 of Jehoshaphat. It is clear, however, that the Lucianic manuscripts did not account to Omri the period preceding the death of Tibni.[35]

From I Kings 22 on, version B is identical to MT and is different from L, which maintains the system it employed previously, and therefore L establishes that Ahaziah son of Ahab was crowned in

---

[32] Thiele prefers the data of MT to those of L (Thiele 1951, 188–189; idem 1974, 179 ff.). This view is shared by Gooding: "The Lucianic Chronology is an unintelligent hotch-potch of the MT and the B Text" (125). Miller and others, in contrast, are of the opinion that some of the data in BL are superior to those in MT (Miller, 283 ff.; Wifall, 320 ff., 325 ff.; Miller and Hayes 229, 264–265, 280). Miller upholds the accuracy of the datum that Elah was crowned in year 20 of Asa, while claiming that most of the other data, including the testimony of the investiture of Omri in year 31 of Asa, are erroneous. He argues that Omri began to rule in year 21 of Asa (such a datum does not appear in any version).

[33] Shenkel, 40.

[34] This point was emphasized also by Gooding, 123.

[35] The question of the reliability of the data of BL for this period has been discussed extensively in the scholarly literature. Begrich (140) maintains that the synchronisms appearing in BL regarding the investiture of Jehoshaphat (in year 11 of

year 24 of Jehoshaphat (in MT; in AB: year 17 of Jehoshaphat).[36] From this point on, the discrepancies between the data of L deepen. The count of the years of Ahaziah and of Joram of Israel, and those of Ahaziah of Judah, are identical in L and in MT. In contrast, there is no precise count of the years of Jehoram: AB maintains 40, undoubtedly a rounded-off number;[37] oe_2 counts 10; and b is identical to MT – 8 years. The investiture of Jehoram should have been established by BL in year 1 or 2 of Ahaziah of Israel, as Shenkel and Miller in fact propose.[38] This datum, however, is absent from the versions of L, and this must remain mere conjecture. The Lucianic manuscripts, in contrast, establish the crowning of Jehoram in year 5 of Joram (II Kings 8:16), thereby clearly contradicting the system of BL. Furthermore, the report in the Lucianic manuscripts of II Kings 1:18a that Joram began to rule in year 2 of Jehoram is incompatible with the system of BL, and contradicts the previous datum. If it is assumed that Joram began to rule in year 2 of Jehoram, this will mean that the latter ruled at least 11 years, in contrast with the lower calculations of L.

The chronological data for this period in MT also are contradictory and difficult. II Kings 3:1 establishes that Joram began to rule in year 18 of Jehoshaphat, while II Kings 1:17 states that he was crowned in year 2 of Jehoram. This datum presumably may be reconciled if it is assumed that year 2 of Jehoram = year 18 of Jehoshaphat his father, i.e., that Jehoram was crowned in year 17 of his father, and that Joram was installed in year 18 of Jehoshaphat = year 2 of Jehoram. The count of the years of reign, however, is at variance with this possibility, for Jehoram and his son Ahaziah (of Judah) ruled together for only 9 years, while Joram reigned 12 years. II Kings 9:24–27 maintains that Joram and Ahaziah (of Judah) were assassinated at the same time; consequently, the years of Jehoram and his son Ahaziah should have totaled 13 years, if Joram was in fact crowned in year 2 of Jehoram. The investiture of Joram in year 2 of Jehoram also contradicts the datum that Jehoram was installed in year 5 of

Omri) and regarding that of Ahab (in year 2 of Jehoshaphat) are not original, but nevertheless are calculated correctly and correspond to the original system of dates. See also: Mowinckel, 263; Jepsen, 41; Tadmor 1962, 289 ff.

[36] For the assumption that the synchronism establishing the investiture of Ahaziah in year 24 of Jehoshaphat lacks historical value, see also: Begrich, 135.

[37] Following Thiele 1951, 178.

[38] Shenkel, 38 ff.; Miller, 285.

Joram (II Kings 8:16); and similarly the contradictory testimonies that Ahaziah (of Judah) was crowned in year 11 or year 12 of Joram (II Kings 8:25; 9:29).

The Lucianic manuscripts contain a repeated accession formula for Joram. The first formula appears in II Kings 1:18a-h, and the second in II Kings 3:1–3 (= the accession formula for Joram in MT). The first includes a synchronism identical to that found in MT of II Kings 1:17 (the coronation of Joram in year 2 of Jehoram), while it is absent in the second. It presumably could be argued that the translator deleted the synchronism from the second formula because it did not suit his system, but this is only an unprovable conjecture, and does not demonstrate the superiority of MT. Nor can the double formula serve as proof of this.

In contrast, the change of the name of the king of Judah in II Kings 3 (Jehoshaphat instead of Ahaziah, or vice versa) may possibly be intentional and not coincidental, and perhaps this holds the key to establishing the superiority of the chronological data in MT over those in BL, or the opposite. Every interpretation of the chronological data in the Lucianic manuscripts shows, beyond any doubt, that Joram did not begin to rule in the time of Jehoshaphat. This is in contradiction to the narrative in II Kings 3 about the joint campaign of Joram, Jehoshaphat, and the Edomite king against King Mesha of Moab. The Lucianic manuscripts make no mention of Jehoshaphat, who is replaced in vv. 7 (twice) and 9, by Ahaziah (of Judah), Jehoshaphat's grandson. This difference matches the chronological data in the accession formula of Joram, for the MT states that the latter began to rule in year 18 of Jehoshaphat, in contrast to the Lucianic manuscripts which establish his coronation in year 2 of Jehoram son of Jehoshaphat.

Shenkel, in his detailed discussion of this point, concludes that the OGT is superior to MT.[39] In his opinion, Jehoshaphat's name was inserted into the original text, which made necessary the emendation of the entire dating system in MT until the coronation of Omri. This was the cause of the considerable differences between the data in BL and those in MT. In order to prove his hypothesis, Shenkel employs two main arguments:[40] the letter sent by Elijah to Jehoram (II Chronicles 21:12–15) indicates that the prophet lived in the time

[39] Shenkel, 43.
[40] Idem, 101 ff.

of Jehoram. Since Elisha is the prophet mentioned in connection with the campaign of Joram against Moab, and since Elijah and Elisha were consecutively, and not concurrently, active, it is clear that the campaign must be dated after the death of Elijah, which followed the death of Jehoshaphat. This argument is weak, however, for it cannot be assumed that the letter was sent by Elijah; the opinion of the majority of researchers is to be accepted: that the letter is not genuine, and was composed by the author of Chronicles, who attributed it to the most important prophet who lived and was active at this time.[41]

Shenkel's second, and in his opinion, the more important argument is that no king ruled Edom in the time of Jehoshaphat, which would preclude dating the campaign to Jehoshaphat's reign. He bases this claim on two testimonies. I Kings 22:48 states: "And there was no king in Edom; a deputy was king"; and II Kings 8:20–22 (= II Chronicles 21:8–10), indicates that Edom shook off the Judean yoke only in the time of Jehoram son of Jehoshaphat, following his unsuccessful campaign against Edom.

During the reign of Jehoram they set a king over themselves, and he threw off the yoke of Judean bondage, defeating Judah on the battlefield. But only a few years later, the Edomite king joined the armies of Israel and Judah in their attack of Moab.[42]

Shenkel's reconstruction is inconceivable. The meaning of "And there was no king in Edom; a deputy was king" is that Edom was not an independent kingdom at the time, but rather a Judahite satellite, a vassal kingdom ruled by a "deputy [who] was king", i.e., a vassal sovereign, a king who was a sort of deputy, a sort of official who served at the pleasure of the king of Judah.[43] The failure of the campaign

[41] Many researchers are of the opinion that the letter was composed by the Chronicler, who attributed it to Elijah. Curtis and Madsen label the letter "A pure product of the imagination" (Curtis and Madsen, 415); see also: Rudolph, 267; Myers, 121–122; Williamson, 306–307; Japhet, 159; Na'aman 1987, 272–273; B. J. Diebner, "Überlegungen zum 'Brief des Elia' (2 Chr 21, 12–15)," *Henoch* 9 (1987), 197–228.

[42] In addition to these two arguments, Shenkel raises a third (105 ff., 111). He claims that the name "Jehoshaphat" was written by "a pious redactor" who sought to justify Elisha's activity during the campaign against Moab and to present it as intervention on behalf of the righteous Jehoshaphat, and not for the wicked Ahaziah (cf. II Kings 3:14 with 8:27). This argument, however, is not convincing; see also the criticism by Gooding, 126–127.

[43] Many commentators have the reading: "And there was no king in Edom, only a viceroy of Jehoshapat; he built . . ." See, e.g., J. Robinson, *The First Book of Kings* (*CB*), Cambridge 1972, 250. This reading, however, is improbable. The subject of

of Joram and Jehoshaphat against Edom apparently was the cause of the Judah-Edom war. It is inconceivable that, after the defeat of Judah against Edom in the time of Jehoram, the king of an independent Edom would suddenly ally himself with Judah and set out with its king against Moab. Furthermore, it is a known fact that the reign of Ahaziah, the grandson of Jehoshaphat, was very short (ca. one year). It is also known that Ahaziah joined Joram son of Ahab in the fighting at Ramoth-gilead, where the combined force suffered a defeat. Joram was wounded and was forced to convalesce in Jezreel, where he was assassinated by Jehu. The question arises, when did Ahaziah and Joram set out on their disastrous campaign against Moab? Clearly, this campaign could not have been conducted after Joram was wounded in the fighting in Gilead, nor is it conceivable that it took place before the battle in Ramoth-gilead, because the description in II Kings 3 indicates that the campaign was a protracted one; it included an offensive through the Edomite desert, extensive punitive actions in Moab, and an extended siege of Kir-Moab (the Moabite capital), which ultimately failed: the Israelites could not capture the city and depose the rebellious Moabite monarch. Moreover, the Bible emphasizes the proximity of the death of Ahab, the ensuing Moabite revolt, and the Israelite response, i.e., the campaign of Joram. Consequently, it may not be assumed that the campaign was conducted, as Shenkel argues, more than 11 years after the death of Ahab.[44]

It follows from this that the system of chronological data in MT is historically conceivable, which is not the case for the data in the BL manuscripts. The data in the latter may be assumed to be a mere emendation of the original data preserved in MT. The name "Jehoshaphat"

v. 48 is Jehoshaphat, and not the "viceroy," as was correctly interpreted by Gray (1970, 457). Gray's translation: "and there was no king in Edom, but a representative of the king" does not do justice to the term "נצב מלך." Better is the translation of Skinner: "a deputy was king" (D. D. Skinner, *Kings* [*NCB*], New York and Edinburgh 1904, 270–271), as it is also rendered by Honor (L. L. Honor, *Book of Kings 1: A Commentary*, New York 1955, 330). A possible alternative reading is "And there was no king in Edom, a royal deputy was [there]," or perhaps it would be preferable to assume that the *hapax legomenon* "נצב מלך" is simply a *terminus technicus* for vassal king, and the meaning of the verse is therefore: And there was no (independent) king in Edom, a vassal king ruled it, and he set forth with Joram and Jehoshaphat to wage war against Moab. See also the recent discussion of Cogan and Tadmor (II Kings, 44–45).

[44] Thiele 1974, 184. For the preference of MT on II Kings 3, see also: Gooding, 126–127, and loc. cit. for additional literature; R. W. Corney, "The Reigns of Omri and Ahab," Th.D. diss., Union Theological Seminary, New York 1970, 74.

was replaced by that of Ahaziah so that the narrative would conform to the BL system. The changes in BL apparently are a function of the different interpretation given to I Kings 16:22–23. BL counts the years of Omri from year 31 of Asa, thus resolving the presumed blatant contradiction in MT, which states that Omri was crowned in year 31 of Asa, ruled 12 years, and was succeeded by his son Ahab in year 38 of Asa. Half of the people did not acknowledge the investiture of Omri in the camp at Gibbethon (which occurred in year 22 of Asa), and the period from the death of Zimri to that of Tibni was not counted to Omri. The reconstruction proposed by BL cannot be original. The king counted his years from his coronation, irregardless of challenges to his authority or of revolts by portions of his kingdom or professions of loyalty to another ruler by the latter.[45] The interpretation of I Kings 16 apparently led to a change in the data pertaining to the coronation of Jehoshaphat and of Ahab. Since this calculation specifies that Jehoshaphat began to rule before Ahab, 22:41–51 was advanced to be placed after 16:28 (the name Ahaziah was deleted from 16:28g [= 22:50 in MT], to be replaced in MS. gi with the name "Ahab"). Since BL states that, Ahaziah began to rule in year 24 of Jehoshaphat, the redactor or translator preferred the datum establishing the coronation of Joram in year 22 of Jehoram (II Kings 1:17) to that establishing the investiture of Joram in year 2 of Jehoram (II Kings 3:1). This preference led to the replacement of the name "Jehoshaphat" in II Kings 3 by "Ahaziah." Similarly, the accession formula of Joram (3:1–3) was advanced, to be inserted before chap. 2, thus resolving an additional difficulty in MT: the insertion of chap. 2 in II Kings after the death and burial formula of Ahaziah and before the accession formula of Joram, as a separate literary unit digressing from the normal order.[46]

[45] Gooding (123) correctly mentions in this context the seven-year reign of David in Hebron during the civil war between the camps of Saul and those of David. Eshbaal son of Saul ruled over portions of the Israelite kingdom at this time, but these years are nevertheless accounted to David.

[46] A possible additional example of the considerable sensitivity exhibited by the Lucianic manuscripts for the problems involved in the arrangement of the Book of Kings may be found in II Kings 13–14. MT includes the last narrative about Elisha, which deals with the wars of Joash against Aram (13:14–25), after the formula concluding the reign of Joash of Israel in II Kings 13:12–13 and before the opening formula of the kingship of Amaziah (14:1 ff.). This is like the first narrative about Elisha (II Kings 2) which also interrupts the normal order of the Book of Kings, which generally is careful not to relate the history of a king after the mention of his death in the usual concluding formula. An additional concluding formula for the

reign of Joash appears after this, in 14:15–16. In both the Lucianic manuscripts and MS. r, 13:12–13 appear at the end of chapter 13 (following v. 25), thus including both the last narrative of Elisha and the wars of Joash against Aram in the body of the description of the latter's reign, before the (first) concluding formula. Accordingly, these manuscripts omit v. 15 from chapter 14 (but not v. 16).

APPENDICES

APPENDIX A

THE DATES OF THE KINGS OF ISRAEL AND JUDAH

Israel		*Judah*	
Jeroboam I	931/30–909	Rehoboam	931/30–914
Nadab	909–908	Abijah	914–911
Baasha	908–885	Asa	911–870
Elah	885–884	Jehoshaphat	870–845
Zimri	884	Jehoram	*851*–843/2
[Tibni	884–880]	Ahaziah	843/2–842/1
Omri	884–873	[Athaliah	842/1–835]
Ahab	873–852	Jehoash	(842/1)–802/1
Ahaziah	852–851	Amaziah	*805/4*–776/5
Joram	851–842/1	Uzziah	*788/7*–736/5
Jehu	842/1–815/4	Jotam	*758/7*–742/1
Jehoahaz	*819*–804/3	Ahaz	*742/1*–726
Joash	*805*–790	Hezekiah	726–697/6
Jeroboam II	790–750/49	Manasseh	697/6–642/1
Zechariah	750/49	Amon	642/1–640/39
Shallum	749	Josiah	640/39–609
Menahem	749–738	Jehoahaz	609
Pekahiah	738–736	Jehoiakim	609–598
Pekah	(750?)–732/1	Jehoiachin	598–597
Hoshea	732/1–722	Zedekiah	597–586

APPENDIX B

THE CHRONOLOGICAL DATA

I. Biblical data

A. *Length of Reigns*

1. *The Kings of Israel*

1. Jeroboam – 22 years (I Kings 14:20).
2. Nadab – 2 years (I Kings 15:25).
3. Baasha – 24 years (I Kings 15:33).
4. Elah – 2 years (I Kings 16:8).
5. Zimri – 7 days (I Kings 16:15).
6. Omri – 12 years (I Kings 16:23).
7. Ahab – 22 years (I Kings 16:29).
8. Ahaziah – 2 years (I Kings 22:52).
9. Joram – 12 years (II Kings 3:1).
10. Jehu – 28 years (II Kings 10:36).
11. Jehoahaz – 17 years (II Kings 13:1).
12. Joash – 16 years (II Kings 13:10).
13. Jeroboam – 41 years (II Kings 14:23).
14. Zechariah – 6 months (II Kings 15:8).
15. Shallum – 1 month (II Kings 15:13).
16. Menahem – 10 years (II Kings 15:17).
17. Pekahiah – 2 years (II Kings 15:23).
18. Pekah – 20 years (II Kings 15:27).
19. Hoshea – 9 years (II Kings 17:1).

2. *The Kings of Judah*

1/20. Rehoboam – 17 years (I Kings 14:21 = II Chronicles 12:13).
2/21. Abijah – 3 years (I Kings 15:2 = II Chronicles 13:1).
3/22. Asa – 41 years (I Kings 15:10 = II Chronicles 16:13).
4/23. Jehoshaphat – 25 years (I Kings 22:42 = II Chronicles 20:31).
5/24. Jehoram – 8 years (II Kings 8:17 = II Chronicles 21:5, 20).
6/25. Ahaziah – 1 year (II Kings 8:26 = II Chronicles 22:2).
7/26. Jehoash – 40 years (II Kings 12:2 = II Chronicles 24:1).
8/27. Amaziah – 29 years (II Kings 14:2 = II Chronicles 25:1).
9/28. Uzziah – 52 years (II Kings 15:2 = II Chronicles 26:3).
10/29. Jotham – 16 years (II Kings 15:33 = II Chronicles 27:1, 8).
11/30. Ahaz – 16 years (II Kings 16:2 = II Chronicles 28:1).
12/31. Hezekiah – 29 years (II Kings 18:2 = II Chronicles 29:1).
13/32. Manasseh – 55 years (II Kings 21:1 = II Chronicles 33:1).
14/33. Amon – 2 years (II Kings 21:19 = II Chronicles 33:21).

15/34. Jósiah – 31 years (II Kings 22:1 = II Chronicles 34:1).
16/35. Jehoahaz – 3 months (II Kings 23:31 = II Chronicles 36:2).
17/36. Jehoiakim – 11 years (II Kings 23:36 = II Chronicles 36:5).
18/37. Jehoiachin – 3 months (II Kings 24:8); 3 months and 10 days (II Chronicles 36:9).
19/38. Zedekiah – 11 years (II Kings 24:18 = II Chronicles 36:11).

B. *Synchronisms*

1. *Israelite Synchronisms*

1/39. 18th year of Jeroboam = coronation of Abijah (I Kings 15:1).
2/40. 20th year of Jeroboam = coronation of Asa (I Kings 15:9).
3/41. 4th year of Ahab = coronation of Jehoshaphat (I Kings 22:41).
4/42. 5th year of Joram = coronation of Jehoram (II Kings 8:16).
5/43. 11th year of Joram = coronation of Ahaziah (II Kings 9:29).
6/44. 12th year of Joram = coronation of Ahaziah (II Kings 8:25).
7/45. 7th year of Jehu = coronation of Jehoash (II Kings 12:2).
8/46. 2nd year of Joash = coronation of Amaziah (II Kings 14:1).
9/47. 27th year of Jeroboam = coronation of Uzziah (II Kings 15:1).
10/48. 2nd year of Pekah = coronation of Jotam (II Kings 15:32).
11/49. 17th year of Pekah = coronation of Ahaz (II Kings 16:1).
12/50. 3rd year of Hoshea = coronation of Hezekiah (II Kings 18:1).

2. *Judaite Synchronisms*

1/51. 2nd year of Asa = coronation of Nadab (I Kings 15:25).
2/52. 3rd year of Asa = coronation of Baasha (I Kings 15:33).
3/53. 26th year of Asa = coronation of Elah (I Kings 16:8).
4/54. 27th year of Asa = coronation of Zimri (I Kings 16:10, 15).
5/55. 27th year of Asa = coronation of Omri (I Kings 16:15–16).
6/56. 31th year of Asa = death of Tibni (I Kings 16:23).
7/57. 38th year of Asa = coronation of Ahab (I Kings 16:29).
8/58. 17th year of Jehoshaphat = coronation of Ahaziah (I Kings 22:52).
9/59. 18th year of Jehoshaphat = coronation of Joram (II Kings 3:1).
10/60. 2nd year of Jehoram = coronation of Joram (II Kings 1:17).
11/61. 23rd year of Jehoash = coronation of Jehoahaz (II Kings 13:1)
12/62. 37th year of Jehoash = coronation of Joash (II Kings 13:10).
13/63. 15th year of Amaziah = coronation of Jeroboam (II Kings 14:23).
14/64. Amaziah died 15 years after Joash's death (II Kings 14:17 = II Chronicles 25:25).
15/65. 38th year of Uzziah = coronation of Zechariah (I Kings 15:8).
16/66. 39th year of Uzziah = coronation of Shallum (II Kings 15:13).
17/67. 39th year of Uzziah = coronation of Menahem (II Kings 15:17).
18/68. 50th year of Uzziah = coronation of Pekahiah (II Kings 15:23).
19/69. 52nd year of Uzziah = coronation of Pekah (II Kings 15:27).
20/70. 20th year of Jotam = coronation of Hoshea (II Kings 15:30).
21/71. 12th year of Ahaz = coronation of Hoshea (II Kings 17:1).
22/72. 4th year of Hezekiah = 7th year of Hoshea (II Kings 18:9).
23/73. 6th year of Hezekiah = 9th year of Hoshea (II Kings 18:10).

C. *Synchronisms of the Kings of Israel and Judah with the Kings of Egypt, Assyria, and Babylonia*

1/74. In year 5 of Rehoboam—the campaign of Shishak (I Kings 14:25 = II Chronicles 12:2).
2/75. Menahem presents tribute to Pul [Tiglath-pileser III] king of Assyria (II Kings 15:19–20).
3/76. In the time of Pekah, Tiglath-pileser [III] king of Assyria exiles Israelites from Galilee and from Transjordan (II Kings 15:29).
4/77. Ahaz requests military aid from Tiglath-pileser [III] in the wake of the attack by Rezin king of Aram and Pekah king of Israel (II Kings 16:7–8 = II Chronicles 28:16–21).
5/78. Hoshea is crowned in the time of Shalmaneser [V]. At first he gives tribute to Assyria; afterwards, however, he rebels, and then Shalmaneser marches against him and imprisons him (II Kings 17:3–6; 18:9–11).
6/79. In year 14 of Hezekiah—the campaign of Sennacherib (II Kings 18:13 = Isaiah 36:1).
7/80. Tirhaka "king of Ethiopia" fights against Assyria during the campaign of Sennacherib against Judah (II Kings 19:9).
8/81. A delegation from Merodach-baladan II visits Jerusalem in the time of Hezekiah (II Kings 20:12 = Isaiah 39:1).
9/82. In his thirty-first year, Josiah dies at Megiddo in battle against Necho king of Egypt (II Kings 23:29 = II Chronicles 35:20).
10/83. The siege of Jerusalem by Nebuchadrezzar king of Babylonia and the exile of Judahites to Babylonia in year 3 of Jehoiakim (Daniel 1:1 ff.).
11/84. Year 4 of Jehoiakim = "the first year" of Nebuchadrezzar (Jeremiah 25:1).
12/85. In year 4 of Jehoiakim, Nebuchadrezzar defeats Egypt at Carchemish (Jeremiah 46:2).
13/86. The servitude of Jehoiakim to Nebuchadrezzar continues for three years, after which he rebels against the Assyrian king (II Kings 24:1).
14/87. The exile of Jehoiachin = year 8 of Nebuchadrezzar (II Kings 24:12); "at the return of the year" (II Chronicles 36:10).
15/88. Year 10 of Zedekiah = year 18 of Nebuchadrezzar (Jeremiah 32:1).
16/89. The destruction of the Temple—on the seventh day of the fifth month of year 11 of Zedekiah = year 19 of Nebuchadrezzar (II Kings 25:2, 8).
17/90. The release of Jehoiachin from his imprisonment in year 37 of his exile = "the year that" Evil-Merodach king of Babylon "began to reign" (II Kings 25:27 = Jeremiah 52:31).

D. *Additional Biblical Data*

1. *The Book of Kings*

1/91. Moab rebels against Israel, after the death of Ahab (II Kings 1:1; 3:5).
2/92. The campaign of Joram and Jehoshaphat against Moab (II Kings 3:4 ff.).
3/93. The assassination of Joram and Ahaziah during the rebellion of

Jehu (II Kings 9:24–28 = II Chronicles 22:7–9).

4/94. The assassination of Athaliah in year 7 of her reign (II Kings 11:4–20 = II Chronicles 23:1–21).

5/95. In year 23 of Jehoash—the repairs to the Temple (II Kings 12:7). "Then" Hazael marched against Gath and Jerusalem (ibid., v. 18).

6/96. In the time of Jotham—the activity of Rezin and Pekah against Judah (II Kings 15:37).

7/97. The war of Rezin and Pekah against Ahaz (II Kings 16:5; Isaiah 7:1; II Chronicles 28:5–15).

8/98. In year 18 of Josiah—the religious reform (II Kings 22:3; II Chronicles 34:8).

9/99. The beginning of the last siege of Jerusalem on the tenth day of the tenth month in year 9 of Zedekiah (II Kings 25:1; Jeremiah 39:1; 52:4).

10/100. The breach of the city on the ninth day of the fourth month in year 11 of Zedekiah (II Kings 25:2–4; Jeremiah 39:2; 52:6; the month is not mentioned in II Kings 25:3).

11/101. The destruction of the Temple and the burning of Jerusalem on the seventh or tenth day of the fifth month in year 11 of Zedekiah (II Kings 25:8; Jeremiah 52:12).

12/102. The assassination of Gedaliah in the seventh month [in the year of the destruction of the Temple] (II Kings 25:25; Jeremiah 41:1–2).

2. *The Book of Jeremiah*

1/103. Jeremiah prophesied "until the end of the eleventh year of Zedekiah . . . until the carrying away of Jerusalem captive in the fifth month" (1:3).

2/104. From year 13 of Josiah to year 4 of Jehoiakim, 23 years elapse (25:3).

3/105. In year 5 of Jehoiakim, in the ninth month—a fast in Jerusalem (36:9).

4/106. In year 7 of Nebuchadrezzar—the deportation of 3,023 Jews (52:28).

5/107. In year 4 of Zedekiah—the anti-Babylonian meeting in Jerusalem (27:1; 28:1).

6/108. In year 4 of Zedekiah, in the seventh month—the death of Hananiah (28:17).

7/109. In year 4 of his reign, Zedekiah goes to Babylon (51:59).

8/110. In year 18 of Nebuchadrezzar—the deportation of 832 people from Jerusalem (52:29).

9/111. In year 23 of Nebuchadrezzar—the deportation of 745 Judahites by Nebuzaradan (52:30).

3. *The Book of Ezekiel*

1/112. The beginning of the prophecy of Ezekiel—the fifth day of the [?] month of the fifth year "of King Jehoiachin's captivity" = the fifth day of the fourth month of the thirtieth year* (1:1–2).

* The dates in the Book of Ezekiel generally refer to the deportation of Jehoiachin, with the exception of datum no. 115, which apparently refers to the reign of Zedekiah. In the first datum, "the thirtieth year" may possibly refer to the reform of Josiah.

2/113. The elders of Judah come to Ezekiel, on the fifth day of the sixth month of the sixth year (8:1).
3/114. The elders of Judah come to Ezekiel to inquire of the Lord, on the tenth day of the fifth month of the seventh year (20:1).
4/115. The beginning of the siege of Jerusalem—the tenth day of the tenth month of the ninth year (24:1–2).
5/116. The prophecy about the king of Egypt—the twelfth day of the tenth month of the tenth year (29:1).
6/117. The prophecy of the breaking of the strength of the king of Egypt—the seventh day of the first month of the eleventh year (30:20).
7/118. The prophecy of destruction to Egypt—the first day of the third month of the eleventh year (31:1).
8/119. A refugee informs Ezekiel of the smiting of the city—the fifth day of the tenth month of the twelfth year "of our captivity" (33:21).
9/120. The lamentation for the king of Egypt—the first day of the twelfth month of the twelfth year (32:1).
10/121. Year 14 after the smiting of the city = the tenth day of the first month of the twenty-fifth year "of our captivity" (40:1).
11/122. The beginning of the siege of Tyre by Nebuchadrezzar—the first day of the first month of the twenty-seventh year (29:17–18).

4. *The Book of Chronicles*
(all the citations are from II Chronicles, except for datum 130)

1/123. Jeroboam dies in the time of Abijam (13:20).
2/124. Until year 10 of Asa—peace in the land (13:23; 14:5) ?**
3/125. In year 15 of Asa, in the third month—religious reform (15:10) ?
4/126. Until year 35 of Asa—peace. In year 36 of Asa—the Asa-Baasha war (15:19; 16:1).
5/127. In year 39 of Asa—the king was diseased in his feet (16:12) ?
6/128. In year 3 of Jehoshaphat—the teaching of the Torah (17:7) ?
7/129. The incurable disease of Jehoram at the end of his days (21:19) ?
8/130. The census in Transjordan, in the time of Jotham and Jeroboam (I Chronicles 5:17).
9/131. Year 1 of Hezekiah, on the first day of the first month—the cleansing of the Temple (29:3, 17).
10/132. In year 8 of Josiah—the king begins to seek after God (34:3) ??
11/133. In year 12 of Josiah—the beginning of the cultic purging (34:3) ??

E. *The Age of the Kings of Judah at Their Coronation*
(for references see above, A 2)

1/134. Rehoboam	41
2/135. Jehoshaphat	35
3/136. Jehoram	32

** The question mark denotes doubt regarding the reliability of the datum.

4/137.	Ahaziah	22
5/138.	Jehoash	7
6/139.	Amaziah	25
7/140.	Uzziah	16
8/141.	Jotham	25
9/142.	Ahaz	20
10/143.	Hezekiah	25
11/144.	Manasseh	12
12/145.	Amon	22
13/146.	Josiah	8
14/147.	Jehoahaz	23
15/148.	Jehoiakim	25
16/149.	Jehoiachin	18
17/150.	Zedekiah	21

II. Extra-Biblical Sources

1/151. Ahab "the Israelite" wars against Assyria in Qarqar = year 6 of Shalmaneser III, king of Assyria (Monolith inscription, II, ll. 91 ff.).

2/152. Jehu "son of Omri" gives tribute to Assyria—year 18 of Shalmaneser III (the "Black obelisk," relief B; IM 55644, the edition of annals of year 20 from the city of Ashur: III, l. 45 – IV, l. 15; the Kurba'il Statue, 29–30).

3/153. J(eh)oash "of Samaria" offers tribute to Adad-nirari III (Tell al-Rimah inscription, l. 8).

4/154. Menahem "of Samaria" offers tribute to Tiglath-pileser III (Iran stele, IIIA, l. 5).

5/155. Menahem "of Samaria" offers tribute to Tiglath-pileser III (Tadmor, *ITP*, Ann. 13*:10; Ann. 27:2).

6/156. Jehoahaz "of Judah" offers tribute to Tiglath-pileser III (K 3751, = Tadmor, *ITP*, Summ. 7: r. 11').

7/157. Deportation from "the land of the house of Omri" to Assyria, in the time of Tiglath-pileser III (Tadmor, *ITP*, Ann. 18; Summ. 4:15'–19').

8/158. The deposal of Pekah and the coronation of Hoshea in the time of Tiglath-pileser III (Tadmor, *ITP*, Summ. 4:17'; Summm. 13:18').

9/159. Hoshea offers tribute to Tiglath-pileser III in the city of Sarabanu (ND 4301+, Tadmor, *ITP*, Summ. 9: r. 9–11).

10/160. Shalmaneser V king of Assyria conquers the Israelite kingdom (Babylonian Chronicle, I, l. 29).

11/161. The conquest of Samaria, the deportation of its inhabitants, and its transformation to a province—in the time of Sargon II (Lie, II.2, l. 10; Calah prism, IV, ll. 25 ff. and others.

12/162. The conquest of Ekron(?) in the time of Hezekiah; and the conquest of Azekah and Ekron(?) by the Assyrian army ("Azekah inscription").

13/163. The campaign of Sannacherib to the west (the "third campaign"); the submission of Hezekiah (Chicago prism, II, ll. 37 ff. and others).

14/164. Manasseh gives tribute to Esarhaddon (Nineveh prism A, V, l. 55).
15/165. Manasseh gives tribute to Ashurbanipal (Nineveh prism C, I, l. 25).
16/166. The conquest of the "city of Judah," the ouster of its king, and the appointment of a successor—2 Adar in year 7 of Nebuchadrezzar II (BM 21946, rev., ll. 11–13).

APPENDIX C

THE AGES OF THE KINGS OF JUDAH

	Date of Birth	*Date of Death*	*Age at Accession*	*Age at birth of Successor*	*Age at Death*
Rehoboam	971	914	41	–	57
Abijah	–	911	–	–	–
Asa	–	870	–	–	–
Jehoshaphat	905	845	35	22	60
Jehoram	883	843/2	32	18	40
Ahaziah	865	842/1	22	23/2	23
Jehoash	843/2	802/1	7	14	41
Amaziah	829	776/5	25	25	53
Uzziah	804	736/5	16	21	68
Jotam	783	742/1	25	21	41
Ahaz	762	726	20 (25–LXX)	21	44
Hezekiah	741	697/6	15 (25–MT)	32	44
Manasseh	709	642/1	12	45	67
Amon	664	640/39	22	16/7	24
Josiah	648/7	609	8	14	39
Jehoahaz	632	–	23	–	–
Jehoiakim	634	598	25	18	36
Jehoiachin	616	after 562/1	18	–	+54
Zedekiah	618	–	21	–	–
average			21.5	22.3	46

APPENDIX D

DATES IN ISRAELITE HISTORY IN THE PERIOD OF THE MONARCHY WHICH MAY BE ESTABLISHED WITH A GREAT DEAL OF CERTAINTY[1]

No.	*Date*[2]	*Event*
1.	*853*	the coalition of the twelve kings of the seacoast, headed by Hadadezer of the land of Damascus, Irhuleni of Hamath, and Ahab of Israel, fights at Qarqar against Assyria, in year 6 of Shalmaneser III king of Assyria
2.	*841*	Jehu (the "son of Omri") king of Israel gives tribute to Assyria in year 18 of Shalmaneser III king of Assyria
3.	*805–796*[3]	Joash ("of Samaria") king of Israel gives tribute to Adad-nirari III king of Assyria
4.	*740*[4]	Menahem ("of Samaria") king of Israel gives tribute to Assyria (in year 6) to Tiglath-pileser III king of Assyria (Iran stele)
5.	*738*	Menahem ("of Samaria") king of Israel gives tribute to Assyria (in year 8) to Tiglath-pileser III king of Assyria
6.	*734*	Ahaz ("Jehoahaz") king of Judah gives tribute to Assyria (in year 12) to Tiglath-pileser III king of Assyria
7.	*733–732*	Tiglath-pileser III conquers Galilee and Transjordan and deports their inhabitants (in year 13–14 of his reign)

[1] Events nos. 1, 2, 12, 15, and 16 are mentioned in the extra-Biblical sources with the year of reign of the ruling Assyrian or Babylonian king (or with mention of the number of the campaign—see no. 12). The synchronisms relating to the other events are not explicitly stated in the Assyrian or Babylonian inscriptions, but they were calculated with a high degree of certainty. Some of the determinations are the subject of controversy (see the following notes).

[2] The reference is to the Assyrian-Babylonian year, which began on 1 Nisan. Thus, e.g., "853" means from Nisan (generally April/May) 853 to Adar (generally March/April) 852. All the years are BCE.

[3] It has not been determined if Joash gave tribute to Assyria at the beginning of Adad-nirari III's campaigns to the West (805), or during the course of these military excursions.

[4] Other scholars are of the opinion that Menahem gave tribute to Assyria for the first time only in 738.

Appendix D (*continuation*)

No.	*Date*	*Event*
8.	*732*	The assassination of Pekah king of Israel by Hoshea and the coronation of Hoshea (year 14 of Tiglath-pileser III)
9.	*731*[5]	Hoshea gives tribute to Tiglath-pileser III in the city of Sarabanu in the land of the Chaldeans (year 15 of Tiglath-pileser III)
10.	*722*[6]	Shalmaneser V king of Assyria conquers the kingdom of Israel, besieges Samaria, and imprisons Hoshea king of Israel (in year 5 of Shalmaneser V)
11.	*720*[6]	The conquest of Samaria and the deportation of its inhabitants by Sargon II king of Assyria (in year 2 of his reign)
12.	*701*	The campaign of Sennacherib king of Assyria to Judah—the "third campaign" (in year 4 of his reign)
13.	*677–676*[7]	Manasseh king of Judah provides forced laborers to Esarhaddon king of Assyria for the construction of the latter's palace in Nineveh (in year 4–5 of Esarhaddon)
14.	*609*	The death of Josiah king of Judah at Megiddo, in battle against Necho king of Egypt. The battle was conducted at the latest in the month of Sivan (in year 17 of Nabopolassar king of Babylon)
15.	*605*	Nebuchadrezzar defeats Egypt at Carchemish in year 21 of Nabopolassar king of Babylon (between Nisan and Ab)—year 4 of Jehoiakim king of Judah

[5] The giving of tribute in the city of Sarabanu could also be dated to 729, but this possibility (which corresponds to the presence of the Assyrian king in southern Babylon in this year as well) is inconsistent with the other data regarding the end of the Israelite kingdom.

[6] Scholarly opinion is divided regarding the time of the siege of Samaria, the conquest of the city, and the deportation of its inhabitants. Most researchers argue that the siege did not begin before 724, and the city was not captured after 720 (see Chapter Five).

[7] This date is not explicitly mentioned in the Assyrian inscriptions, but is calculated with a high degree of probability. Manasseh is included in the list of 22 "sea-coast, and sea kings," who are to be dated to ca. 677–676 (at any rate, this list does not predate the conquest of Sidon, which occurred in year 4 of Esarhaddon = 677). Manasseh apparently also was one of the kings who were required to build the "port of Esarhaddon," the city established in the time of Esarhaddon on the ruins of Sidon. Esarhaddon reigned until 669.

Appendix D (continuation)

No.	*Date*	*Event*
16.	*2 Adar (by the Babylonian calendar) 597*	The conquest of Jerusalem by Nebuchadrezzar II king of Babylonia in year 7 of his reign; the submission and deposal of Jehoiachin; the deportation of 3,023 Jews
17.	*after 1 Nisan 597*[8]	The exile of Jehoiachin, in year 8 of Nebuchadrezzar II king of Babylonia
18.	*10 Tebeth 587*[9]	The beginning of the last siege of Jerusalem, in year 17 of Nebuchadrezzar II = year 9 of Zedekiah king of Judah
19.	*587*	The deportation of 832 people from Jerusalem in year 17 of Nebuchadrezzar II = year 10 of Zedekiah
20.	*9 Tammuz 586*[9]	The breaching of the walls of Jerusalem in year 19 of Nebuchadrezzar II = year 11 of Zedekiah
21.	*7 or 10 Ab 586*[9]	The destruction of Jerusalem and the Temple and the exile of Judah to Babylonia, in year 19 of Nebuchadrezzar II king of Babylonia
22.	*582*	The deportation of 745 Jews by Nebuzaradan, in year 23 of Nebuchadrezzar II king of Babylonia
23.	*25 or 27 Adar 561*	The release from prison of Jehoiachin in the accession year of Evil-Merodach king of Babylonia

[8] Some researchers establish the exile of Jehoiachin in year 7 of Nebuchadrezzar II, before 1 Nisan 597.

[9] According to other scholars, the last siege of Jerusalem began in 588, and the city was destroyed in 587.

APPENDIX E

THE CHRONOLOGICAL DATA IN THE GREEK TEXT OF THE BOOK OF KINGS[1]

I. Length of Reigns

A. *The Kings of Judah*[2]

					The Luc. manuscripts					
No.	*King*	*Source*	*MT*	*A*	c_2	*b*	e_2	*o*	*B*	*Notes*
1.	Rehoboam	1 Kings 12:24a	–	–	17	17	17	17	12	–
		1 Kings 14:21	17	17	17	17	17	17	17	3
2.	Abijah	1 Kings 15:2	3	16	3	6	6	6	6	4
3.	Asa	1 Kings 15:10	41	41	41	41	41	41	41	5
4.	Jehoshaphat	1 Kings 16:28a	–	–	25	25	25	25	25	–
		1 Kings 22:42	25	25	–	–	–	–	25	–
5.	Jehoram	2 Kings 8:17	8	40	10	8	10	10	40	6
6.	Ahaziahu	2 Kings 8:26	1	1	1	1	1	1	1	–

[1] A. E. Brooke, N. McLean, and H. St. J. Thackeray (ed.), *The Old Testament in Greek*, vol. II, part II, Cambridge 1930.

[2] The data appearing in the Septuagint regarding the age of the kings of Judah at the time of their coronation were not included in this table, because the majority of them are identical to those of MT, with two exceptions: Rehoboam was 16 years old when he was crowned (B on I Kings 12:24a, contrast MT – 41), and Jehoram was 9 years of age when he was crowned (N on II Kings 8:17; or 10 years – oc_2e_2, contrast MT – 32).

[3] MS. x maintains that Rehoboam ruled 11 years.

[4] MS. i maintains that Abijam reigned "six and three years." This is a strange combination of the versions of the MT (three) and BL (six). The count of 16 years of reign for Abijam in version A apparently is a corruption, ensuing from the number 6 in MS. BL.

[5] The Septuagint on II Chronicles 16:13 counts 30 years for Asa (B), or 31 years (A, b, c_2).

[6] The other Greek manuscripts count for Jehoram 8 (N) or 40 (d_2 and others) years of reign.

B. *The Kings of Israel*

					The Luc. manuscripts					
No.	*King*	*Source*	*MT*	*A*	c_2	*b*	e_2	*o*	*B*	*Notes*
1.	Jeroboam	1 Kings 14:20	22	22	22	–	–	–	–	–
2.	Nadab	1 Kings 15:25	2	2	2	2	2	2	2	–
3.	Baasha	1 Kings 15:33	24	24	24	24	24	24	24	–
4.	Elah	1 Kings 16:8	2	2	2	2	2	2	2	–
5.	Zimri	1 Kings 16:15	7 days	7 days	7 days	7 days	7 days	7 days	7 years	7
6.	Omri	1 Kings 16:23	12	12	12	12	12	12	12	–
7.	Ahab	1 Kings 16:29	22	22	22	22	22	22	22	8
8.	Ahaziah	1 Kings 22:52	2	2	2	2	2	2	2	–
9.	Joram	2 Kings 1:18a	–	2	–	12	12	12	12	–
		2 Kings 3:1	12	12	11	12	12	12	12	–

[7] MSS. E, a_2 also maintain 7 years.

[8] Other MT manuscripts count 20 or 24 years.

[9] A number of MT manuscripts maintain that Nadab was crowned in year 10 of Asa, while MS. a_2 maintains that he was crowned in year 12 of Asa.

[10] Cf. MSS. d, e, y, and z that maintain that Elah was crowned in year 28 of Asa.

[11] According to MSS. N, x, and y, Omri was crowned in year 27 of Asa (as is also maintained by MS. A on I Kings 16:10, 15).

[12] In contrast with the other Septuagint manuscripts, MS. N establishes the coronation of Ahab in year 38 of Asa.

[13] According to N and other manuscripts, Joram was crowned in year 21 of Jehoshaphat.

[14] A datum identical to that in MT also appears in MSS. x, y.

II. Synchronisms

A. *Judaite Synchronisms*

No.	*Synchronism*	*Source*	*MT*	*The Luc. manuscripts*							
				A	c_2	*b*	e_2	*o*	*B*	*Notes*	
		I Kings									
1.	Coronation of Nadab	15:25	2	2	3	2	2	2	2	9	
	=year X of Asa										
		I Kings									
2.	Coronation of Baasha	15:28	3	3	4	4	3	3	3	–	
	=year X of Asa	15:33	3	3	5	5	3	3	3	–	
		I Kings									
3.	Coronation of Elah	16:6	–	20	29	20	20	20	20	10	
	=year X of Asa	16:8	26	26	–	–	–	–	–	–	
		I Kings									
4.	Coronation of Zimri	16:10	27	27	–	–	–	–	–	–	
	=year X of Asa	16:15	27	27	31	22	22	–	–	–	
		I Kings									
5.	Coronation of Omri	16:23	31	31	31	31	31	31	31	11	
	=year X of Asa										
		I Kings									
6.	Coronation of Ahab	16:29	38	–	Year 2 of Jehoshaphat					12	
	=year X of Asa										
		I Kings									
7.	Coronation of Ahaziah	22:52	17	17	24	24	24	24	17	–	
	=year X of Jehoshaphat										
8.	Coronation of Joram	II Kings									
	=year X of Jehoshaphat	1:18a	–	18	–	–	–	–	18	13	
	=year X of Jehoram	1:18a	–	–	1	2	2	2	–	–	
	=year X of Jehoshaphat	3:1	18	–	–	–	–	–	18	–	
		II Kings									
9.	Coronation of Joram	1:17	2	–	–	–	–	–	–	14	
	=year X of Jehoram										

B. *Israelite Synchronisms*

No.	*Synchronism*	*Source*	*MT*	*A*	*The Luc. manuscripts* c_2	*b*	e_2	*o*	*B*	*Notes*
1.	Coronation of Abijah =year X of Jeroboam	I Kings 15:1	18	18	18	18	18	18	18	–
2.	Death of Abijah =year X of Jeroboam	I Kings 15:8	–	–	20	24	24	24	24	–
3.	Coronation of Asa =year X of Jeroboam	I Kings 15:9	20	20	21	24	24	24	24	–
4.	Coronation of Jehoshaphat =year X of Omri	I Kings 16:28a	–	–	12	11	11	11	11	15
	=year X of Ahab	22:41	4	4	–	–	–	–	4	–
5.	Coronation of Jehoram =year X of Joram	II Kings 8:16	5	5	5	5	5	5	5	16
6.	Coronation of Ahaziah	II Kings 8:25	12	12	11	11	11	10	12	–
	=year X of Joram	9:29	11	11	11	11	11	11	11	17

[15] According to E, Jehoshaphat was crowned in year 10 of Omri while N, as MT, establishes this in year 4 of Ahab.

[16] The words "and Jehoshaphat the king of Judah" are absent from a number of MT manuscripts, and from MS. N in the Vulgate and the Peshitta.

[17] According to MS. e, Ahaziah was crowned in year 10 of Joram, as is also maintained by MS. o on 8:25.

APPENDIX F

THE KINGS OF TYRE

I. The Chronological Data[1]

	Name of the king	*Reconstruction of the original*	*The Laurentianus Codex*	*Cassiodorus*	*Eusebius*	*Theophilus of Antioch*
1	Hiram (I)[2]	34 53	34 53	34 53	34 53	– 53
2	Baʿal-ʿezer (I)	17 43	7 43	7 43	17 43	7 43
3	ʿAbd-ʿAshtart[3]	9 29	9 29	9 20	9 39	– –
4	ʿAshtart[4]	[20] –	12 –	– –	– –	– –
5	Dalay-ʿAshtart[5]	12 54	12 54	12 53	12 54	12 54
6	ʿAshtar-rom	9 58	9 54	9 54	9 58	9 58
7	Phelles	8 months 50	8 months 50	8 months 50	8 months 50	8 months 50
8	Itto-Baʿal (I)	32 68	32 68	32 48	32 48	12 40
9	Baʿal-ʿezer (II)	6 45	6 45	6 45	8 45	7 45

[1] The upper number in each column denotes the years of reign and the lower number the lifetime of the king. E.g., Hiram I ruled 34 years, and he lived 53 years.

[2] An additional datum: Solomon's Temple was established in year 12 of Hiram, 143 years before the establishment of Carthage.

[3] The name of ʿAbd-ʿAshtart is absent from the manuscript of Theophilus of Antioch.

[4] The Laurentianus Codex states: "The elder brother ruled 12 years," as is also maintained by the Armenian recension of Eusebius, without mention of the years in which he reigned.

[5] The distinction between ʿAshtart and Dalay-ʿAshtart follows the proposal of F. M. Cross. In the Laurentianus Codex: "ʿAshtart son of Dalay-ʿAshtart," while Theophilus states: "ʿAshtart died."

Chronological data (*continuation*)

	Name of the king	*Reconstruction of the original*	*The Laurentianus Codex*	*Cassiodorus*	*Eusebius*	*Theophilus of Antioch*
10	Matan (I)	9 32	9 32	9 32	29 32	29 32
11	Pigmalion	47 56	47 56	40 56	47 58	7 56
	Summary[6]	155+ 8 months	155+ 8 months	155+ 8 months	155+ 8 months	155+ 8 months

[6] The total refers to the count of years from the crowning of Hiram I to year 7 of Pigmalion. Each manuscript contains the same sum (155 years and 8 months). In fact, however, the detailed count totals 125 years and 8 months (Cassiodorus); 137 years and 8 months (Laurentianus); or 157 years and 8 months (Eusebius).

II. A Chronological Table of the Kings of Tyre

The dynasty of Abi-Baʿal

Abi-Baʿal	?–980
Hiram I	980–946
Baʿal-ʿezer I	946–929
ʿAbd-ʿAshtart	929–920

ʿAshtart and his brothers

ʿAshtart	920–900
Dalay-ʿAshtart	900–888
ʿAshtar-rom	888–879
Phelles	879

The dynasty of Itto-Baʿal

Itto-Baʿal I	878–847
Baʿal-ʿezer II	847–841
Matan I	841–832
Pigmalion	832–785

Itto-Baʿal II	?–740
Hiram II	739–731
Matan II	730–729
Eluli	729–701
Baʿal I	701–660?

Itto-Baʿal III	591–573
Baʿal II	573–564

INDEXES

INDEX OF SUBJECTS

INDEX OF SOURCES

1. Old Testament

2. Northwest Semitic Inscriptions

3. Cuneiform Sources

4. Rabbinic Literature

5. Classical Literature

INDEX OF AUTHORS

Gershon Galil, Ph. D., Hebrew University, Jerusalem, is Senior Lecturer in Biblical History in the Department of Jewish History at the University of Haifa.